Under Scan
Rafael Lozano-H

East Midlands Development Agency *(emda)*
Apex Court, City Link, Nottingham NG2 4LA
www.emda.org.uk

Antimodular Research
4040 Blvd. St-Laurent, studio 5
Montréal, Québec H2W 1Y8 Canada
www.antimodular.com

Edited by Rafael Lozano-Hemmer and David Hill

ISBN 0-9781347-0-2

Designed and typeset by Graphic Thought Facility
Printed by Graphicom, Italy

Contents

Section 1

Foreword, Introduction and Concept

Foreword
Ross Willmott
emda Board Member
April 2006

When East Midlands Development Agency (*emda*) set out its vision for the East Midlands, to be a top 20 region in Europe by 2010, we set ourselves an ambitious and challenging target. Our commissioning of Rafael Lozano-Hemmer to deliver *Under Scan* reflects both this ambition and the challenge we set.

The East Midlands is undergoing a quiet cultural renaissance. The region has five major population centres and a host of smaller towns, many of which are creating dynamic cultural facilities fit for the 21st century. This programme of development includes over £140 million invested in new buildings for culture and creative work. *Under Scan* celebrates this investment though its imaginative and creative use of arts and technology.

emda and many of our partners recognise that if we are to achieve our ambitions not only do we need enterprising and entrepreneurial businesses, we also need to attract and retain the best and most talented people. As people like Richard Florida (*The Rise of the Creative Class*) and Charles Landry (*The Creative City*) have pointed out, to succeed in achieving this we need to have a vibrant cultural offer in our cities, towns and villages.

We believe the East Midlands region has such an offer. One of our challenges is to tell the world about it. Our vision was to commission a work of genuine international quality that would help communicate better what the East Midlands is really like— a flourishing region with a diverse and dynamic culture and a rich pool of talented people. Our fervent hope is that many other cities around the world will host *Under Scan* and through it gain a better understanding of this region, its culture and its people.

Already the Creative Industries contribute over £6.9 billion to the region's economy. We want to see that grow. We want to inspire our people to take risks and to think internationally. We want to inspire people from all over the world to visit the region and to do business with us.

This publication tells the story of *Under Scan* and of some of the exciting developments that are already taking place in the East Midlands. Through it we hope that you will appreciate not only the fantastic piece of work that Rafael created for the region, but some of the inspirational places and people in the East Midlands.

Foreword
François Matarasso

Chair, Arts Council England East Midlands
April 2006

It is a commonplace that we live in a globalising world, and a somewhat misleading one if it suggests that international connections are new: people have always travelled and interacted with others from distant lands. But the current ease and extraordinary speed of those connections, facilitated by low-cost air travel, mobile telephony and computer technology, is changing our lives profoundly, and not only for the better.

It is therefore very apposite that the first major artistic commission undertaken by *emda* with Arts Council England should focus on just these questions. The invitation to Rafael Lozano-Hemmer to work in the East Midlands, in partnership with regional artists, filmmakers and audiences, was a clear signal of interest in international partnerships. It also showed a commitment to exploring how new technologies might bring people from different places and with different backgrounds together in artistic development. Lozano-Hemmer's innovative use of new media in public spaces, and his approach to opening up shared processes of creation with his audience, made him the ideal choice for this commission.

The project succeeded in breaking new ground technologically, and that will be important for the future work of all those involved. But its success was more significant in creating a space for playful interaction between people, and in framing suggestive questions about the meaning of such mediated relationships. *Under Scan* offered its audience—its participants—a strange, magical and elusive experience that will be remembered for many years to come.

Under Scan also established many new routes and connections. The professional and social relationships that resulted will continue to develop, while the technological resources acquired for the project and the skills and ideas of the region's participating artists will and lead to further new work.

At the same time, *Under Scan* will tour internationally, taking something of the East Midlands and its people abroad. The web of connections will grow, at a human pace, and help all those drawn into it to reflect on and respond to their own globalising world.

Introduction
David Hill and Rafael Lozano-Hemmer

This book and accompanying DVD have been created to document the public art project *Under Scan,* commissioned by East Midlands Development Agency (*emda)* to transform pedestrian areas in Derby, Leicester, Lincoln, Northampton and Nottingham.

The book is divided into four sections: section one explores the background to and concept for the piece; section two provides critical essays that see the work through historical, contextual and theoretical approaches; section three focuses on location reports, with information on each one, including comments from the public; the last section encompasses biographies and credits.

The DVD comprises a main, twelve minute-long documentary illustrating the project; video interviews with people who experienced the piece; and a section with unedited "raw" footage of interaction in each of the five locations. Whilst the DVD is in the PAL format commonly used in Europe, it does play back in many NTSC players and from all computers equipped with a DVD player.

As the producers of *Under Scan* we would like to acknowledge the key organisations and people that made the artwork possible: *emda*; Arts Council England East Midlands (ACE EM); the participating Local Authorities; Lincoln University; the local participants whose portraits are the core of the project; the production team that is credited at the end of the book—in particular the ArtReach Production Manager, Emma Jones; and finally, the public in the five locations, who made the piece come alive.

As co-editors of the publication we would like to thank the authors, copy editor Susie Ramsay, the design team at GTF, video and DVD editor Matthew Biederman, and for their support the key partners *emda*, ACE EM and Lincoln University.

Under Scan Concept
Rafael Lozano-Hemmer

Under Scan was a large-scale video art installation for public space, featuring 1000 interactive portraits that were activated by the shadows of passers-by. The piece was intended as a public takeover of a city by its inhabitants, linking high technology with strategies of self-representation, connective engagement and urban entitlement.

Video-portraits of local people recorded in Derby, Leicester, Lincoln, Northampton and Nottingham were projected at night on the ground of busy squares and pedestrian thoroughfares of these cities. The world's brightest projector was used to completely flood the area in a white light that hid from view the projected portraits. As people walked around the area, their shadow was cast on the floor and within it characters appeared and interacted. The video-portraits were short animated sequences, mostly of young people, "chilling-out," resting, dancing, making signs with their hands, some euphoric, others standoffish, always relational and complicit. The sequences typically began with the subject static, aloof, turned away from the camera. As they were revealed, the projected bodies began to move, turning to look straight at the pedestrian, and a variety of attitudes and contacts were established. The video portraits were taken in universities, rock concerts, community centres and other gathering places, by a team of local filmmakers and facilitators who introduced and workshopped the production. People were free to represent themselves in whichever way they desired—the only request was that they look directly at the camera at some point so that there could be a moment of eye contact. The portraits varied in length from 5 seconds to several minutes, and they were completely uncensored.

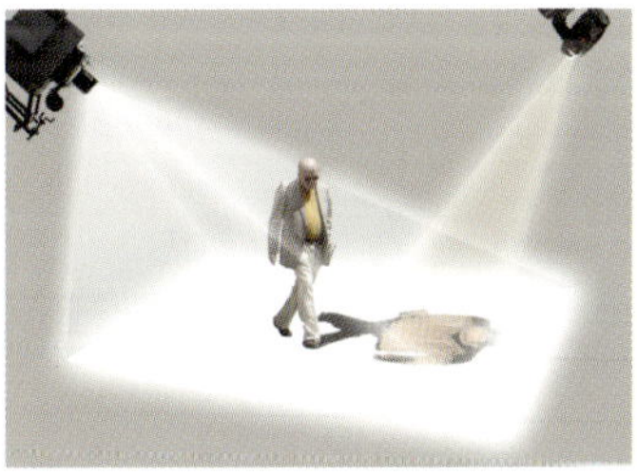

The behaviour of the project was as follows:

1. As you walked into the piece a powerful projector would cast your shadow on the ground and you would encounter the image of a person lying inside your shadow.

2. As soon as you fully uncovered the person with your shadow the portrait would "come alive" and begin moving until he or she was looking straight at you. At this point the portraits would make hand gestures, send you kisses, take off their clothes,

show you written statements, invite you to dance, take a photo of you, communicate by sign language, nod for you to go away, try to touch you, etc.

3. For as long as you were looking at the portrait it would remain engaged, as if suspended, repeating actions at different speeds and making eye contact.
4. As you walked away the portrait would likewise lose interest in you and go back to sleep and, after a while of not being activated, would fade away and disappear.
5. Portraits appeared at random and in different places of the interactive area, so it was impossible to predict where, when and who would appear to a participant.
6. Every seven minutes the entire project would stop and reset, with the tracking mechanism revealed in a brief "interlude" lighting sequence, which would project all of the calibration grids used by the computerised surveillance system.
7. At all times people could see the tracking system interface to understand how the project worked; this was publicly shown in a small monitor next to the explanation of the piece.

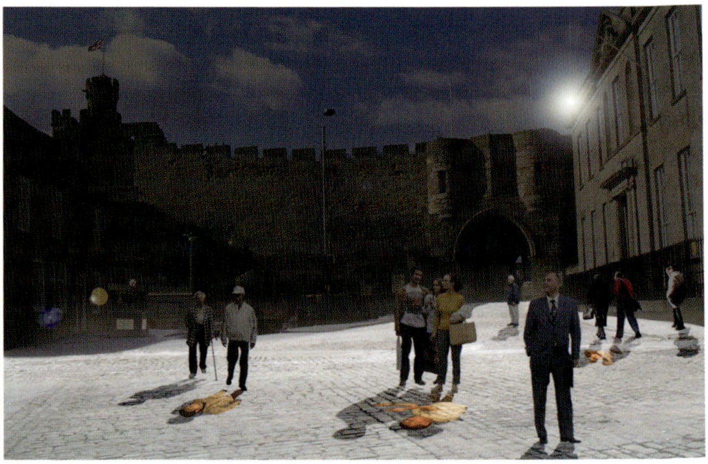

Early concept sketches for the project: Lincoln and Nottingham

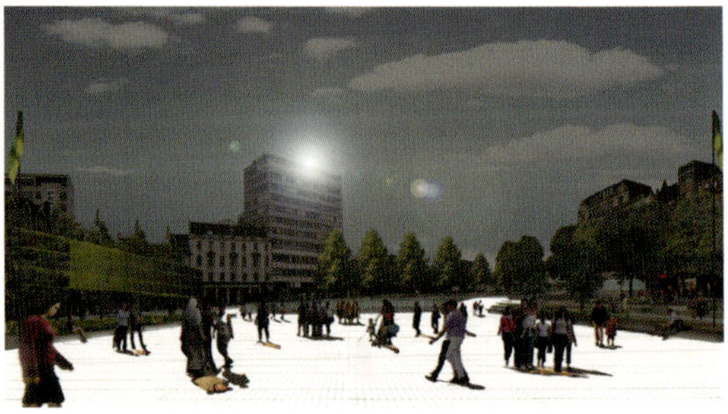

Under Scan could cover any public area between 500 and 2,000 m^2 and spread 14 different portraits simultaneously over that area. The design for the project called for a flexible staging so that very different urban layouts could be accommodated. The staging also needed to be low-key so that in the daytime the installation could "disappear" as much as possible. This provided contrast to the transformation afforded by the night time projections. Aesthetically, this was also important because often the sites chosen were already emblematic of the towns; logistically, this allowed the space to be utilised in the day by market vendors, delivery vehicles, pedestrian traffic and other everyday functions.

The project was conceived as an ongoing installation that would operate for ten nights in each city, from dusk to midnight. The idea was to work with very different strategies than a traditional son-et-lumière or fireworks spectacle would employ. For example:

Spectacle	***Under Scan***
Pre-programmed	Interactive
Spectacular	Intimate
Linear: has start and ending times	Non-linear: no beginning nor end
One narrative (often didactic)	Thousands of mini-narratives
Cathartic	Critical
Passive spectators	Actors and complicit participants
Privileged viewpoint/proscenium	Distributed, partial experiences
Special effects	Special causes and effects
Top-down	Side-by-side
One to many	One to one
Technology as novelty	Technology as language
Monumental/memorial	Alien memories
Site crucial for theme	Relationships crucial for themes
Representation	Self-representation

One of the objectives of *Under Scan* was to attempt to invert the logic of surveillance that is widespread in our cities. Critical questions informing the project included: What would happen if every single camera in public space became a projector? What if instead of taking images of us, and assume we are suspicious, tracking systems offered us images? How can we construct exceptions to trends of globalising urban homogenisation?

Inspiration and Precedents
Rafael Lozano-Hemmer

Under Scan **as a Shadow Play**

Victor Stoichita's wonderful book, *A Short History of the Shadow,* outlines different relationships to shadows in art; the shadow as a metaphor for being (Plato); the birth of representation and painting (by Butades' daughter, according to the ancient Greeks); the mysterious expression of the self (Shadowgrammes) and, most importantly, the expression of a hidden monstrosity or otherness.[1] It is hard to find an artist in the history of art that has not explored shadows. As an interface for electronic art, a shadow is a very intuitive device—one that is expressive, self-evident and that has a vast vocabulary of interaction. This is due, in part, to the personal experience that everyone has with his or her shadow and also to the sophisticated shadow puppet traditions that are found in most cultures. It is no coincidence that many electronic artists have worked with shadows, including Steina and Woody Vasulka, Myron Krueger, Christian Möller, Doug Back, Camille Utterback, Scott Snibbe, Ron Kuivila, Masaki Fujihata, Ken Goldberg, Golan Levin, minim++, Electronic Shadow, Motoshi Chikamori, Wolfgang Münch and Maurice Benayoun.

I have used shadows as an interface in four previous large-scale public art installations, starting with *Re:Positioning Fear* on the façade of the Landeszeughaus Arsenal building in Graz, Austria in 1997 (in collaboration with Will Bauer).

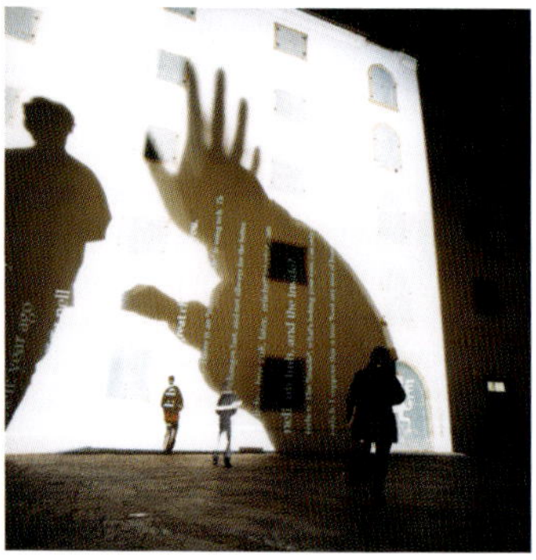

Rafael Lozano-Hemmer, *Re:Positioning Fear* (1997). *Landeszeughaus*, Graz, Austria. Produced for the Biennial on Media and Architecture.

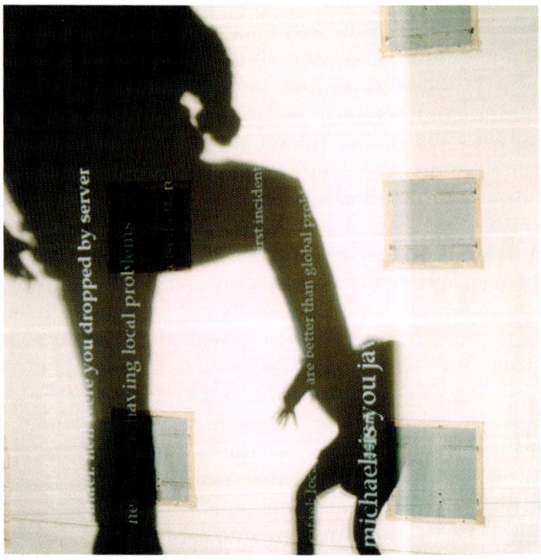

1. Stoichita, Victor I. (1997) *A Short History of the Shadow* (Essays in Art and Culture). London, England: Reaktion Books Ltd.

This project allowed passers-by to use their shadow to reveal and read a live Internet discussion on the transformation of the concept of fear, featuring thirty artists and theorists from seventeen countries. Originally I wanted the installation to create an environment inspired by the films of Murnau, with long distorted shadows that could be seen as metaphors of the threats documented inside the arsenal. The unexpectedly playful interaction that resulted from that installation inspired my next shadow work, *Body Movies*, which was designed specifically to tap into the expressive public behaviour witnessed in Austria. Instead of uncovering text with their shadow, in *Body Movies* participants revealed still portraits projected twenty-five metres high on buildings surrounding a public square. Once all the portraits in a given scene were revealed, a new slide would automatically be queued, inviting people to embody new representations. The piece was commissioned by V2 for the European Cultural Capital in Rotterdam in 2001 and has since been shown in several countries in Europe and Asia. In *Two Origins*, presented in Toulouse in 2002, shadows were used again to read texts, this time overlapping Cathar manuscripts from the heretic *Book of Two Origins*. Finally, in *Frequency and Volume*, premiered in Mexico in 2003, shadows became antennas that allowed participants to tune in audio and video signals from the radio spectrum.

Conceptually, the most similar project to *Under Scan* is *Body Movies,* as they both deal with embodying portraiture. However, in *Body Movies* the portraits were extracted from photographs of crowds taken on the streets, while in *Under Scan* there was a concerted effort to involve the community to participate in the video recordings, seeking their complicity. Another key difference between the projects is that in *Body*

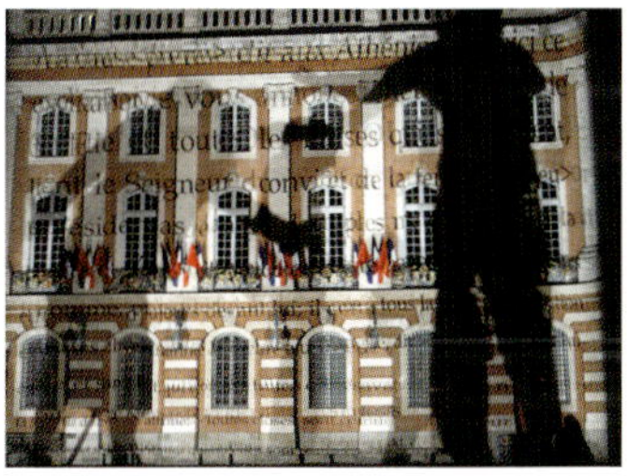

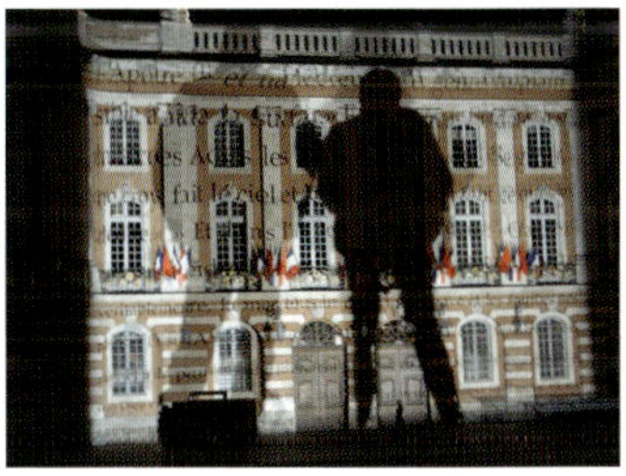

Rafael Lozano-Hemmer, *Two Origins* (2002). Place du Capitole, Toulouse, France. Produced for Festival Printemps de Septembre.

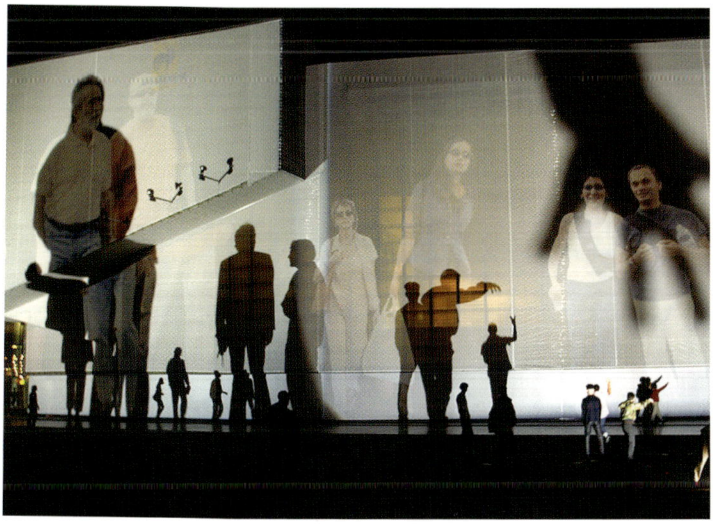

Rafael Lozano-Hemmer, *Body Movies* (2001-2006). First shown at the Schouwburgplein, Rotterdam, Netherlands. Produced for Cultural Capital of Europe by V2.

Movies the portrait is a huge static "field" that is matched and animated by the shadows of individuals, in a game of mimicry that I call reverse-puppetry. In *Under Scan* the portraits are not a passive canvas, they are animated and have agency: they are the ones that take over the shadow and look out at the public. Furthermore, the scale is intimate and life-sized, creating a far more uncanny effect. The intention is to attain what Brecht called a "noticing of the knots": the moment of complicity between the representation and reality.

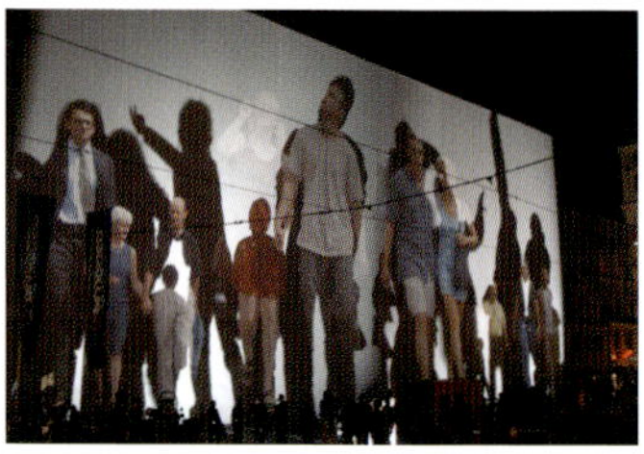

Rafael Lozano-Hemmer, *Body Movies* (2001-2006). Shown here at the Hauptplatz, Linz, Austria, during the Ars Electronica Festival 2002.

Under Scan as Surveillance Feedback

The work of painters such as Van Eyck, Parmigianino, Velázquez and, more recently, Leon Golub and Attila Lukacs show scenes where vectors of glances precisely pin the viewer in complicity with what is being seen. Who is the viewer? Who is the subject in these works? These are also pertinent questions as we deal with the disappearance of public space. Video-portraits as seen in Gary Hill's installation *Tall Ships* or in the work of pioneering media artists such as Luc Courchesne, Lynn Hershmann, Sharon Grace, Tony Dove and Paul Sermon take these questions to the next level of intimacy. Inspired by the *mise en abime* described by Michel Foucault in *The Order of Things*, which dismantles the presumed objectivity of the viewer, *Under Scan* makes use of eye contact as a way to establish an endless mirror between the representation and the public.[2]

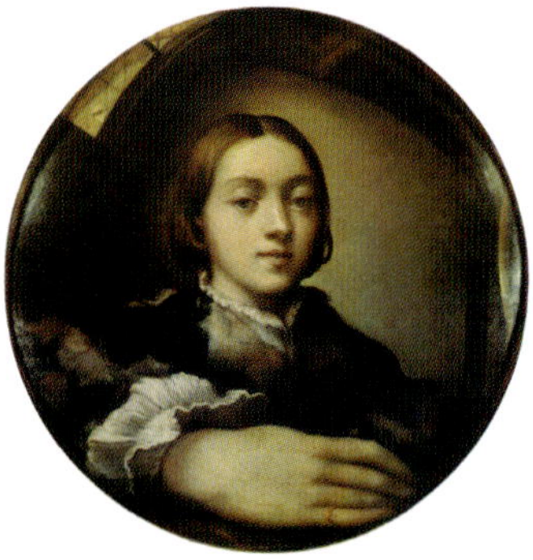

Girolamo Francesco Maria Mazzola "Parmigianino," *Self-portrait in a Convex Mirror* (c.1524); Oil on wood, diameter 24,4 cm; Kunsthistorisches Museum, Vienna.

In 1991, in collaboration with Will Bauer, I started developing *Surface Tension*, an interactive staging module for a technological theatre, which consisted of a human eye that followed people on a stage by means of a 3D tracking system. This Orwellian experience has since been reworked by several artists, perhaps motivated as I was, to question the predatory nature of visual technology or to invert the paradigm where the virtual takes place on the other side of the mirror and instead invades our own corporeal space. Surveillance technologies establish a fundamental power asymmetry that has been skilfully exposed, deconstructed and parodied in the work of modern artists such as Dan Graham, Nam June Paik, Julia Scher and Bruce Nauman. A new generation of machine vision technologies used for ethnic profiling, for automated searches in criminal databases, for recording and quantifying public movement and other "Homeland Security" priorities, is now being addressed by a new generation of artists: David Rokeby, Natalie Jeremijenko, the Institute for Applied Autonomy, Harun Farocki, Christian Moeller, Jordan Crandall, Marie Sester and the Surveillance Camera Players have examples of exciting developments in this field.

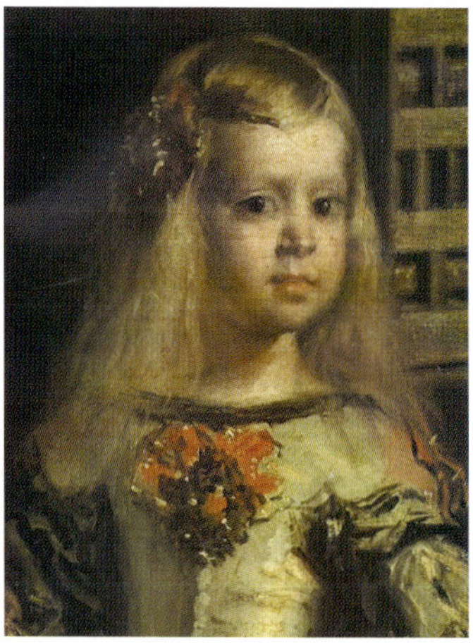

Diego Velázquez, *Las Meninas* (1656); Oil on canvas, 318 x 276 cm; Museo del Prado, Madrid.

2. Foucault, Michel (1994) (1966– French version). *The Order of Things: An Archaeology of the Human Sciences.* New York: Vintage Books.

Other References

The work of performative photographers such as Daniel Canogar, Spencer Tunick, Gerardo Suter and Karla Solano has been inspiring when thinking about the human body as a visual field. The idea of technologically concealing and revealing representation is derived from, among others, the work of César Martínez Silva who, in the 1980s, used a low-power slide projector to show outrageous imagery on religious and political buildings in Mexico (the images were so faint that they could only be seen through long exposure photography). Fairground cinematographs as popularized in Britain between 1900–1913, quite notably in the Midlands, by Sagar Mitchell and James Kenyon, was an important historical reference as we sought to portray at least 1,000 people from the East Midlands. Although I learnt about Mitchell and Kenyon once the project was already being developed, it is now impossible to think about *Under Scan* without referring to their work.[3]

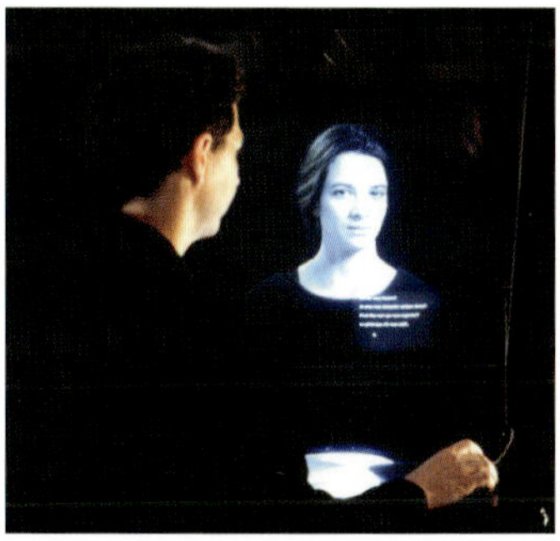

Luc Courchesne, *Portrait One* (1988-1990). First presented in TED2, Monterrey, California.

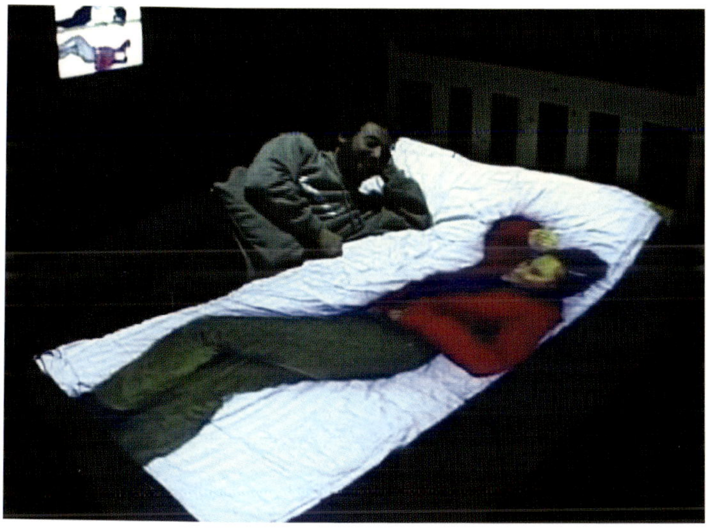

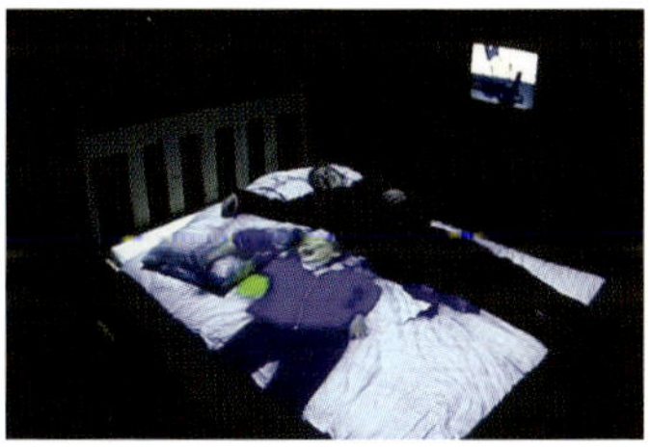

Paul Sermon, *Telematic Dreaming* (1992). First shown in Finland at Kajaani Art and Helsinki Telegalleria.

3. Two excellent DVDs are available:
The Lost World of Mitchell and Kenyon BBC, UK 2004.
Electric Edwardians: The Films of Mitchell & Kenyon BFI, UK 2005

Technology
Rafael Lozano-Hemmer

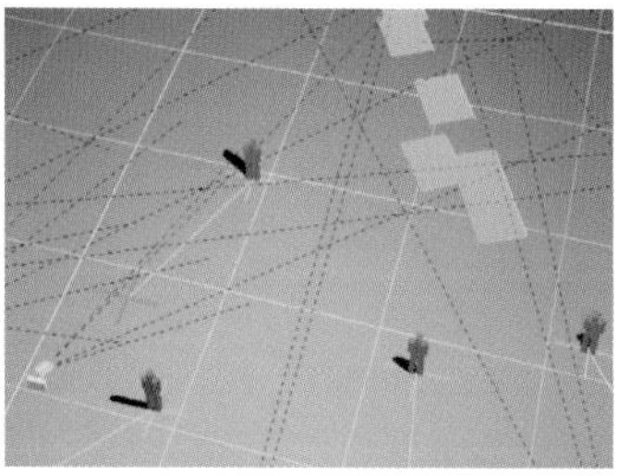
Live 3D view of tracking system

The technology for *Under Scan* was developed and implemented by a production team from Canada, the US, Austria and the UK. There were four key technologies used in the project:

Computer Vision Tracking System
Developed by APR inc. in Canada, a computerised surveillance system detected the presence of everyone in the public space by analysing the feed from a digital camera. The software was programmed in Delphi and C on open computer vision libraries, but was specifically customised for the project with automatic routines that would allow the system to adapt to changing lighting conditions in the public space, to compensate for uneven lighting and to avoid interference from the projections themselves. The system had an extrapolation algorithm so that it could predict where people would be in the near future: the system would automatically point the robotically controlled projectors to the locations where they would be likely intercept the trajectory of pedestrians and then cue a sequence of video for them.

The tracking system was connected to the robotic projectors using DMX, to the media servers using Ethernet (both UDP and TCP/IP), to the camera using a fire wire interface, to an external public monitor via VGA and to the internet for remote maintenance using a second Ethernet port.

Digital Lights
Fourteen DL1 digital lights by High End Systems were used for projecting the portraits. These are video projectors mounted on a robotic pan and tilt platform that can be controlled by DMX. The lights were calibrated so that the control system had knowledge of the precise 3D location and orientation of each of these so it could automatically point them to match the location of people's shadows.

By using projectors on motorised pan-tilt platforms, very large areas could be covered by a small number of projectors, and varying urban layouts could be accommodated.

Custom made Media Servers

Each DL1 was connected to a Mac-mini computer that had the entire database of video portraits in its hard drive. The video server software running in the minis was programmed in Xcode and it allowed the video to be rotated, keystoned, scaled and scrubbed using OpenGL so that the portrait was always oriented in relation to the shadow and with the appropriate geometry corrections. The minis were networked over wireless links or ethernet to the main control room, from where the videos were queued, triggered and controlled. Apple remote desktop was used to manage each Macintosh and robust network error handling was implemented. The server would also automatically gamma correct the videos so that darker portraits could be seen with more detail.

12kW HMI Projector

One PANI BP12 Platin II HMI projector with wide-angle optics was used to generate the shadows, with 120,000 ANSI lumens of power and a coverage area of up to 4,000 square metres. The projector was lifted twenty metres high over the interactive area, often by means of a scissor lift. The projector was masked to avoid spilling light that could distract drivers, hit neighbouring windows or otherwise disrupt the safety of the environment. A DMX controlled douser allowed the system to automatically fade out the projector during the interlude sequence.

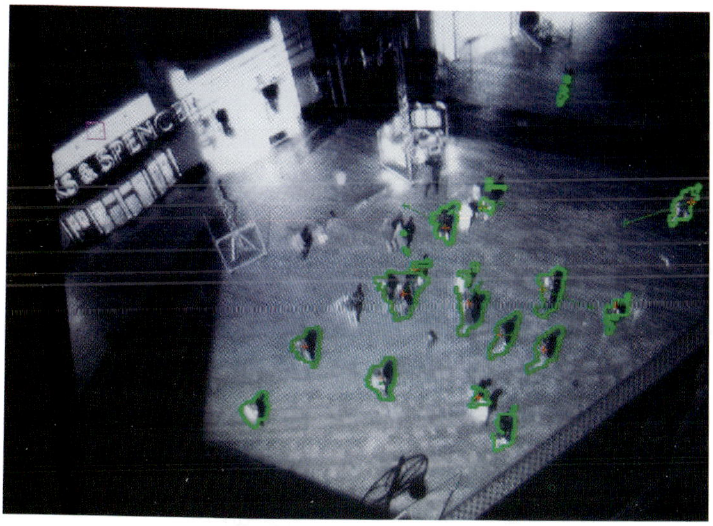

Live camera view of tracking system

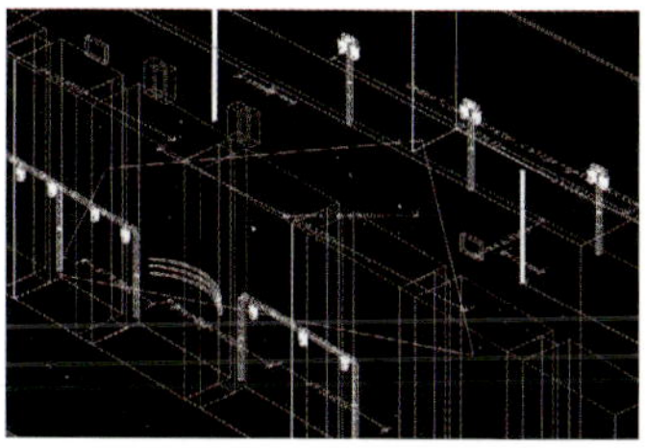

CAD plans for projector placement

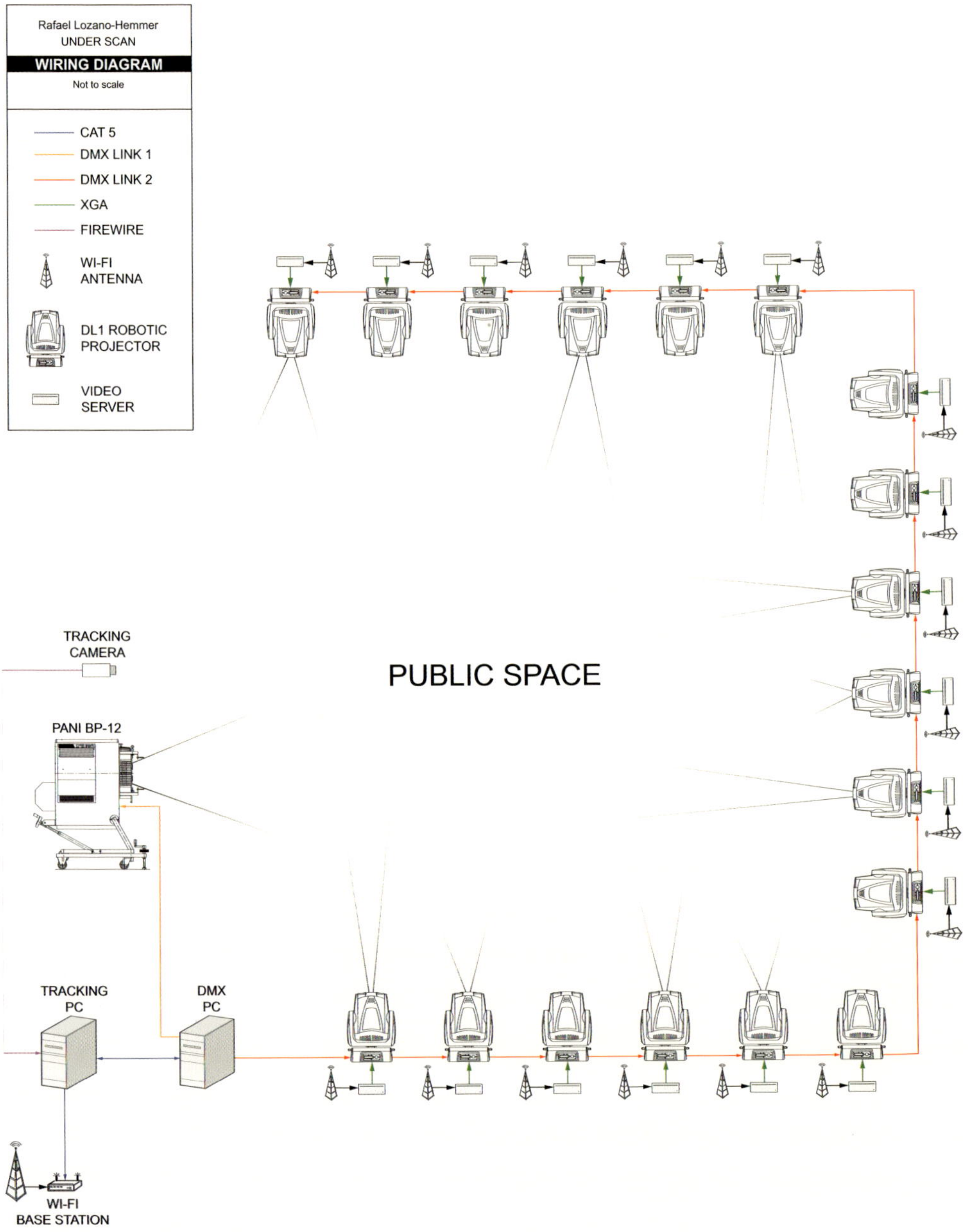

Rafael Lozano-Hemmer
UNDER SCAN
WIRING DIAGRAM
Not to scale
CAT 5
DMX LINK 1
DMX LINK 2
XGA
FIREWIRE
WI-FI ANTENNA
DL1 ROBOTIC PROJECTOR
VIDEO SERVER
TRACKING CAMERA
PANI BP-12
PUBLIC SPACE
TRACKING PC
DMX PC
WI-FI BASE STATION

Commissioning *Under Scan*
David Hill

Following a competitive tendering process *emda* appointed ArtReach (a specialist arts consultant and events company) in November 2004, with a Brief to recruit an appropriate artist(s) and to produce delivery of a "Cultural Quarters' Star Prize" public art commission.

A clear Artist Brief was distilled and articulated and the commission opportunity was advertised internationally through the arts press, curator and artist networks and the internet. The project was subject to European procurement law and as required was advertised through the EU Journal.

Whilst Expressions of Interest were sought, ArtReach took the opportunity to consult with a range of potential stakeholders in each of Derby, Leicester, Lincoln, Northampton and Nottingham. Those consulted included Local Authority officers and Members, representatives of arts organisations, educationalists (including those involved with delivery of higher education visual arts courses) and City/Town Centre Managers.

In January 2005 ninety Expressions of Interest were received from artists all over the world with responses from Asia, North America, Australia, Europe, many parts of the UK and the East Midlands region itself.

A Commissioning Body was established to manage the artist selection, to include representatives from *emda*, ACE EM and each of the five Local Authorities providing a location for the proposed work. Curators and artists were also invited to participate.

Following a thorough initial selection process six artists were short-listed in February 2005 and awarded funding to carry out a period of research and development leading to a detailed Proposal and Tender. As part of this process the short-listed artists were invited to visit the East Midlands in early March to spend a week with ArtReach, visiting the key locations and meeting people in the region.

Short-listed artists were given an opportunity to comment on the full Tender document prior to its finalisation. The Tender deadline was 31 March 2005 and five detailed Proposals were received and then presented, by the artists, to the Commissioning Body.

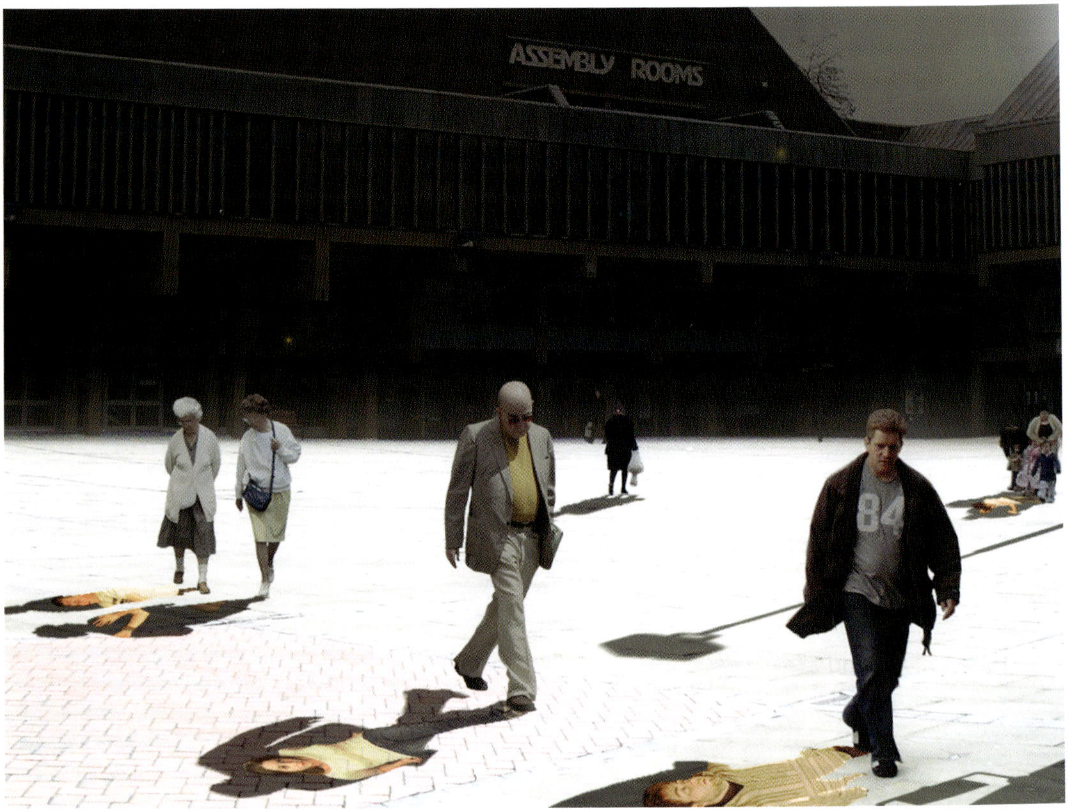

Early concept sketch for the project: Derby

Rafael Lozano-Hemmer's Proposal for *Under Scan* was selected as the concept that most closely fulfilled the Commission Brief, by using an appropriate combination of thought-provoking artwork, interactive engagement and sophisticated technology.

Rafael was appointed to deliver the Commission in April 2006. His team would include two Canadian companies, Antimodular and APR, to provide the necessary specialist expertise to develop and deliver an appropriate video database and a sophisticated computer tracking system.

Production
David Hill and Emma Jones

By June 2006 the production team for *Under Scan* was in place, following a further tender process that led to the appointment of Stage Right Productions from Northampton to take responsibility for equipment management, installation and staging delivery.

The first task for the team was to work with Local Authorities and identify the most appropriate and suitable site in each location. Sites needed to be chosen that would provide large pedestrian space with clear, accessible ground surfaces, and that were in close proximity to areas of cultural redevelopment. Timing also had to be taken into consideration, with particular regard for other activities already programmed into busy city and town centres.

It was agreed that the Commission should be presented for ten nights in each location (encompassing two full weekends) and allowing a set up period of one week. A further three days was allowed at the end of each installation to strike the work. This schedule would allow *Under Scan* to be delivered within the period November 2005 – March 2006, as required by the Brief.

In Derby and Northampton it quickly became clear that the main Market Square areas were the most appropriate locations for the installation of *Under Scan.* In Leicester there was no large-scale pedestrian area available in the St George's Cultural Quarter and it was agreed to focus on the busy Humberstone Gate West pedestrian thoroughfare. The options in Nottingham were reduced as a result of the already contracted refurbishment of Old Market Square. Following site visits and SWOT analysis, Canal Side, adjacent to the Magistrate's Court, became the preferred location in Nottingham. In Lincoln there was considerable enthusiasm to site the work within the University Campus, supporting the new cultural developments taking place on the campus, and enabling the installation to be presented simultaneously with the city's popular, annual Christmas Market.

A schedule for the tour was agreed as follows:
Lincoln: University of Lincoln, November 25 to December 4, 2005
Leicester: Humberstone Gate West, January 12–22, 2006
Northampton: Market Square, February 3–12, 2006
Derby: Market Place, February 24 to March 5, 2006
Nottigham: Canal Side at Castle Wharf, March 16–26, 2006

Following agreement to the framework schedule a detailed Project Delivery Plan was prepared in late June 2006.

Under Scan required:

- A bespoke design for the installation in each location, created to work successfully within the specific architecture and urban space that had been chosen.
- An assessment of infrastructure needs and permission requirements to facilitate the installation in each location.
- The creation of a database of 1,000 video portraits of local people. The intention was to film 200 people from each of the five locations.
- The purchase and preparation of specialist equipment required to deliver the work.
- Marketing and promotion to disseminate the project to arts communities and the wider public, and to ensure the potential legacy of *Under Scan* could be maximised.
- A detailed installation plan.

Installation design

An individual design was created for each location by Rafael Lozano-Hemmer and the *Under Scan* production team using 3D simulation software. The final design was then used as a template to facilitate work with the Local Authorities, relevant public bodies and local agencies/business to gain licenses and permissions required for the installation to be built and operated in public space.

Infrastructure needs and permissions

Each location brought its own challenges. Early in the process it was determined that as much as possible *Under Scan* should be self-contained, with specially constructed equipment towers to site the video projectors at the optimum height and spacing, without relying on suitable sites within the external structure of adjacent buildings. Similarly the requirement for the single, large PANI projector was such that introducing a temporary scissor lift to the space was often a more appropriate solution than trying to mount the projector on the roof of a surrounding building.

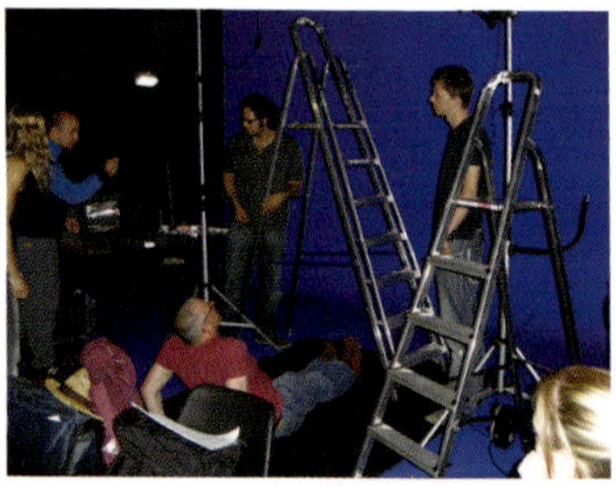

Video portraiture

The production of *Under Scan* required the creation of a database of video portraits to be filmed across the East Midlands. This approach to engaging the public within the creative process was fundamental to Lozano-Hemmer's vision, with the content of the installation to be centred on self-representation by local people. Their movements and gestures would provide the unique visual material for *Under Scan.*

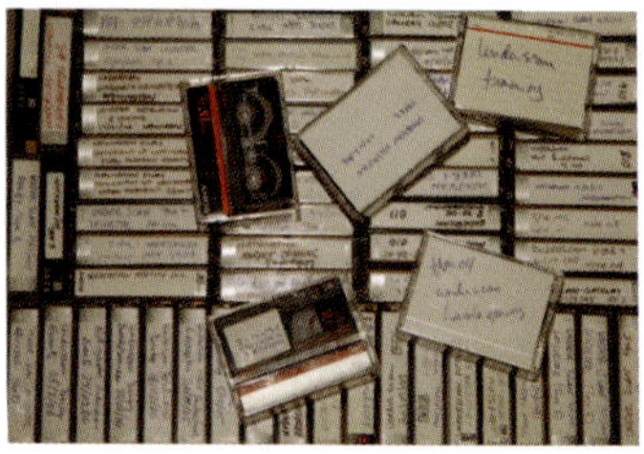

Potential regional camera operators were identified via the East Midland's network of creative capillaries with five personnel (a representative from each city in which the installation would eventually be realised) employed and trained by Lozano-Hemmer for the commission.

A compact touring rig was devised, enabling the portraits to be shot from an aerial perspective of 2.5 metres as members of the public lay beneath the suspended camera and lights. This mobile film studio ensured optimum lighting conditions including temperature and intensity. Final measurements for the rig's structure were agreed and recorded to ensure accurate replication by all five crews to create visual consistency.

Arrangements were made to take the mobile film studio to arts venues, community centres and other public spaces in Derby, Lincoln, Leicester, Northampton and Nottingham. People were invited to take part from the local network of community organisations, but at each venue the public also "discovered," unexpectedly, the filming opportunity. It was necessary for all participants to be sixteen years old or above in order to legally consent to the use of their image. Every individual signed a release form, permitting their image to be edited and used in *Under Scan.*

Each individual had full responsibility for their own portraiture and content—the filming was totally open to be used as they wished, without censorship. A monitor was placed on the ground directly beside the participant in which they could see themselves and therefore self-direct. It was not possible for individuals to view their portraits once they had been filmed, so there was some technical directorial input from the camera operator.

The creation of the *Under Scan* portraiture database was a key part of the creative process which handed over authorship of the portraits to local camera operators and self elected members of the public. Filming commenced in July 2005 and was completed by October 2005. A limited edition of 1000 *Under Scan* prints was created featuring all the people who were filmed. These were distributed to each participant during the installation as a gift.

Equipment purchase and preparation

The PANI projector and fourteen DL1 video projectors were imported from Austria and the US. The equipment was purchased in time for tests to be undertaken to ensure the equipment could perform in the way required to deliver the installation. Special casing was constructed in order to protect the equipment from whatever weather conditions an English winter might impose.

Marketing and promotion

Before promoting wide public awareness of the forthcoming installation it was essential to disseminate information to artists, curators, students, and interested organisations and business. In October 2005 Rafael Lozano-Hemmer delivered a free public lecture in each city that would subsequently show *Under Scan.* The lectures were open to anyone interested in his work or public art in general. The artist's insight into producing highly complex artwork in public spaces offered an important opportunity for the arts community and wider audiences to engage in debate about contemporary ideas the role of visual art in cities and communities.

The journey of the project was well documented in local and regional press. Television, radio and the press covered the video portraiture process, installation planning, the lecture tour and then the work itself. The press interest developed on a national and international scale once *Under Scan* was installed. Awareness of *Under Scan* was promoted using flyers, small posters, large-scale bus shelter posters and banners. Primarily interest was developed through press and word of mouth.

Installation of *Under Scan*

Each presentation of *Under Scan* involved an installation period of five days. In Lincoln, the first location for the work, this period was extended to ten days. The process commenced with Stage Right Productions delivering equipment and rigging infrastructure. The computer control room was assembled whilst equipment was safely rigged, powered and calibrated. ArtReach attended to issues such as ensuring that light pollution from nearby shops, buildings and streetlights was reduced as much as possible. Preparations were also made for a launch event in each location. The artist and his team arrived on the second day of installation to programme the control systems and ensure that the computer tracking system enabled video portraits to be placed in the path of pedestrians crossing the space. The light projector, at an elevation of over 20 metres, was focused to create the required "interactive space" within which the portraits would appear.

During the presentation of *Under Scan*, there was an opportunity for practicing artists to meet and work with Lozano-Hemmer, ensuring that the techniques used in *Under Scan* could be replicated or developed in other artwork within a variety of contexts.

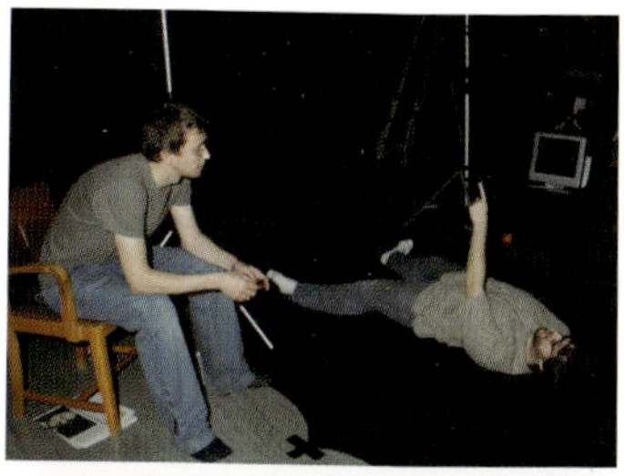
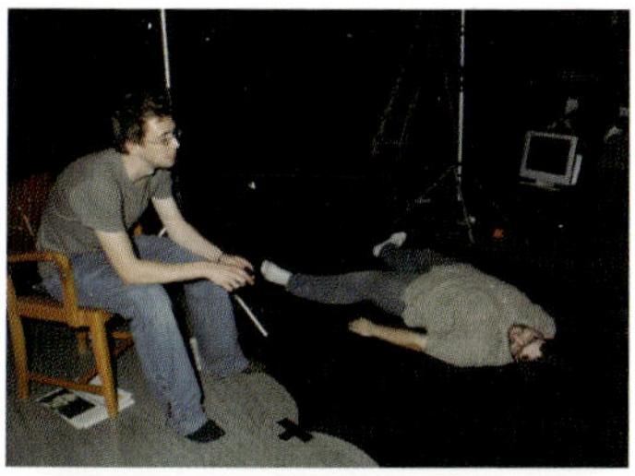
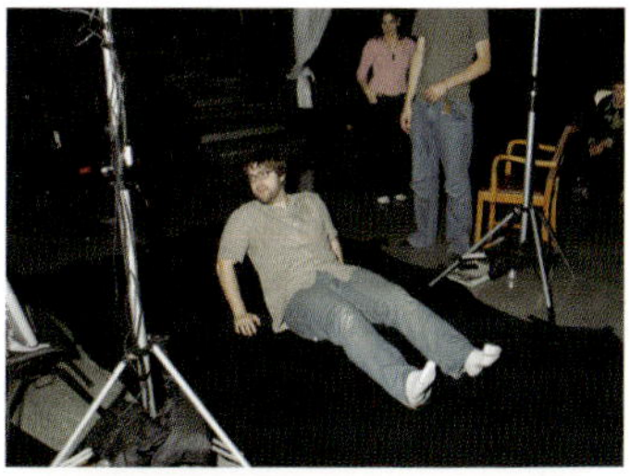
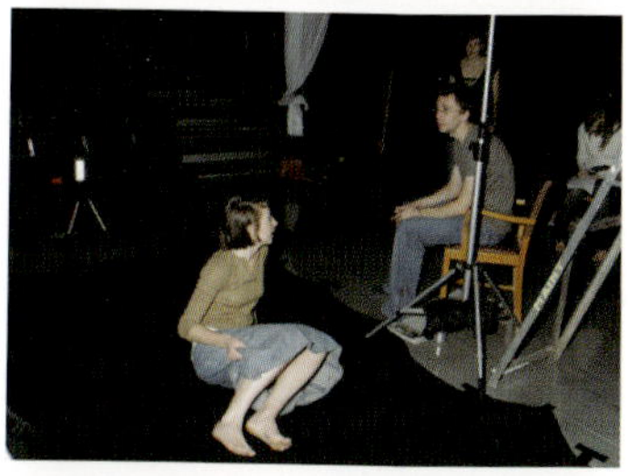
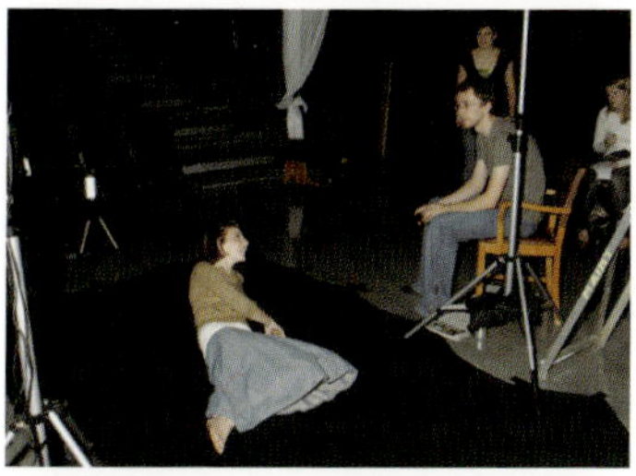
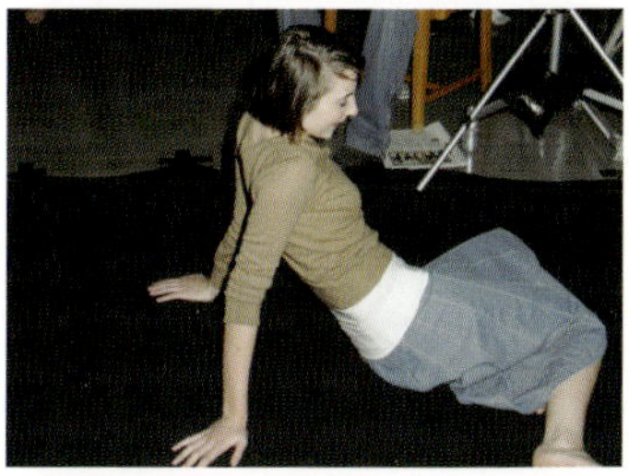
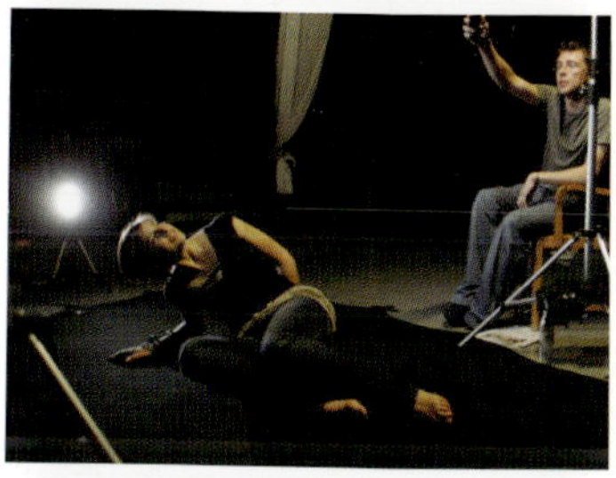
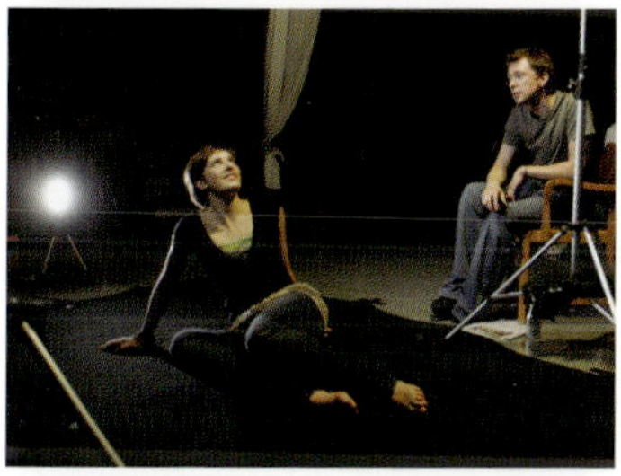
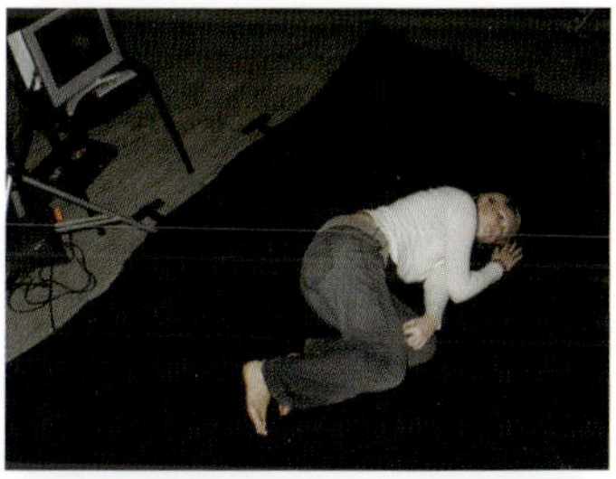
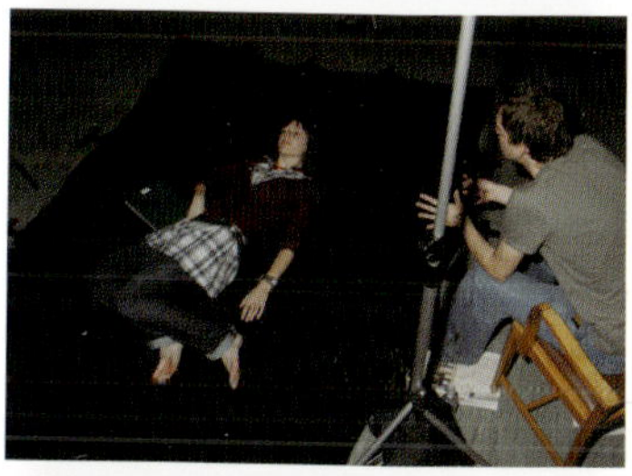
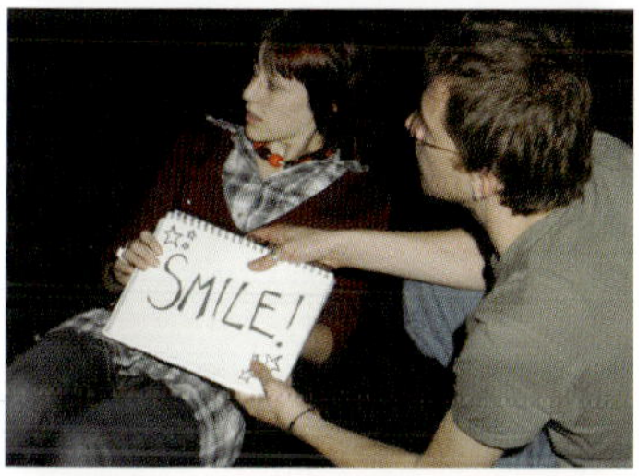
SMILE!
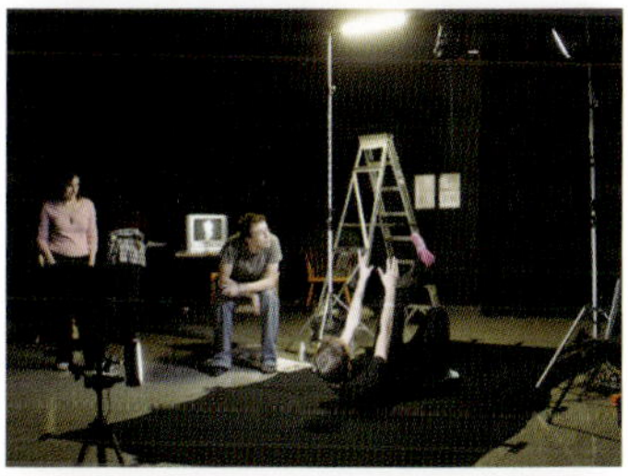
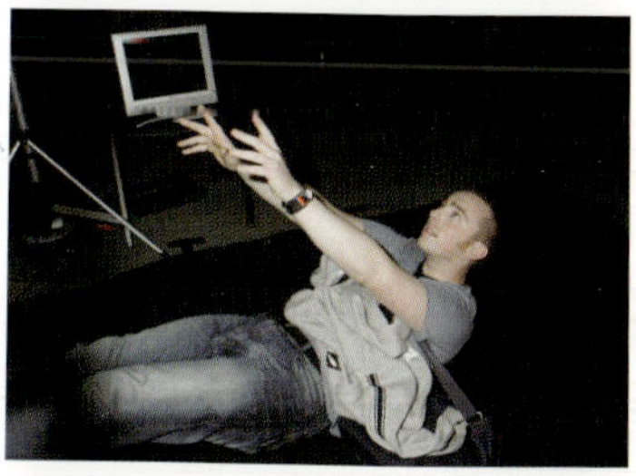
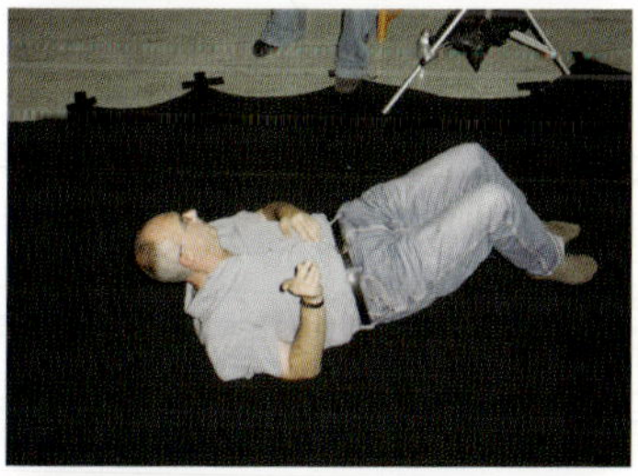
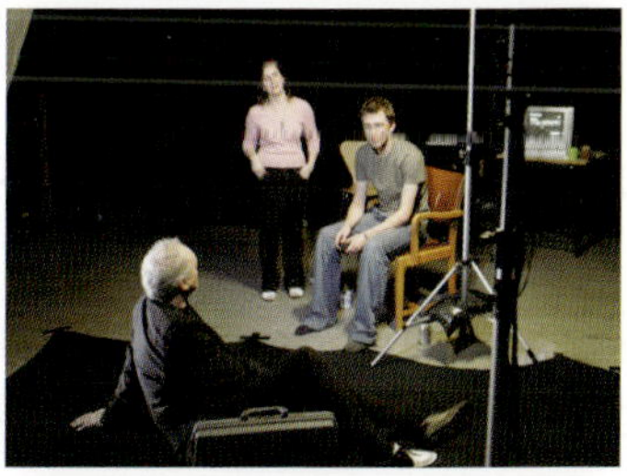
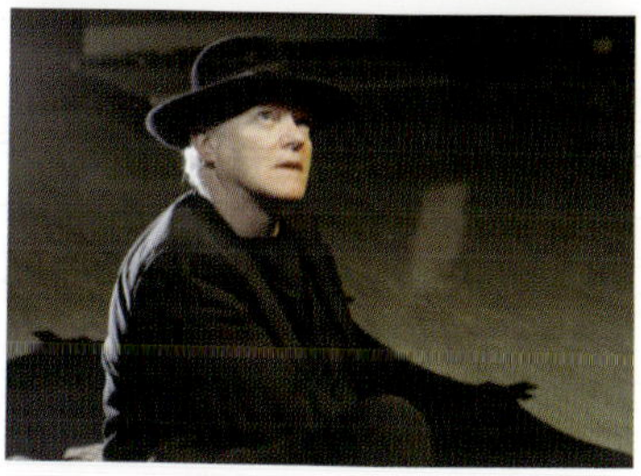
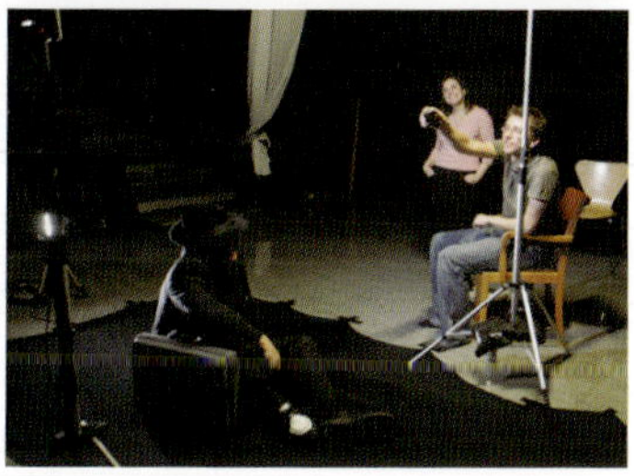
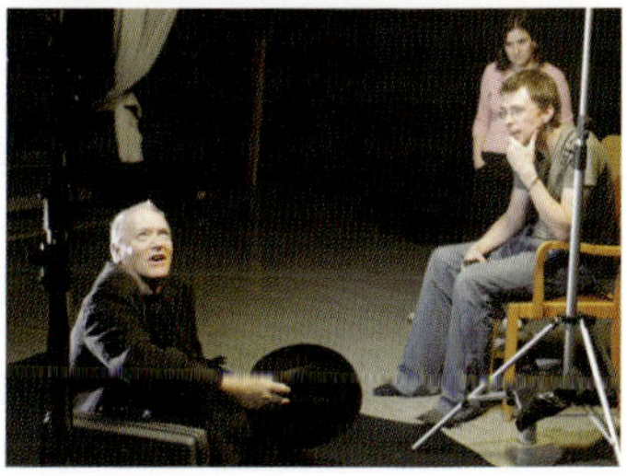

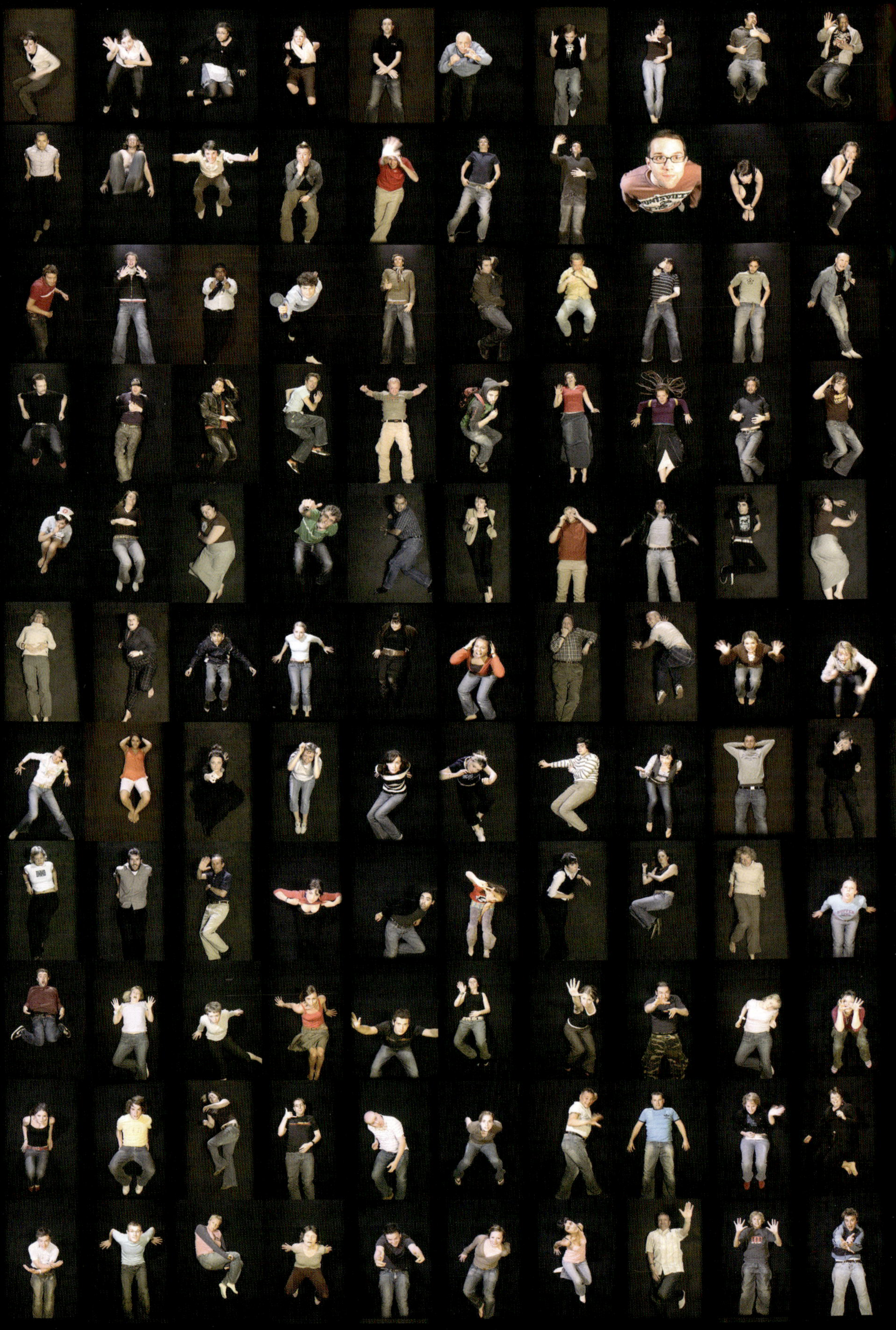

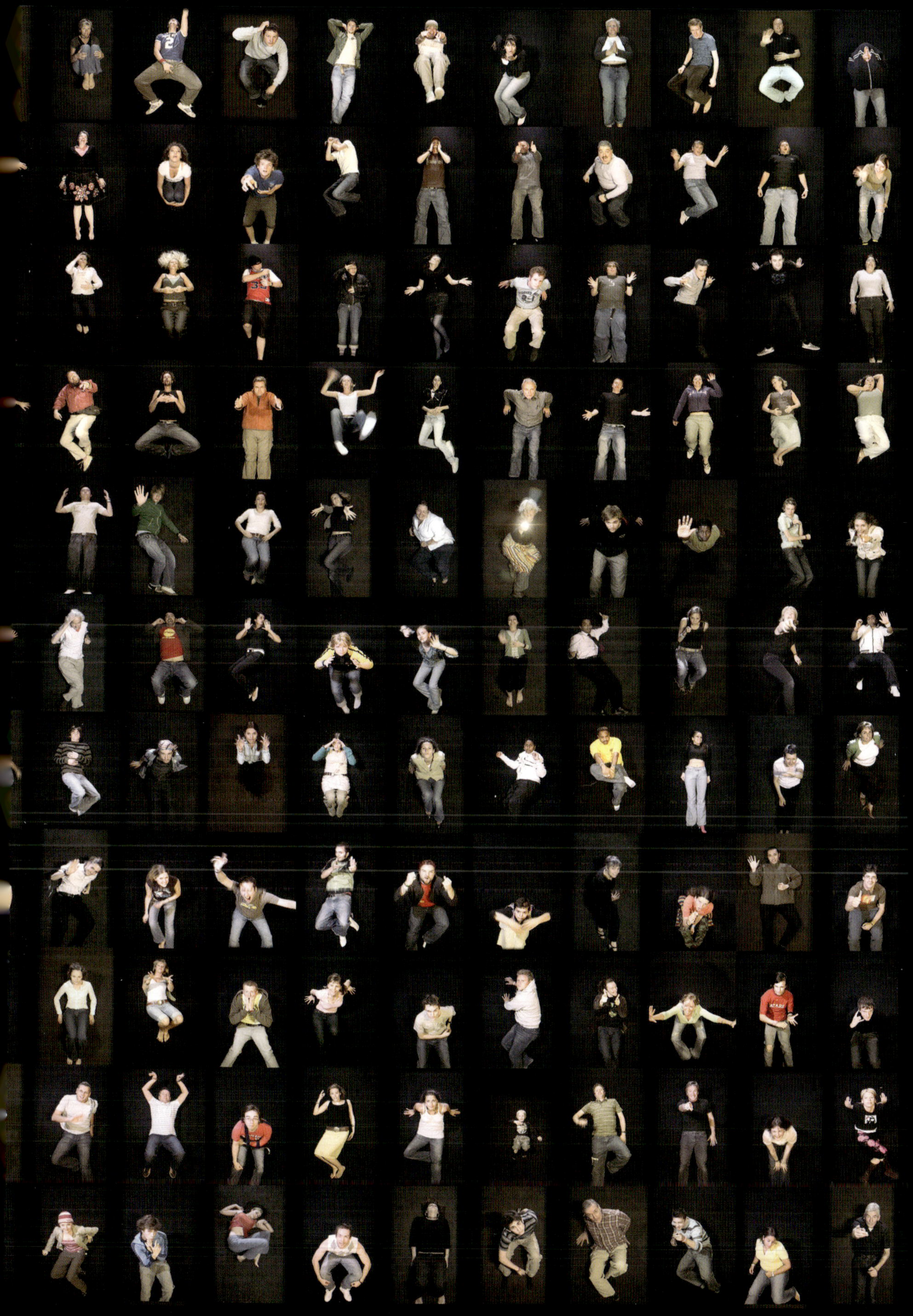

Interview with Rafael Lozano-Hemmer
Nadja Mounajjed

Nadja Mounajjed: Did *Under Scan* turn out as you expected? Did you get the interaction you were aiming for?

Rafael Lozano-Hemmer: The only thing that can be predicted about interaction in public space is that there will always be a very wide range of behaviours: some people spent half an hour interacting with the installation, some 10 seconds; some would come in big groups and reveal portraits together, others would just walk alone and have a quiet experience; some found it fun, while others found it frightening or perverse. We had all sorts of participants in the installation, from vintage punk-rockers to members of the "Army of Christ,"—even though it sounds cliché, we had people of all ages, classes and ethnic groups. In addition, the piece changed a lot depending on the city, the time of night, the day of the week, and so on. Typically we would see a lot of people come during the weekends and this made the environment more festive; during weekdays it would be calmer and often people would run into the installation as they went home from the office or had to go across town to do some shopping or go to the pub.

It often took people a while to figure out that the portraits were interactive. But it was preferable in my opinion to have them discover this interaction rather than having someone tell them what to do. I think some people were expecting that the portraits would appear in their shadow wherever they were standing. But I conceived the project specifically so that people had to promenade in the space and walk toward the portraits, which would appear in their path, rather than the portraits chasing after the public. I am happy with this decision even if the other way may have been easier to understand or more fun.

NM: How were the sites chosen? In Lincoln I talked to people who wondered why it was located outside the city centre.

RLH: The site had to be a large area with many pedestrians and without car traffic; for projection, we needed the ground to be even and with a light-coloured tone. Finally, the commission's aim was to highlight the new cultural quarters of cities in the East Midlands so that's where we looked for locations. In Lincoln the site at the University was chosen mostly because all the other large public spaces had a very dark cobblestone, which is an extremely difficult surface to

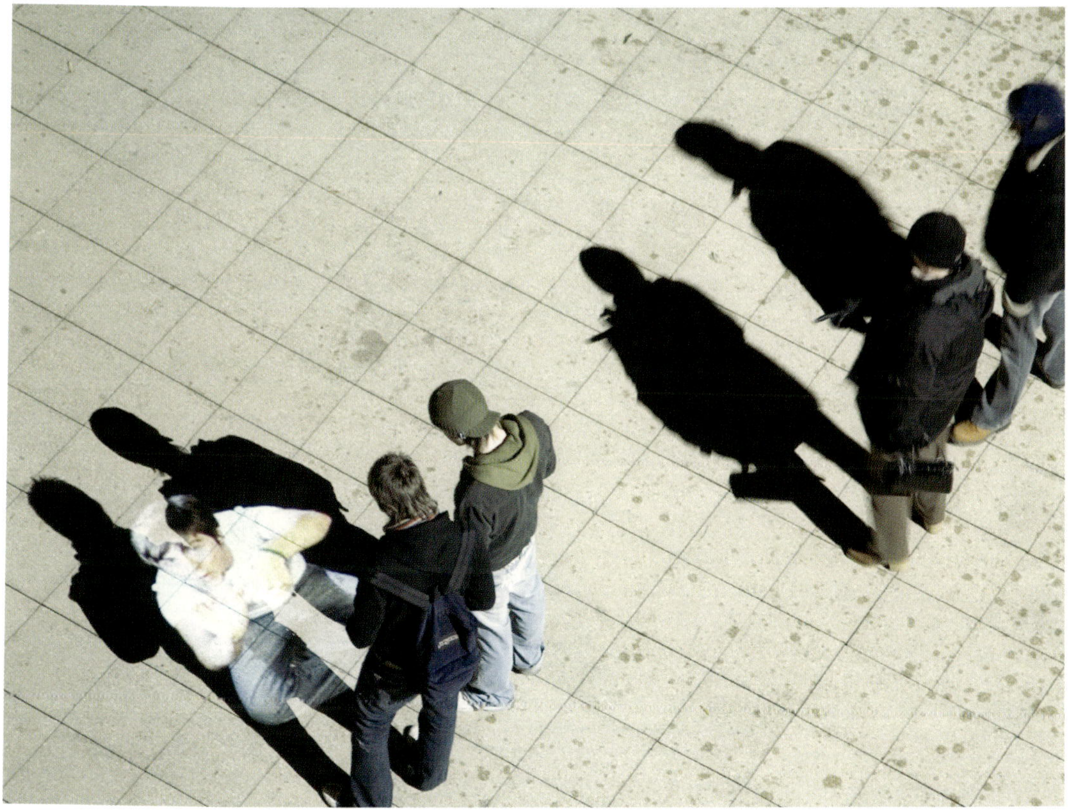

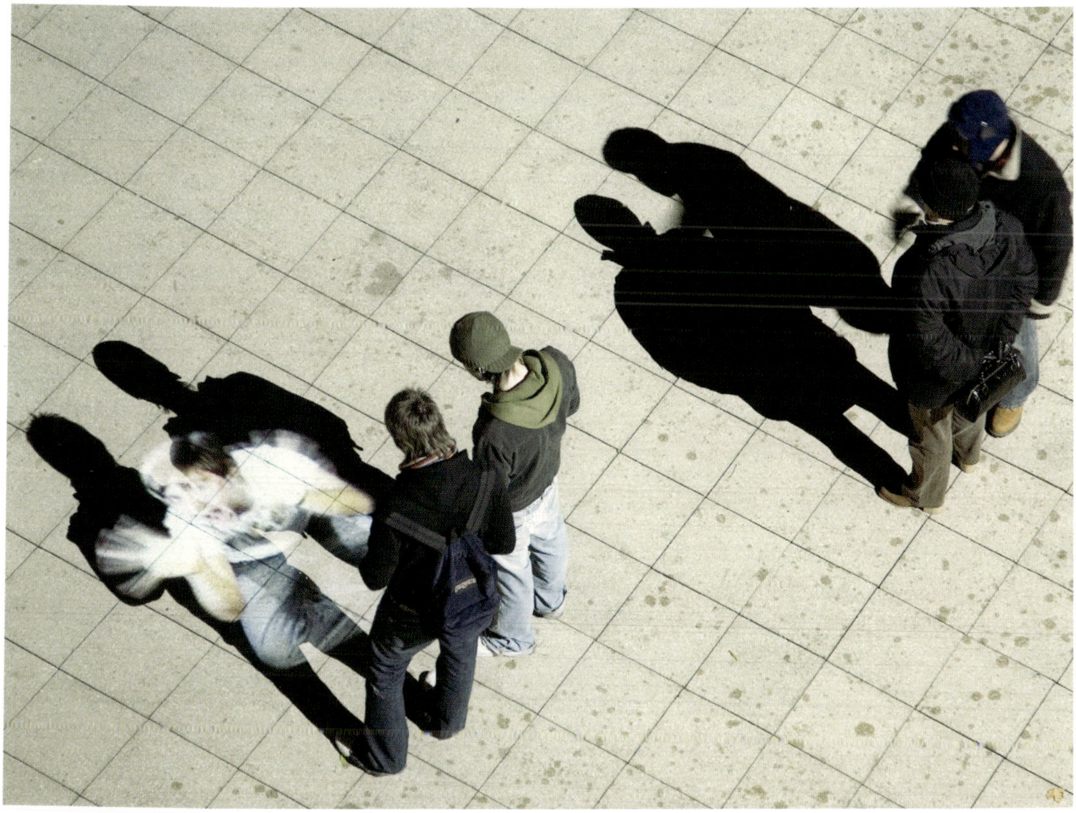

project on. In Nottingham the perfect site would have been Old Market Square but it was being renovated during our tour so the alternative Canal Side site was quite picturesque but a bit out of the way.

NM: Did the site affect the feedback you got from participants?

RLH: Sure. I think people enjoyed the project more when they just encountered it in their normal activities in town, as a surprise. If the site was further away then often people would go there expecting some kind of son-et-lumière show or a fireworks display, and they would be disappointed because *Under Scan* was not a cathartic spectacle. I like to think of my work as being closer to landscaping in a park, or to a public fountain, than to a pre-programmed show.

NM: In my interviews I found that many people actually preferred the interlude light animation shown every 7 minutes rather than interacting with portraits. In almost every interview I heard "I liked when the lights shut down and the grids show on the ground." Do you have an explanation for this?

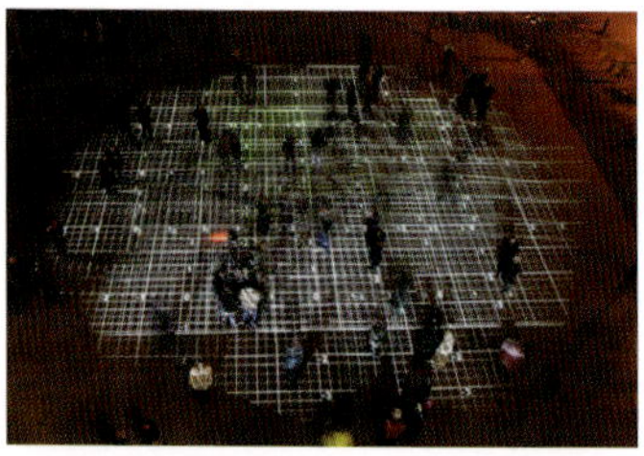

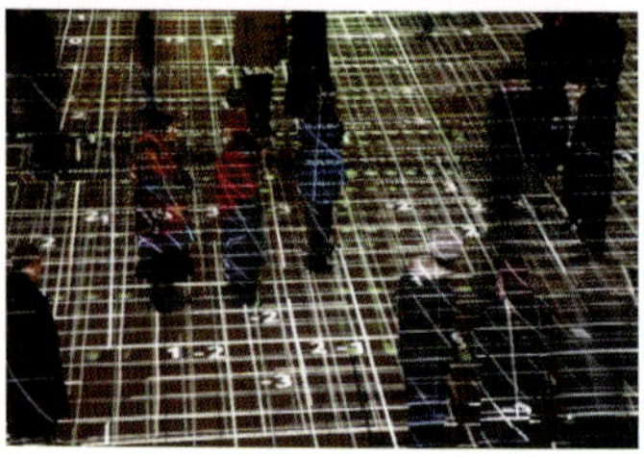

The interlude lighting sequence revealed the tracking mechanism every 7 minutes.

RLH: Yes, that was a really big surprise for me! Originally I expected the exact opposite: I thought the interlude was going to be this scary moment when all of the tracking mechanisms would be revealed, creating an Orwellian environment that would make people aware that they were being scanned with predatorial technology. I wanted something that would break the game of representation, like in a Brecht play when all the actors stop suddenly and say "wait, this is only a play" and thus make people aware of themselves, of the theatre, of the whole artificiality of the construct. Instead, every time the grids came out people laughed and ran and often danced.

I think this happened because interacting with the portraits turned out to be quite an eerie experience, — where someone you don't know was in your shadow making eye contact and maybe sending you kisses or waving or trying to tell you something or frowning at you. The portraits had a lot of power, they had agency, and they could be quite invasive. But during the interlude people were relieved from that gaze, they instead related to one another, to a more familiar situation. This is one of the things that I love about developing this kind of artwork: the piece is really out of my control and I can't predict how people will end up experiencing it.

NM: In *Under Scan,* you used the video-portrait as a visual stimulus to produce interaction. Can you tell us a bit more on how the idea came about?

RLH: In 2001 I did a project called *Body Movies* where people could reveal still, photographic portraits within their shadow projected on a wall. The portraits were "every day"

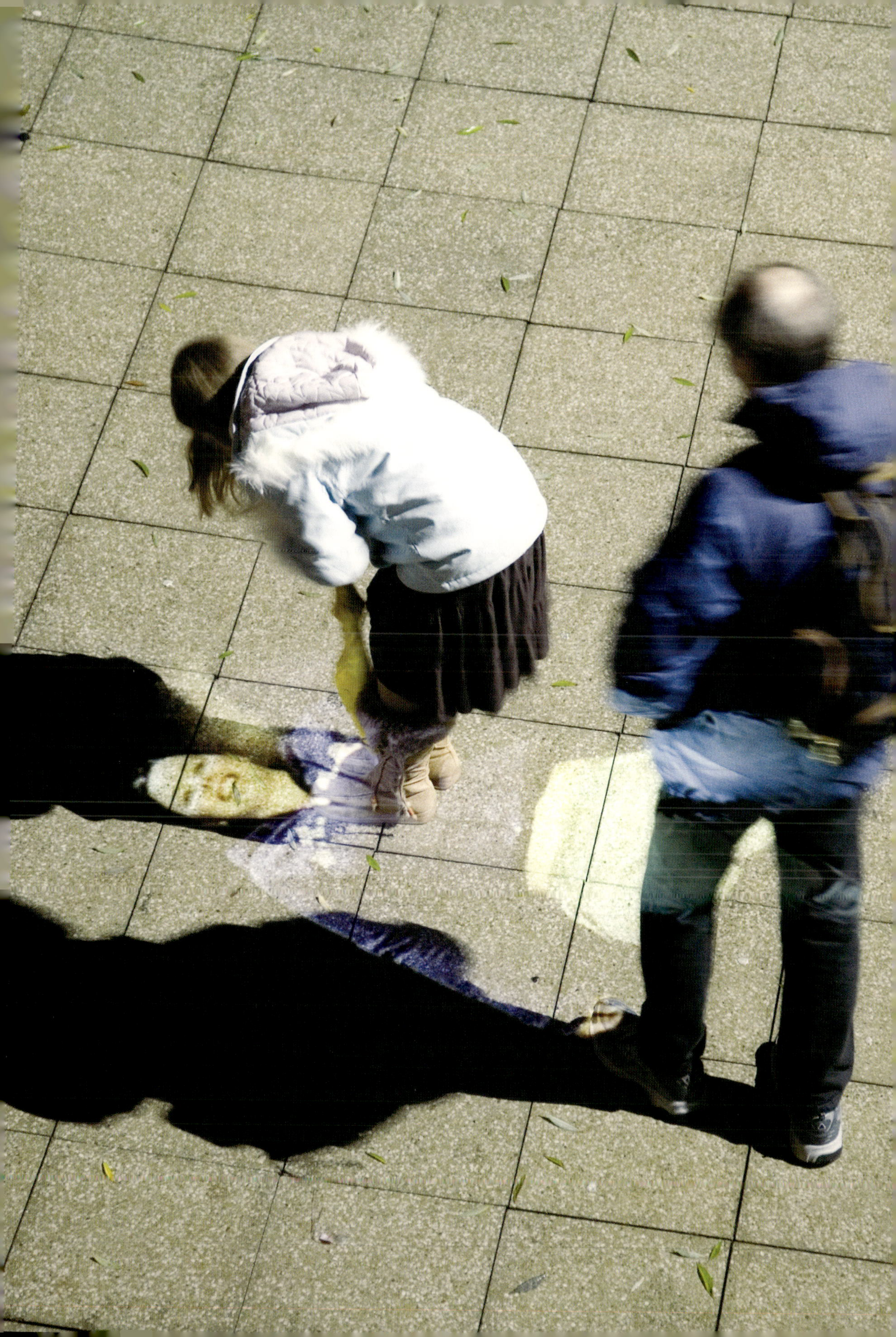

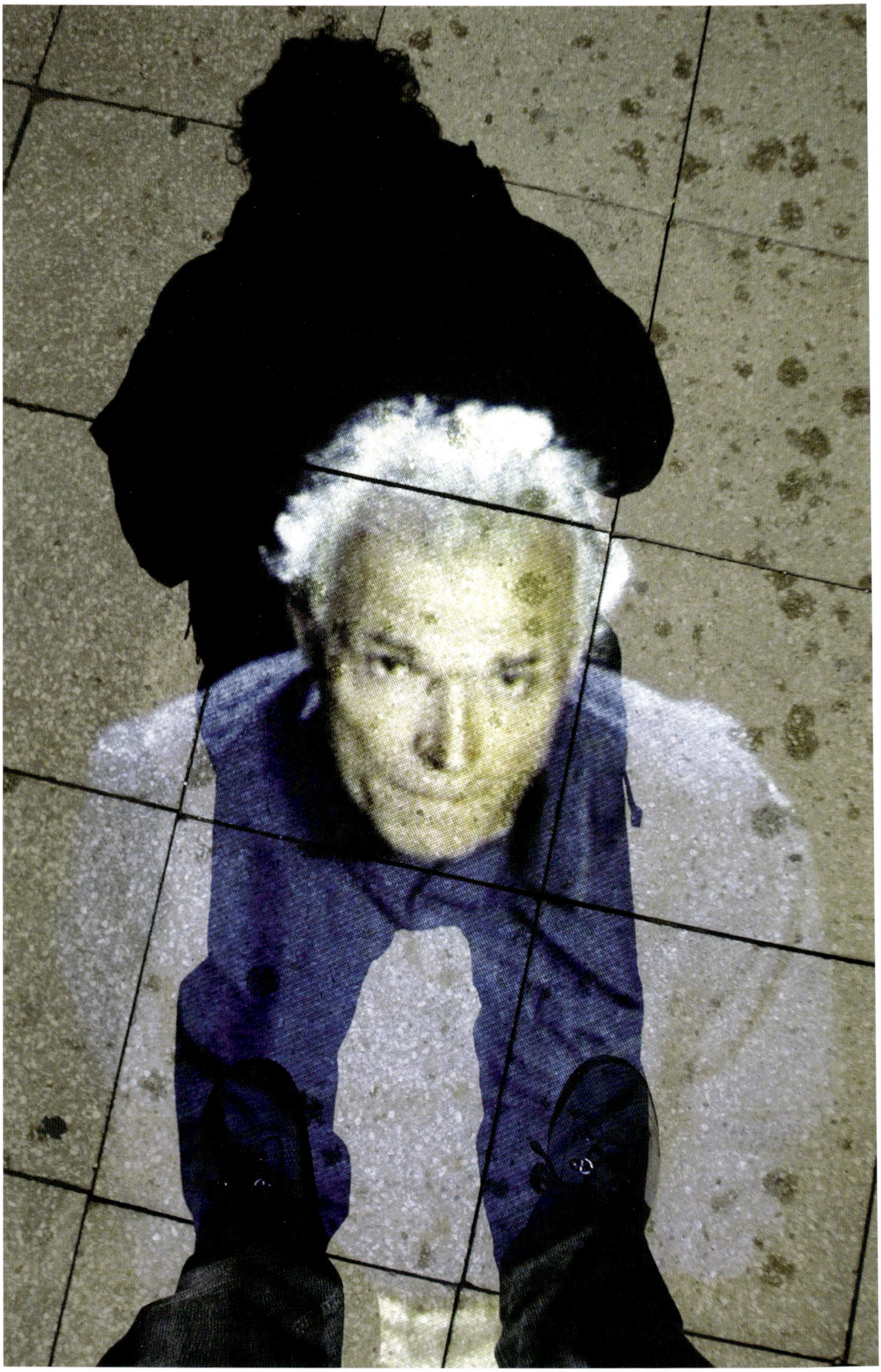

people taken on the streets by a team of photographers. The installation was very successful because passers-by would basically "animate" the stills by moving around and gesticulating. But I felt that the portraits did not have agency, they could not look back and be active. So *Under Scan* is an attempt to make the interactive experience more bi-directional. The people portrayed in *Under Scan* knew exactly what the project was about and they were free to do anything they wanted to self-represent as long as at one point they made eye contact with the camera. Portraiture is a direct way of acting out identity. For me it is crucial to refer to it as "acting," because self-representation done in a conscious way can be very theatrical and unnatural. I was interested in phantasmagorias, or ghost-like presences that would react to people in an intimate way.

NM: Why did you not use sound?

RLH: There have been some great interactive portraits by Luc Courchesne, Lynn Hershman, Tony Dove, Sharon Grace and others that talk back to you. One problem is that if portraits can talk it is reasonable to expect them to listen and understand you, and this level of simulation is not what I am good at. Plus, for *Under Scan*, playback would have been a problem because what would work is for the sound to originate at the projection itself and technologically this was not easy to solve. In art history, except for the examples I just mentioned, portraits seldom talk. So in this case they didn't either. This added a certain distance, highlighting the ghost-like qualities of the project, the fact that this piece is in a way about loneliness. When people were portrayed you got this sense of the desire to communicate: some were doing sign language, others pulled out little cards with writing on them, others are speaking very slowly so that you can read their lips, and I like that, it is as though they are trying to bridge the distance that the piece creates. Of course this failure to communicate was often intensely poetic.

NM: What I find particularly interesting in your work is the way you approach the interface. It seems to me that there is an attempt in your work to look at the interface beyond its technical dimension and more into the conceptual level, can you tell me more about this?

RLH: The interface is central to interactive art because it is the platform for participation. I don't like to think of the interface as a window between two worlds—the view of it as inputs and outputs between the virtual and the real—but rather as a place where disparate realities co-exist and often relate. I tend to prefer intuitive or self-evident interfaces that just disappear and don't need too much explanation, like a shadow. This adds theatricality to the pieces because already people have a sophisticated vocabulary of what can be done with a shadow. At the same time, I like to always have a Brechtian

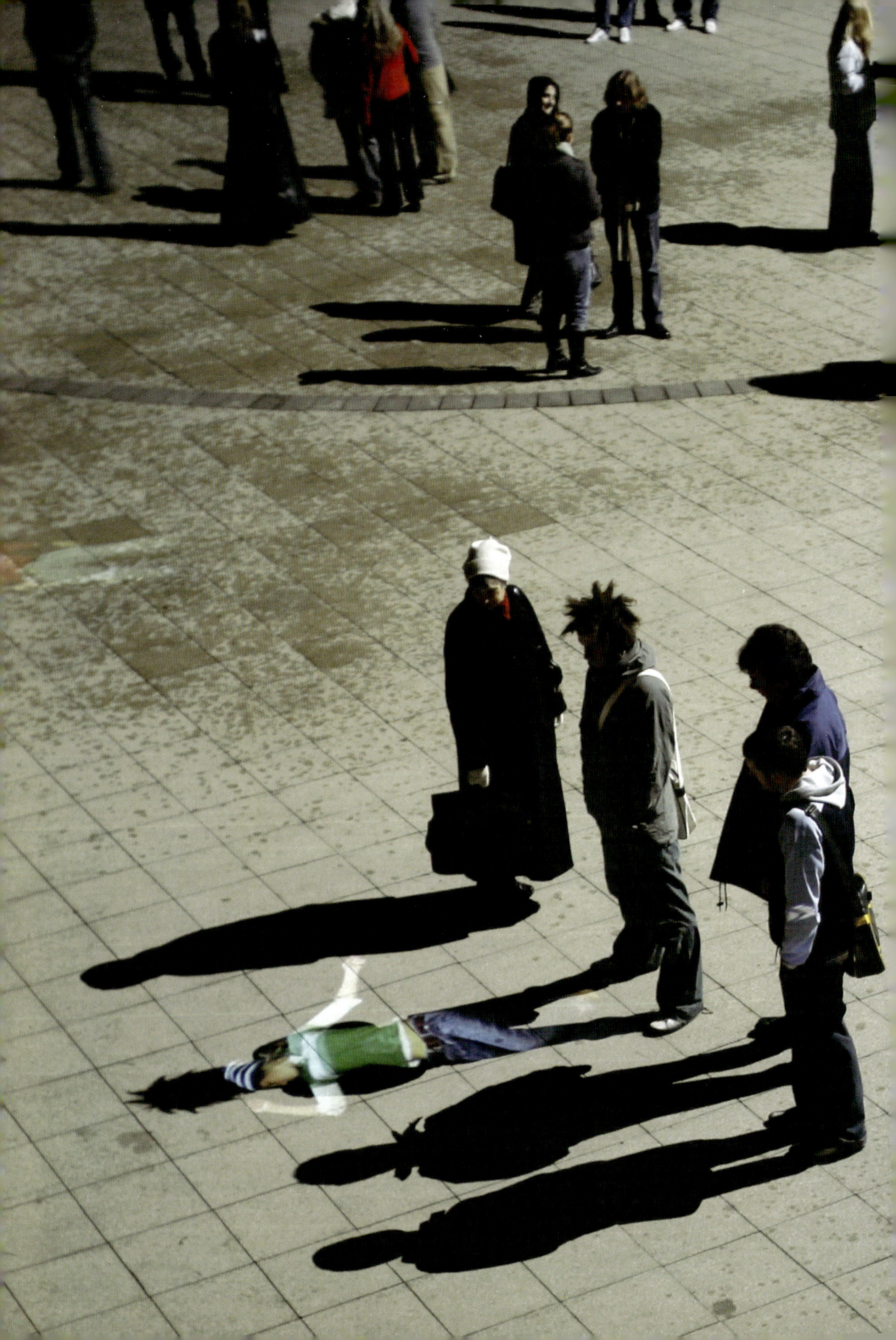

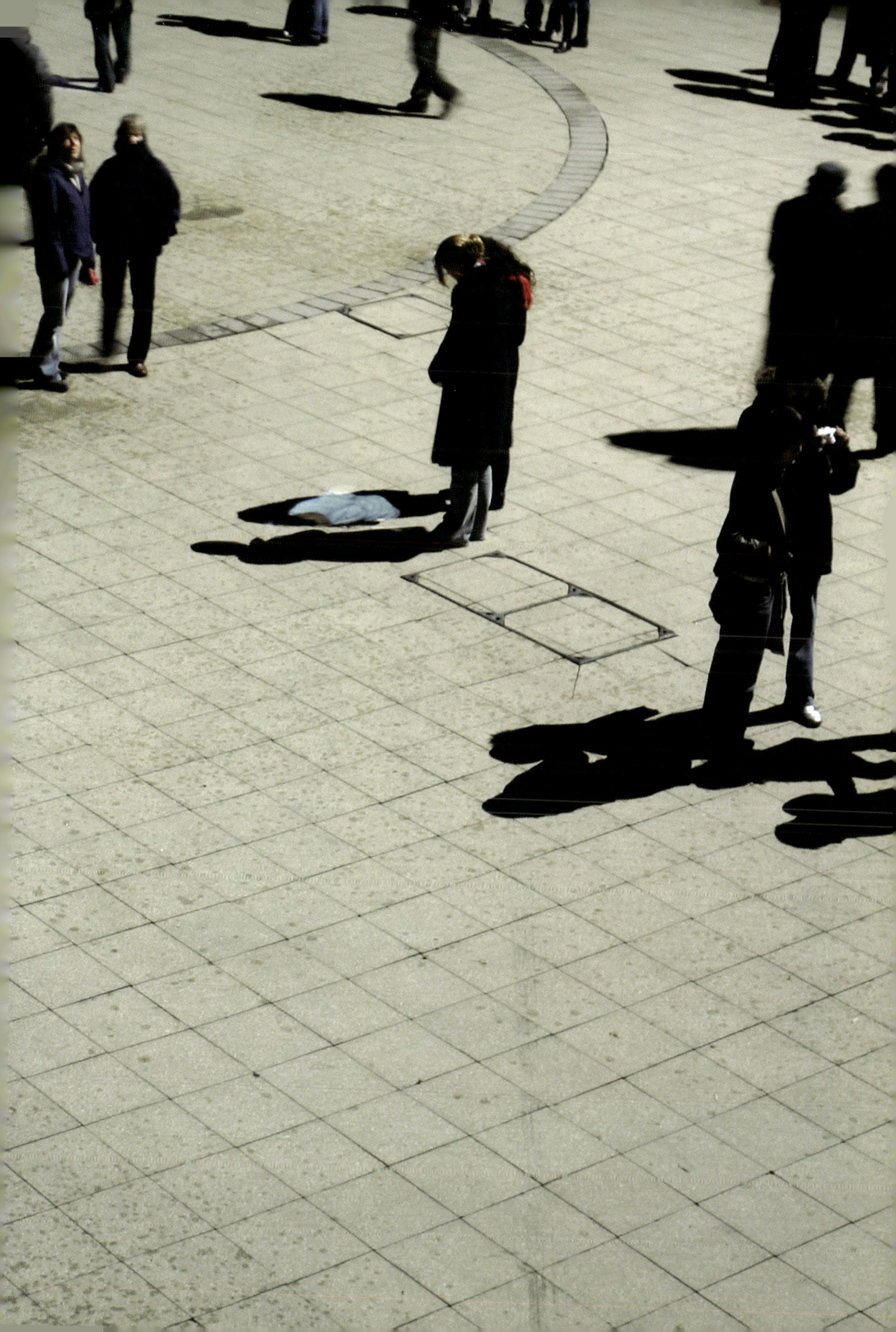

moment where the simulations stop and people are asked to confront the mechanism for the deceit,—the periodic "interlude sequence" in the case of *Under Scan*.

NM: Is it fair to say that *Under Scan* is an elitist work? Some people found it to be too complicated technically and others felt that the public information panels with historical references were too dense. Do people need to be familiar with Plato to fully engage in the work?

RLH: Reading Plato is absolutely not essential for the work. I saw 5 year-olds enjoying the piece and that makes me happy because to me an artwork should have multiple entry points: it should be able to appeal on different levels to different people. My decision to state philosophical and artistic precedents is because I like to connect the piece to debates and experiments that have been going on for ages. I don't like to emphasise that the work is "new" but rather the idea of ongoing research. If people don't care about research that's fine with me too, and I believe the work can engage on other levels.

NM: I also felt children were amongst the most engaged participants, they just go there and they experiment with it instinctively.

RLH: Exactly! Children have fewer reservations in a social context. As we get older we are taught to maintain a physical and psychological space around people: if I am too close to you, you will be uncomfortable because you want your "living space": people go out of their way to maintain that *lebensraum*. *Under Scan* challenges this concept of *lebensraum* because you are over the person in the video portrait and that is quite charged politically, socially and sexually. So this makes adults feel very uncomfortable. Children don't have that to the same extent. They are like: "oh, there is somebody. I am going up to them!"

NM: In your work, is there a particular perception or representation of the body you are trying to explore?

RLH: I am interested in the body as a performance,—as a process of becoming, of change—and less interested in physiognomy, anatomy, forensics or physical ergonomics. I have worked a lot with choreographers and dancers and I am sensitive to the idea that a body is always out of balance, always in motion, even when it is static. When people uncover a portrait they align themselves to it and there is a certain puppetry that ensues, an embodiment of the representation. But this embodiment is in a dynamic equilibrium, where the actors are suspended in an artificial dependency. If people don't use their body to match the representations, these disappear.

NM: Does that also go further to question the relationship with architecture and the environment?

RLH: That is different. I have a cursory interest in architecture, especially when it involves utilitarian issues of permanence, symbolism or style. But if architecture is understood more widely as comprising the architecture of social relations, of surveillance, of fleeting exceptions, then count me in. I have often said that my work is not "site-specific" but rather "relationship-specific." Contrary to many artists working in public space I am not trying to understand or criticise the underlying political, aesthetic or historical structures of a specific building, but rather I am seeking to explore the temporary micro-politics of relationships that emerge in an environment that dissimulates being something other than itself. That is why most of my pieces tour. I always look forward to seeing how the same platform will behave in a new architectural context.

NM: What is the potential for relationships between physical architecture and the virtual dimension?

RLH: I think every architect working today considers electronic media to be as fundamental and as inevitable as, say, an elevator. The impact that elevators had on architecture is evident, but what is or will be the impact of media? Hopefully not the so-called "intelligent buildings" that have been designed since the seventies! When architects speak of intelligent buildings they mean using climate control subsystems that save energy, or fuzzy logic algorithms for the efficient dispatch of elevators, or surveillance technologies that track occupants, and so on. As artist Emilio López-Galiacho noted, this intelligence is always towards the inside of the building and deployed in order to optimise worker output. My hope is that we can see what media theorist Derrick de Kerckhove calls "connective intelligence" and can ask ourselves how a building can be connected to the outside, to people, to other buildings, to other stories. Clearly, at any given point disparate realities coexist and I think there are some fascinating architects and artists who are working in interfacing these. The field of architecture is evolving into understanding itself as a processor of all these different connections.

NM: One final question: You previously talked a lot in your work about memory. Was memory present in *Under Scan* in particular?

RLH: Yes! Many years ago I read Francis Yates' "The Art of Memory" and really got into Giulio Camillo, Giordano Bruno, and the idea of memory as a place. But *Under Scan* was specifically not mnemonic: I decided that the portraits should be able to appear anywhere within the public space and in a way that was not repeatable. A video portrait captured a sequence in time, which in fact became a memory in our database; this memory was activated by passers-by who

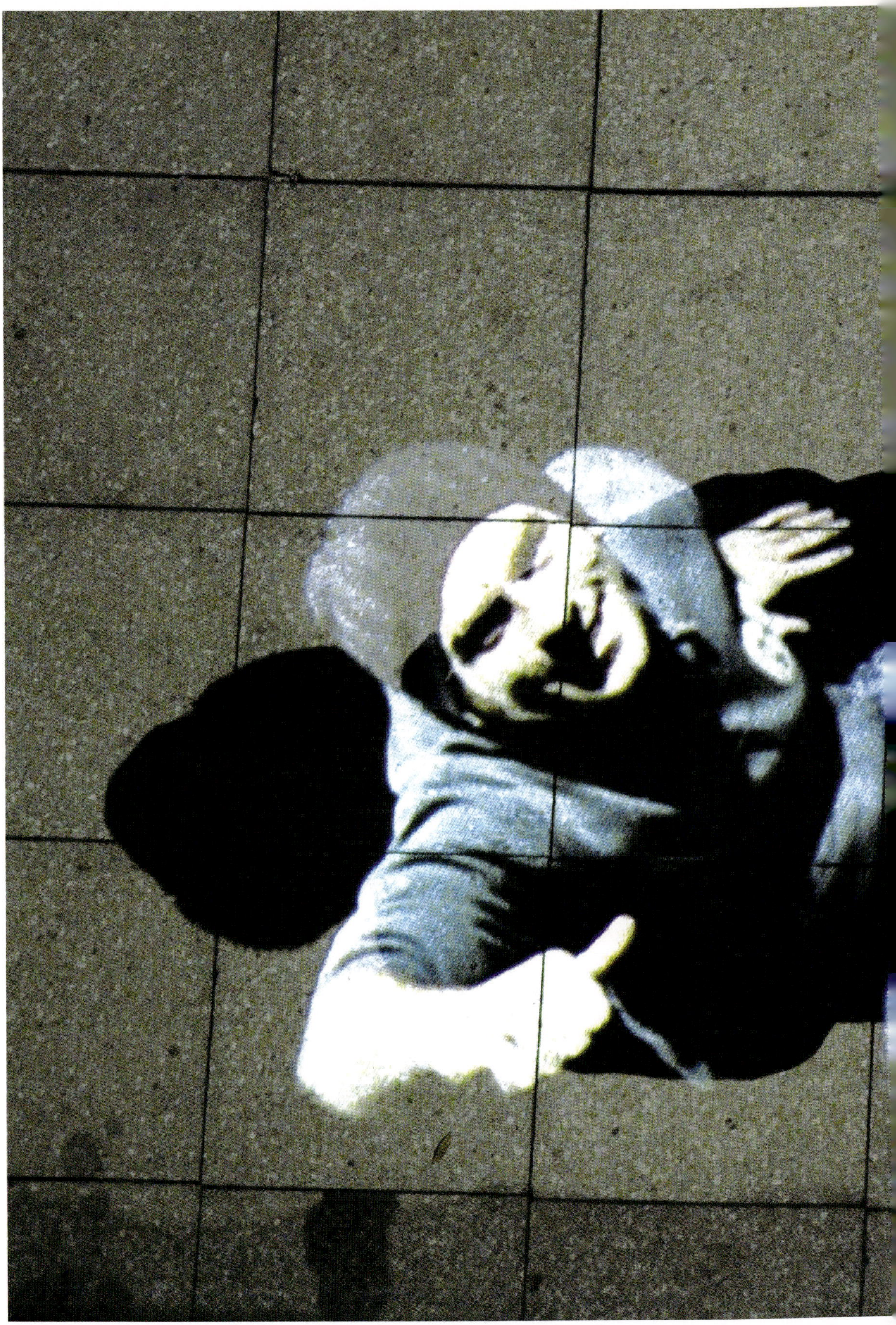

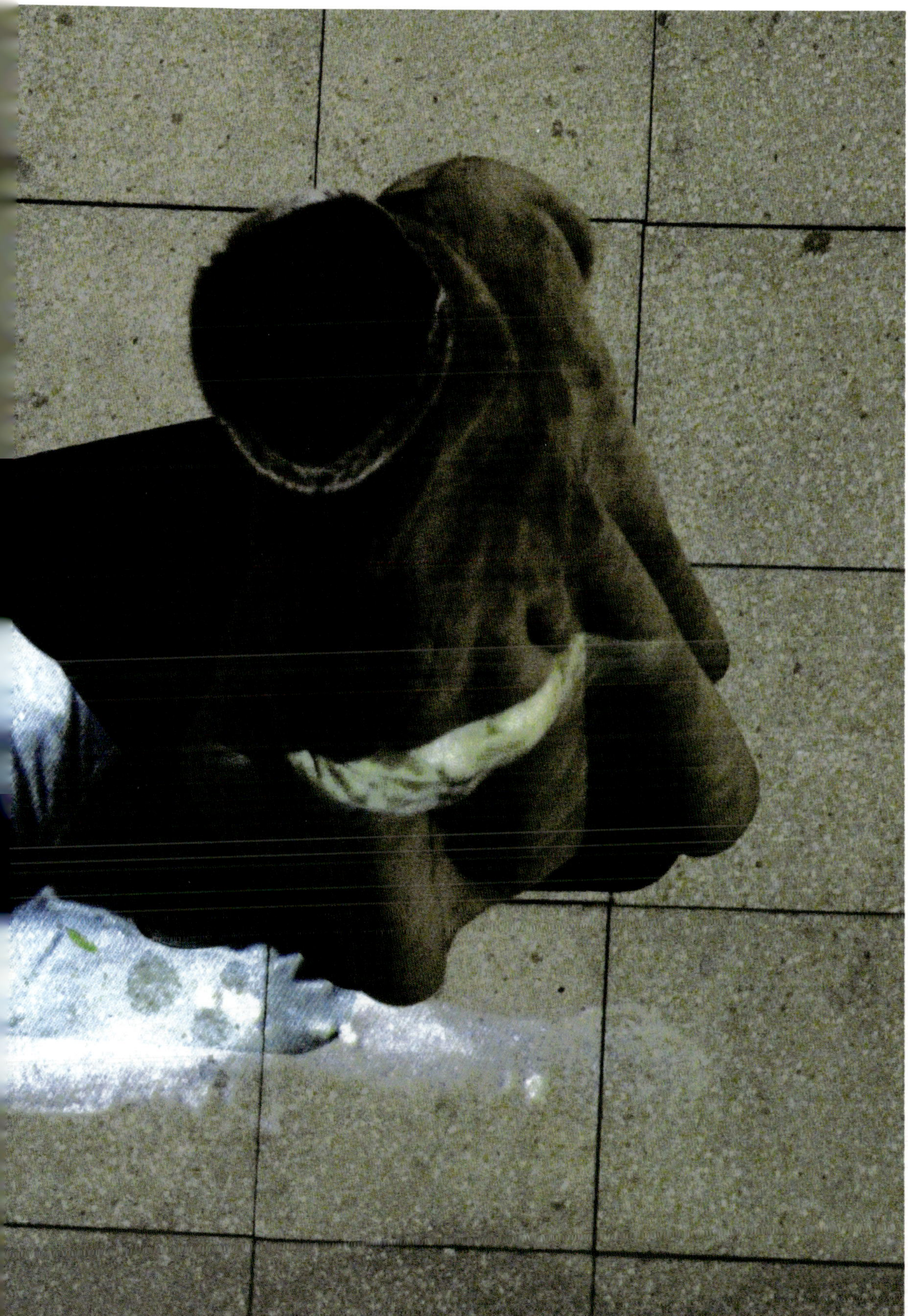

then shared an experience with a presence from another time. The memories were perpetrated, not preserved, as they played back differently depending on how they were triggered and engaged. Of course the reading is very different if it is a family triggering the portrait or a policeman or the recorded person himself or herself (which was very uncanny thing to see, by the way). The singularity comes not from the memory but from the way it is read and by whom.

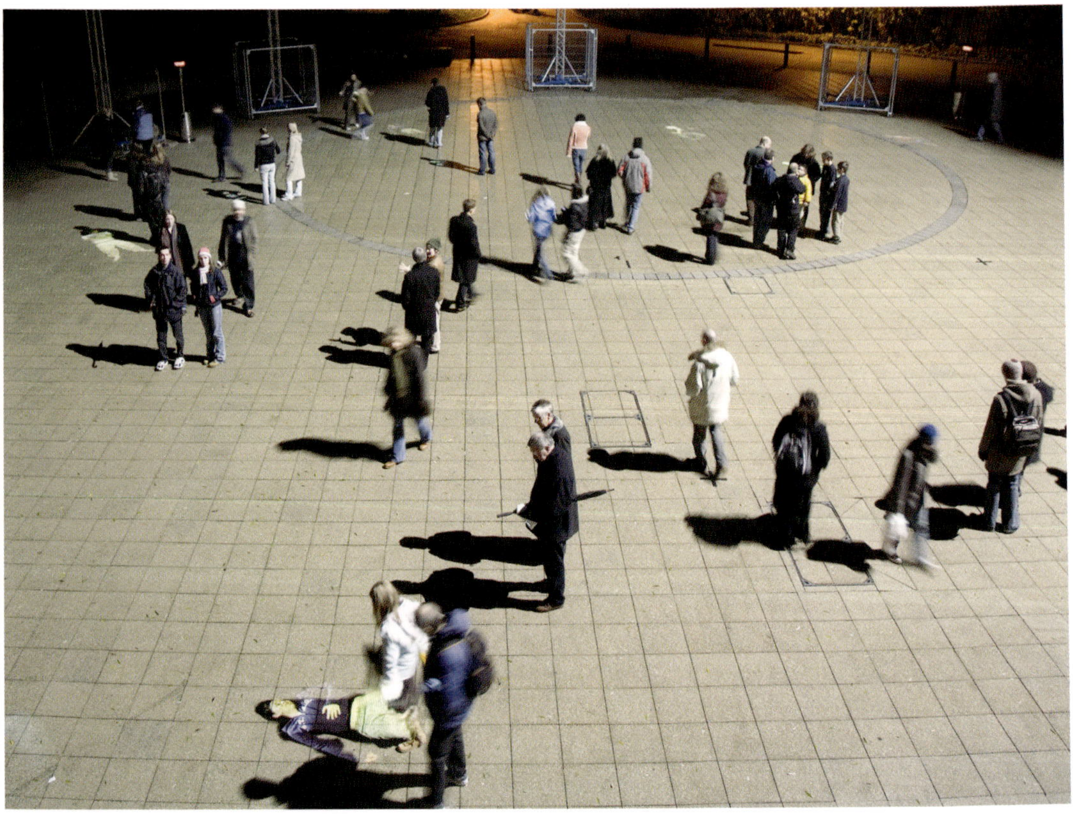

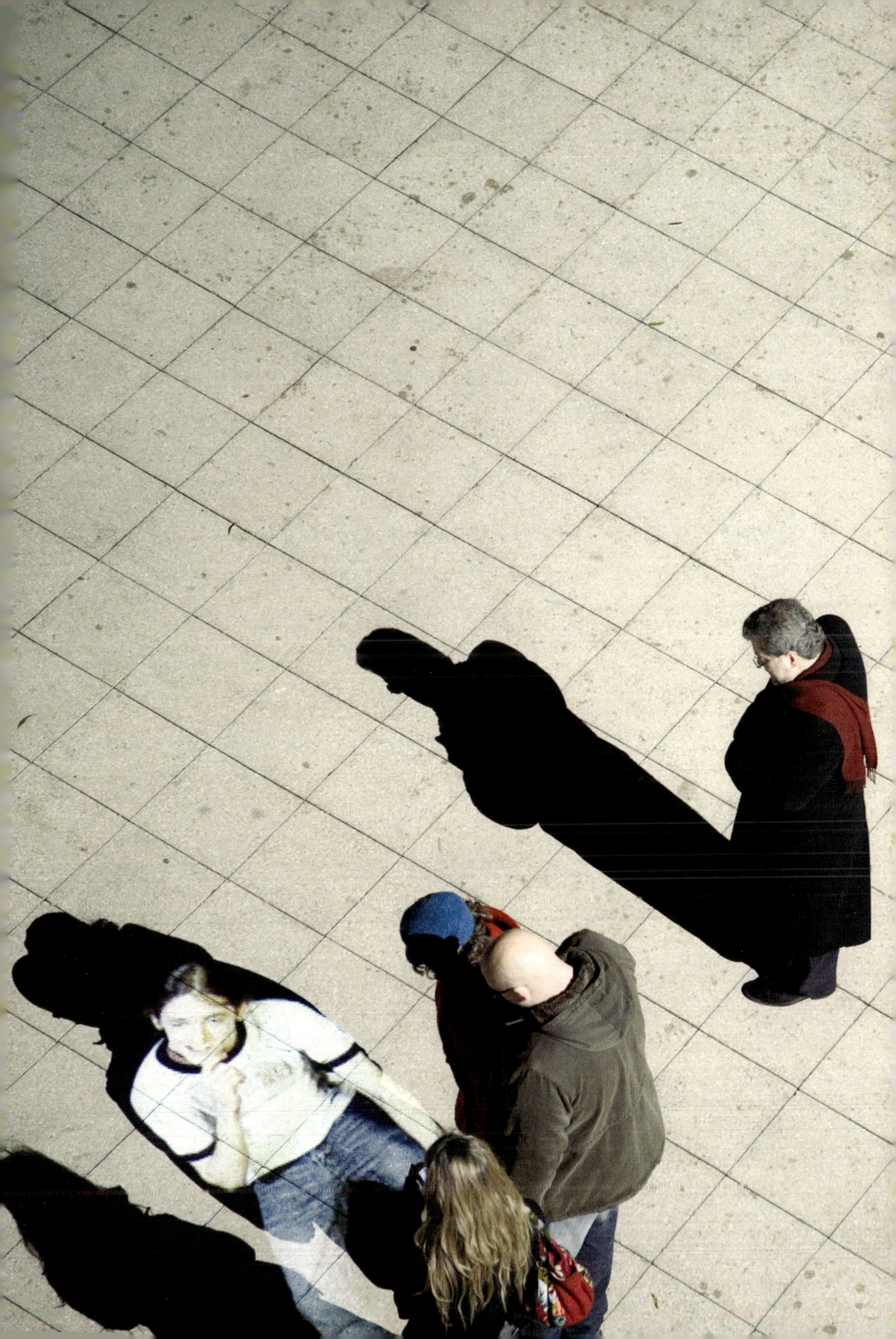

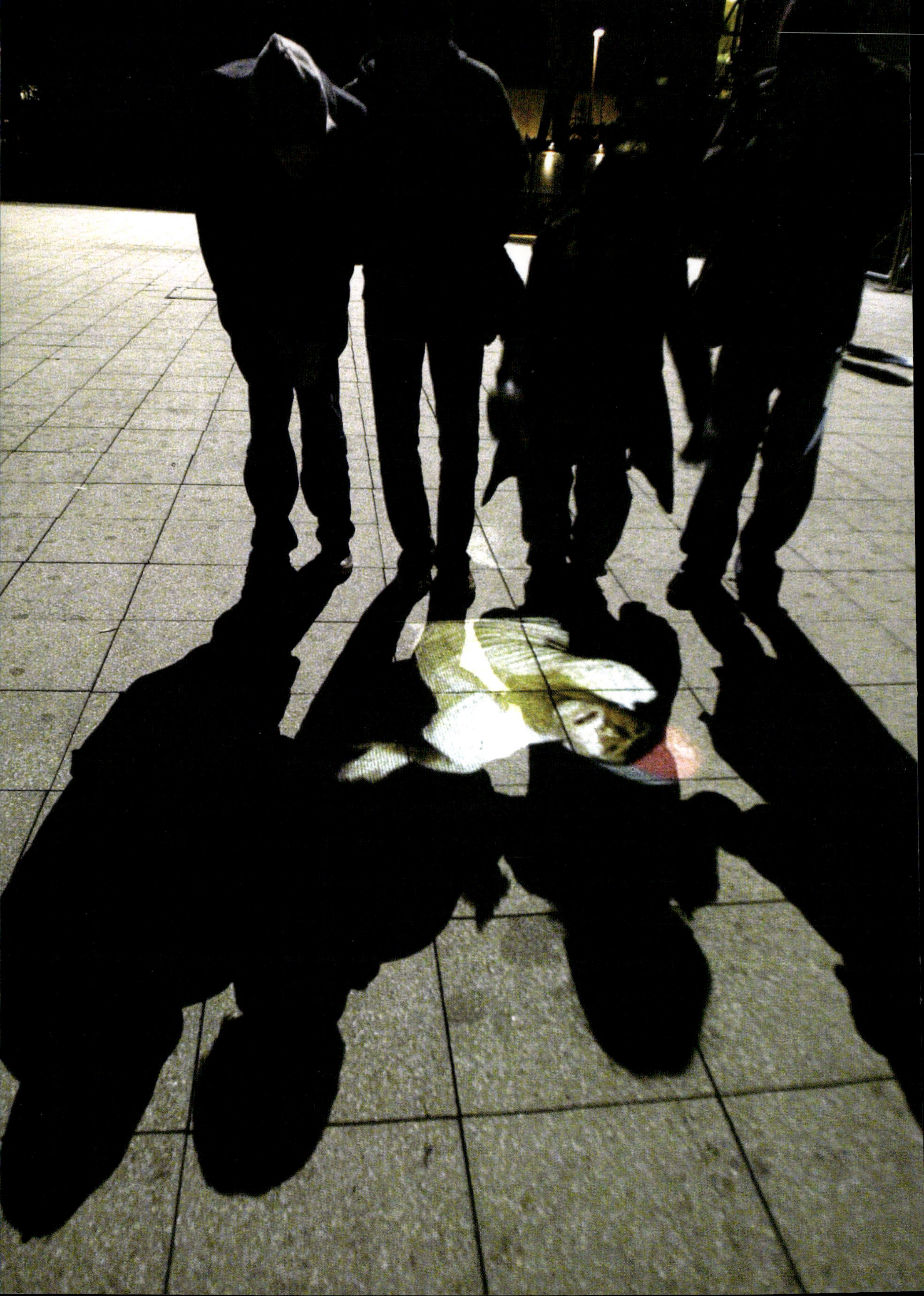

Section 2
Critical Essays

Taking Place
Timothy Druckrey

"The objective tendency of the Enlightenment, to wipe out the power of images over man, is not matched by any subjective progress on the part of enlightened thinking towards freedom from images..." (Theoror Adorno, Minima Moralia)

Our theatres of the artificial have generated phantasmagoric experiences straining to induce illusions of affinity with our omnivorous "realities." Indeed the long history of the apparatus "advanced" along several lines that oscillated wildly between substitution and spectacle, surrogacy and sensation, seduction and speculation. Even a cursory glance into the history of the optical apparatus, from the magic lantern to the phantasmagoria, from the peep show to the zoetrope, from photography to the cinema, will surely demonstrate that modernity's "frenzy" for "scopic regimes" (Comolli), the "optical unconscious" (Benjamin), the "spectacle" (Debord), the "simulated" (Baudrillard), or the "virtual" has undergone astonishing transformation, but that has largely failed to shatter the "objective tendency" and liberate representation from its parasitic dependence on inscription or imitation.

So deeply has the relationship to imitation (a kind of epistemological plateau) ingrained itself in the imaginary that even "virtual" worlds readily substitute themselves—if fleetingly—for existing ones. Untethered from history, unfettered by the forces of physics, freed from material consequence, this is a realm of symptomatic satisfactions and special effects, a realm of little, or no, material consequence, little or no human pathos. And while the fragile illusions of the apparatus are extraordinary, they remind us that the imaginary is a special condition (increasingly a social one), one in which we can jettison the clumsy obstacles of the world "as-is" (the photographic illusion), the world "as-if" (the virtual illusion) in favor of the less stable possibility of the world as "what if," or "why not."

As our media continually hunt for the "real," reality insistently becomes a variable with the image as one of its momentary states. In this sense our task is to reconsider representation as itself an unfinished project, one in which the progressive "retreat" from the presumptive link between an image and a real will continue to dissolve into an epistemological discourse. This approach can only be sustained by resolute—and unrepentant—deconstruction of imaged realities, the conditions of which are hopelessly confined with the now collapsed assumption that what we see is merely the effect of a cause, rather than it's opposite. In contemporary terms we must refigure the notion of representation as itself an interface into "realities" *only possible as images.* In this sense, our representations no longer endure as signifiers but as ciphers.

Made possible by the shift from optical to electronic apparatuses, analogue to digital processing, our representational technologics have penetrated the glacial surfaces that have so epitomized modernity. So instead of bleak mnemonic traces, loss signified by artifacts, fetishism veiled by sentiment, our understanding (and production) of images now serves more complex analytical purposes, the panoptic supplanted by the post-optic, by a gaze no longer just omnipresent but omniscient. The archive assimilated into the database, the image turned logistical, nostalgia turned forensic, our mutable images now serve imperatives unimagined only decades ago. Liberated from any banal correspondence to actuality, representation has exploded passivity and instead proposes itself as participatory, contingent, mutable.

Only recently has the reassessment of the history of the visible become the subject of close deconstruction. Of the many attempts to "de-phenomenologize" representation, the works of Norman Klein and Siegfried Zielinski serve to persuasively underscore the issues. In *The Vatican to Vegas*: *A History of Special Effects* Klein highlights "The scripting of illusions" that characterize the "virtualization" of reception as a shifting terrain of the experiential and the perceptual. For Klein the "scripting of illusion" has been written into the very space of experience. He both assesses and diagnoses the continuing consequences in linking illusion and architecture: "from 1550 to 1780, then on toward cinema and amusement parks, and finally, to our era, when both architecture and film coexist inside the same moment." Only, he continues, "by decoding scripted space, we learn how power was brokered between the classes in the form of special effects."[1]

In a related way, Zielinski identified the evolving "triumph" of representation from the 19th Century:

"The first seventy years of the nineteenth century gave expression to the growing need and technical ability to grasp

1. Norman Klein, *The Vatican to Vegas: A History of Special Effects* (The New Press, New York, 2004) p. 11.

and appropriate the visible surface of the world through its re-visualization and the ability to play around with it: the cinematisation of the eye and of perception as a counterpart and complement to the extensive acquisition of natural and technical processes for other areas of the production of commodities and meaning."[2]

"Scripted illusions" and "the cinematization of the eye" come among many other phrases that drive so much of the rethinking of the history of the subjectification of representational practices. The look, the glance, the gaze, the momentary, were increasingly affective—a tangled reciprocity between objective and subjective, phenomena and signification. Enveloped in the "script," the logic of modernity's compulsive mastery of the visual subtly shifted from imitation to calculation to substitution. Embedded in technique, the "script" is also related to the systemization of the image as a repository of calculated intention, one that turns the observer into a target for whom illusion triumphs over rationality. This strategic shift, where, in Virilio's word, the image is "logistical," signals both a deep crisis and a radical possibility.

In *The Production of Space* Henri Lefebvre asks "What occupies the interstices between representations of space and representational spaces. A culture, perhaps? Certainly—but the word has less content than it seems to have. The work of artistic creation? No doubt—but that leaves unanswered the queries "By whom?" and "How?" Imagination? Perhaps—but why? and for whom?"

Rafael Lozano-Hemmer's sweeping interrogation of these very questions posits an alternative to the "inevitable" assimilation of representation into the unilateral circuits of globalization. Resolutely working in a kind of "anti-illusion," his work is no longer dependent on primitive modes of recognition or reflexivity. Instead, the works tackle a far more cunning reversal by integrating the "interference" of the public as the vital dynamic in anti-spectacle, anti-narrative and as an abandonment of the "regime" of illusions.

The successive works in the series *Relational Architecture* posits the interface as more than just a portal into an illusion; it stands against illusion in favor of developing a unique relationship with a distributed public without losing site of either identity, locality, or with the delicate meanings of interactivity. To do this under the rubric of architecture is neither ironic nor paradoxical. To transpose interior and exterior space, to reclaim the public square as a site of public discourse,

2. Siegfried Zielinski, *Audiovisions: Cinema and Television as Entre'actes in History* (University of Amsterdam Press, Amsterdam, 1999) p. 27.

of the social imaginary, of the "projection" of the public will, is an act at once defiant and compelling. To "write" into the surfaces of the sky, onto the exterior walls of buildings that stand as a repository of cultural history, to "write" the body into the "social text" of the physical world, suggests collisions of meaning that, on the one hand, embeds this work in specific histories and, on the other, extends from the passive confrontation of space into that of time (both historical and experiential).

In this sense, *Relational Architecture* is neither attempting to "build" consensus or to conjure up a useless interactive-cinema. It is an evocation of the kind of social space in which active participation is not a by-product, but the driving force in the creation of dynamic agora in which every position is established in an open system that ruptures hierarchies and dismantles the notion that the public is an undifferentiated mass, the media not the harbinger of a utopian global village, interactivity not the opiate of shoppers.

In carefully balancing often vast spaces with individual actions, the works that have been developed by Lozano-Hemmer conspire to reverse-engineer the looming, phantasmatic, or cultish extravaganzas whose effects were created to overwhelm the senses, to evoke false unity, or to provide a backdrop for mob rallies. Instead, *Relational Architecture* relinquishes the crowd in favor of the assembly. It simultaneously integrates the use of the net as more than a delocalized enclave and reconsiders it as an arena for communication rather than distribution.

Relational Architecture reminds us that our social spaces are never neutral, that they are inhabited by memories of all sorts, that ephemerality is not inconsequential, that interactivity is not merely a catchphrase for media art. It also proposes a social "architecture" that should, in Virilio's wonderful phrase, "take place."

Discovering the Interrelation of Public Space, Interaction and New Media

Mirjam Struppek

"Public space is the city's medium for communication with itself, with the new and unknown, with the history and with the contradictions and conflicts that arise from all those. Public space is urban planning's moderator in a city of free players." (Prof. Wolfgang Christ, 2000)

In the last ten years, interactive media installations and performances have emerged as a new art form in public space. This genre of interactive art, with its playfulness, its focus on communication and its reflection on the power of new technologies, has proven to be well suited to public space. Rafael Lozano-Hemmer's artworks, in particular his *Relational Architecture* series, explore this interconnectedness of public space, interaction and new media. They represent an urban phenomenon that has been increasingly investigated by both media artists and architects, encouraged by the mobilization of digital technologies and new wireless and wearable gadgets.

Public space understood as open, civic space is a key element in the development of European urbanism. It is in this role as a space for representation, culture, encounter through trade, and discussion, that public space has always come alive. Interactivity, in turn, is an important characteristic of digital media. It offers new forms of exchange and collaborative production and has revived discussions about the development of public sphere based on civic negotiation. The possibilities of complex data processing and the accumulation of information generated through these interactions are having an increasing influence on our daily lives. Our modern culture has been dominated by the idea of using technology as a tool to enhance our standard of living, yet many of these technologies were designed for military purposes. Artists like Rafael Lozano-Hemmer point out the increasing ubiquity of new media that is crystallising in urban space, such as surveillance infrastructures, mobile telephony, and digital screens. By connecting the virtual world with urban space, and by exploring the participatory and interactive potential of new technologies to generate new exchanges, these artists are part of a counter-movement against the paralysing dominance of mass media in the last century.

Recent ideas in urban planning and sociology help to understand the possible role of interactive art works in public space. Increasingly, public space is being rediscovered as a unique arena for communication, for the performance of ritual, and for constantly evolving social interactions. European urban culture originated in ideal conceptions of an inclusive, connective space, based on social justice and tolerance, accessible to rich and poor, to locals and strangers, and controlled by a notion of common rules. Through a rich variety of exchanges, which constitute local culture, an urban space comes alive and a collective urban memory emerges. In contrast to the private space, public space is where the individual presents himself to the community and where his confrontation with the unknown helps determine his place in a complex society. Since the rise of digital media, the possibilities of human interaction have been clearly widened and the perception and definition of the strange, as well as concepts of the private and public sphere, are being redefined. Interactions between people are becoming more complex but also more distant and detached from physical experience. New media experiments revive the importance of public space as a space for interaction and direct confrontation with the unknown and the new. Learning to encounter the unexpected helps to shape our social competence. Rafael Lozano-Hemmer's *Under Scan* creatively recalls the sudden alien encounter with the urban stranger that crosses your path, an occurrence less likely within the growing segregation of modern social structures.

Public space has always been a complex network of spaces for various functions yet recently we can observe a problematic segregation of urban society into separated public spheres that is destroying the traditional rhythms of a city and its varied social contexts. For example, people seem to feel less rooted in and responsible for their neighbourhoods. Gated communities, which try to minimise unexpected conflicts, represent a growing fear and scepticism towards the idea of a diverse urban community. The success of private transportation has helped to recast public space as merely one of transit from one place to another. And as a reaction to growing fears of a city's potential dangers, we face increasing surveillance in controlled spaces of organised urban entertainment. In this globalised world threatened by diffuse and complex fears of instability and lack of strong local roots, we need creative ideas on how to find a new urban balance while integrating technological developments.

In its early stages, the Internet was explored as an alternative public sphere. Starting with virtual cities and chat rooms, a variety of tools has been developed to connect people who share common interests. More recently, communal experiments like collaborative wikis, blogs, mobile phone networks, and cross-media platforms are emerging in the growing field of social computing. Using these nascent technologies, media artists, through unusual experiences, can bring new, thought-provoking elements to this process of re-negotiating public space and contribute to the re-emergence of public space as a space for positive and inspiring friction.

The term "urban hacking" represents an attitude derived from computer hackers who explore the use of technology in ways not intended by the developer and who experiment with the limits and possibilities of new media. The Chaos Computer Club of the German hacker scene produced the project *Blinkenlights,* one of the most popular interactive facade installations in public space. This project exemplifies how, by disrupting everyday urban activities and consumption patterns, the emerging ubiquity of media in urban spaces can be used alternatively as a tool to explore the richness of public space, to create new social interactions and to imprint vivid spatial memories. In fact the renewal of a civic society can be positively linked with the development of the Internet, which is strongly based on cooperative exchange and shared engagement through the openness of systems. New media art in urban space can be understood in the context of this ideology of "open source," applying this idea of sharing and collective thinking to a wider audience in public space. Media artists can help to discover more sustainable ways to revitalise urban spaces by actively involving its inhabitants, often through playful or humorous elements. Artworks that clearly depend on active participation and that repeatedly question the necessity of controlling their openness represent an attitude of treating inhabitants not as mere consumers but as responsible citizens. Various projects, including Rafael Lozano-Hemmer's works, have investigated the idea of free expression in public space, using the mobile phone or the Internet as input devices, provoking discussions about censorship while revealing how participants tend towards self-organisation.

Various typologies of media art in public space are currently crystallising and being recognised in the art world. An overview of projects developed in the last ten years reveals how various new technologies have been utilised in challenging ways. Special events and contests such as Fusedspace and ISEA 2006 Interactive City demonstrate the upsurge of projects in the last three years. New genres such as "locative media" and "urban screens" are being established. "Locative media" originated in the growth of mobile technologies and are media of communication bound to a location through location-oriented content. Artists such as Teri Rueb and Masaki Fujihata explore these new possibilities of experiencing and documenting space inspired by GPS technology. "Urban Screens" combines various strategies in order to engage a growing infrastructure of screens and moving images already integrated in architecture and urban settings. Since 1992, Christian Möller has experimented with architecture and urban space as interface, creating interactions with images, light and sound. Artist Giselle Beiguelman explores the utilisation of large LED boards in urban spaces for participatory art, while Johannes Gees experiments with laser text projections onto various locations in his series of interfacing landscapes. The publication www.interactionfield.de gives an overview of numerous interactive media projects on its "open list" and describes their potential for:

- Promoting interaction, fearless confrontation and contact with strangers.
- Promoting formation of the public sphere through criticism, reflection on society.
- Promoting social interaction and integration in neighbourhoods.
- Supporting understanding of current developments in our high-tech society.
- Supporting conscious participation in the creation of public space.

Artists like O+A (Bruce Odland and Sam Auinger), Iain Mott, Achim Wollscheid, Greyworld, Noriyuki Fujimura, and Usman Haque have explored extensively media-related interactions in urban space and shaped the development of new experiments based on different technologies. Some of the work includes interactive installations that use surveillance technologies such as CCTV or RFID or that includes light and sound-triggering or sound-recording elements. Other works use various forms of digital public message boards, and image projections or sculptures that function as communication catalysts between strangers. Building facades, digital screens, or the pavement has been used as canvas and shop windows have functioned as an extended gallery space.

Some projects explore and reveal the invisible information sphere, such as the electromagnetic environment circulating in public space, by using mobile technologies such as cell phones, PDAs, and laptops.

Artists like Katherine Moriwaki working with wearable media question the growing ubiquity of technologies embedded in everyday objects and clothing. These artists explore the moving body as interface and develop artistic tools for social networking. WIFI art uses the new invisible infrastructure of wireless hotspots that increasingly cover cities. Space annotations and place-based storytelling localise invisible data by using GPS or graffiti like barcodes called semacodes, which augment public space with digital information from the Internet. New interpretations of psychogeographic performances, experimental cartographic explorations, location-based mobile games and its predecessors of outdoor mixed-reality games, explore public space as a playground of the urban phenomenon.

In today's world, where moving billboards can detect and respond to our behaviours and where consumer preferences and individual concerns seem to dominate, public space needs to be recalled as the glue that holds urban society together. Experiments of art in public space serve as an inspiration and testing ground for rediscovering a communicative urban environment. They call for an urgent social enhancement of our media saturated cities in order to achieve a more inclusive and sustainable urban society. These art projects are a step towards the implementation of Wolfgang Christ's definition of public space.

Reference Projects

Bins and Benches **(Cambridge, UK 2004)**
Greyworld
www.junction.co.uk/publicartve/greyworld.html
Bins and Benches involve active street furniture. Intelligent bins and benches will roam the new piazza in front of The Junction and respond to the needs of the humans that share their habitat: when it rains, they head for shelter; when the sun comes out they burst into song; at night, they move to provide seating for queuing crowds.

Biomapping **(2004–2006)**
Christian Nold
www.biomapping.net
Instead of security technologies that are designed to control our behaviour, this project envisages a new tool that allows people to selectively share and collaboratively make use of this information. The Bio Mapping tool allows the wearer to record their Galvanic Skin Response (GSR), which is a simple indicator of emotional arousal in conjunction with their geographical location. This can be used to plot a map that highlights point of high and low arousal. By sharing this data we can construct maps that visualise where we as a community feel stressed and excited.

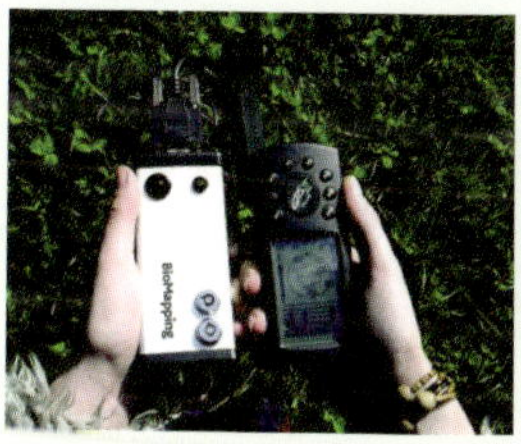

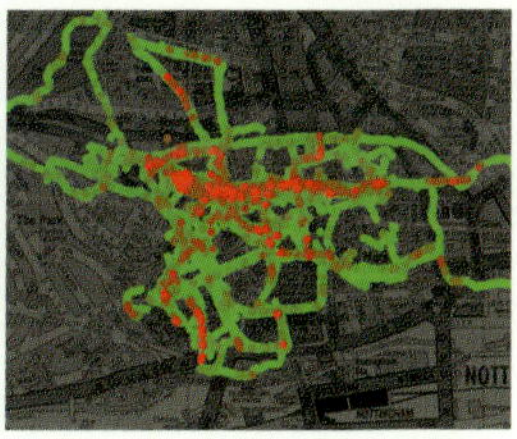

Blinkenlights **(Image shown by Susanne Schuricht 2001 – 2002)**
Chaos Computer Club
www.blinkenlights.de
Blinkenlights was a large abstract interactive computer display. The lights of each window could be animated with the program "Blinkenpaint." Everybody could send one's creations to the editor. Additionally, standing in front of the building with a mobile phone one could play Pong on the cladding and call up a prepared animation to let one run one's own love letters.

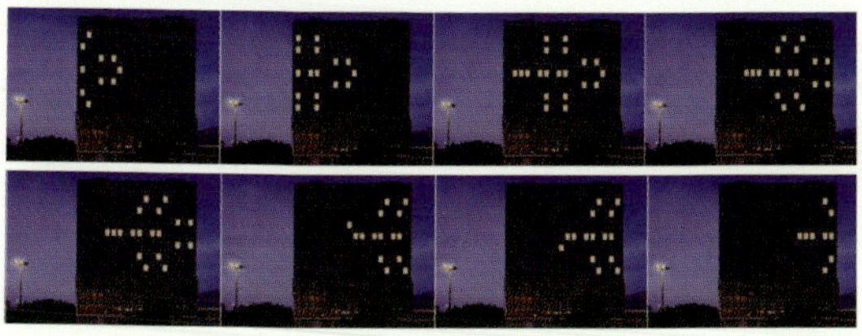

Clickscape '98 **– Clickable Public Space**
Stadtwerkstatt
www.servus.at/clickscape98
Clickscape '98 is a meeting area between material and virtual worlds. By mouse clicking, the lights of the windows of the EA-Generali building can be switched on and off and the Nibelungen bridge can be fed with tones. The sounds are sent into the urban space over loudspeakers at each lantern mast on the bridge. The scrolling text at the building of the Stadtwerkstatt serves as a display for texts, which are addressed to this area.

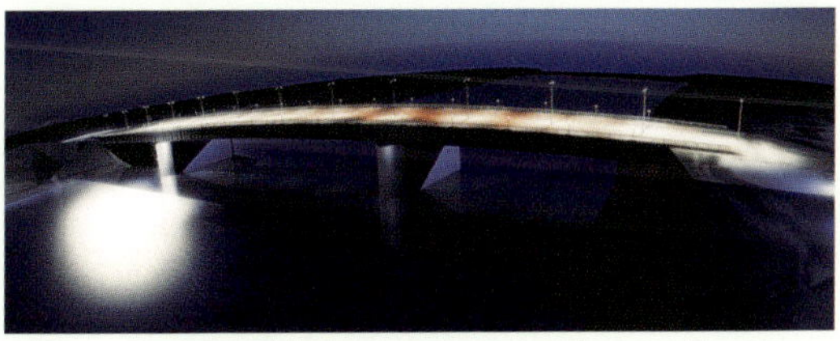

Energie_Passagen **(Munich 2004)**
Monika Fleischmann & Wolfgang Strauss
www.energie-passagen.de
The project "Energie_Passagen" reproduces the linguistic space of the city in form of a data flow. Hundreds of catchwords taken from current newspaper reports appear in a projected "information flow" and are spoken by artificial computer voices. As soon as passers-by select individual words, thematically related networks of terms start to perform in this flow, which can also be experienced as an audiovisual echo. The text is thus detached from its linear context and staged as a medial reading in urban space.

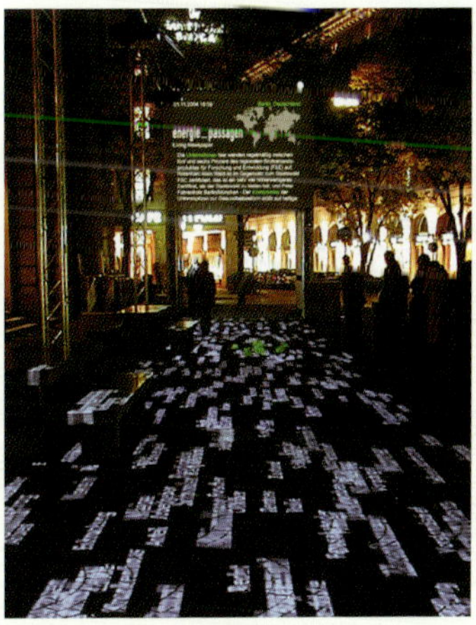

***Face Your World* (Columbus, 2002)**
Jeanne van Heeswijk
www.faceyourworld.net
In a special bus children were given access to a multi-user computer game to redesign their communities as they envisaged them. The children's creations were displayed on special screen sculptures at three bus stops, presenting the results proudly to the urban community. Digital media were utilized here as interaction catalysts for the participation and engagement of young people in their local community.

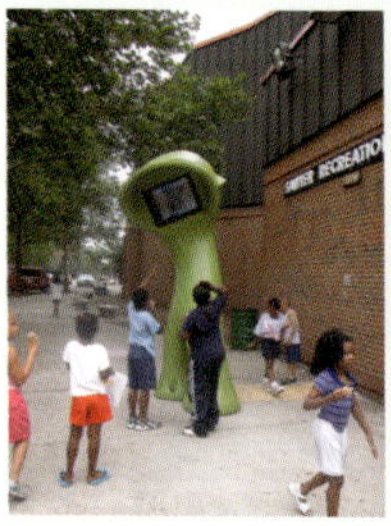

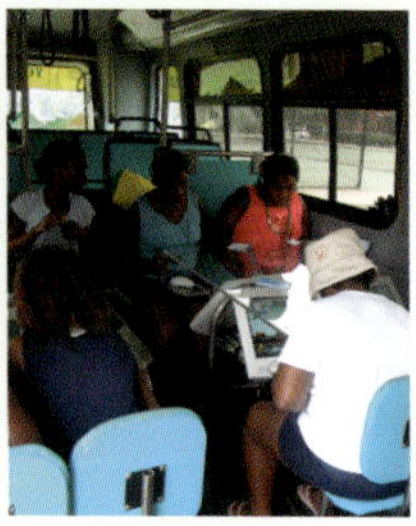

Johannes Gees
www.johannesgees.com
Messages are beamed with laser onto giant walls in four cities, during the UN World Summit on the Information Society in Geneva. People are invited to participate by contributing their own messages as well. During the International Human Rights Day messages about human rights are shown.

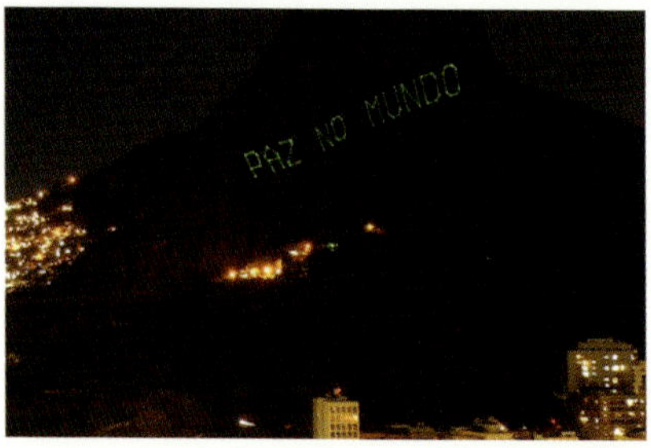

***Hole in the Earth* (2003/2004)**
Maki Ueda
www.ueda.nl
An installation that takes place on the two sides of the earth simultaneously, Rotterdam and Bandung, Indonesia. Through this "virtual hole," people can see and hear the other side of the earth. The "hole" is made with computers, monitors, web cameras, speakers, and microphones. Through the Internet, real-time audio and visual connection is made.

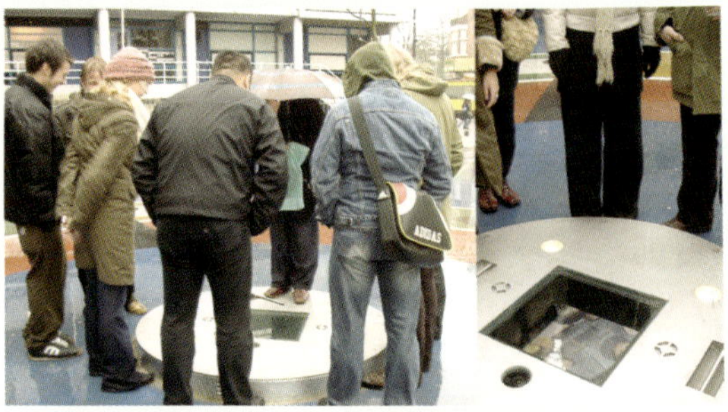

Les-Lignes-Mobiles
Antoine Schmitt
www.gratin.org/as/txts/leslignesmobiles.html
Surveillance camera based projection installation.

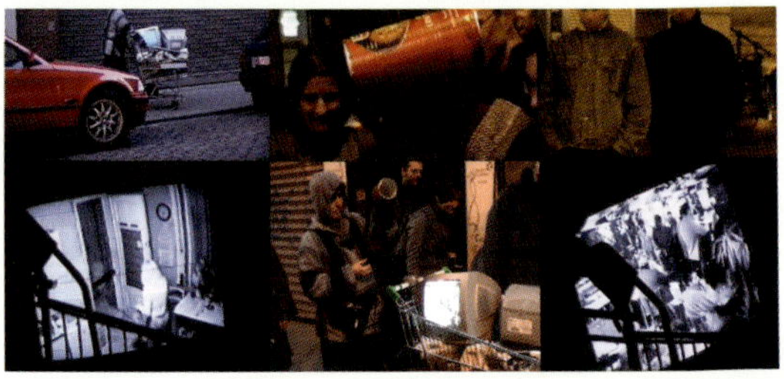

One Free Minute
www.onefreeminute.net
One Free Minute is a mobile sculpture designed to allow for instances of anonymous public speech. When you call the cell phone inside One Free Minute, you get connected for exactly one minute to a 200-watt amplifier and speaker.

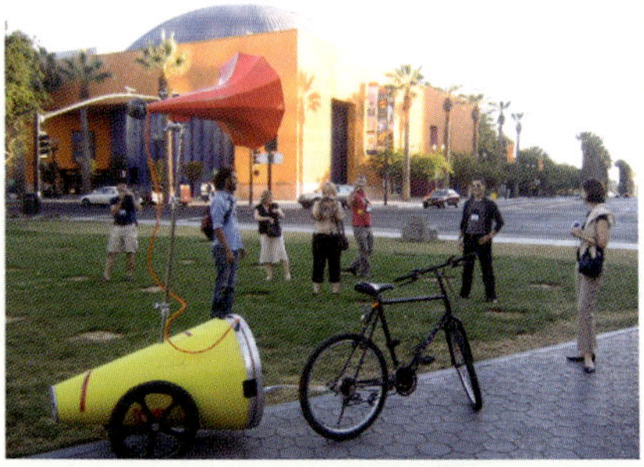

The Peoples' Portrait **(New York, 2004)**
Zhang Ga
www.people.apiece.net
The Peoples' Portrait uses the Internet to produce a global series of portraits, thus making a connection between people of greatly varying cultural and ethnic backgrounds. In cities such as Rotterdam, New York, Brisbane or Singapore passers-by can enter special photo booths to have their picture taken, which is then instantly and simultaneously displayed on large screens in all of these cities, including the large Reuters screen in New York's Times Square.

Radioscape
Edwin van der Heide
www.evdh.net
Catching sounds from twelve radio transmitters.

Raindance **(Image shown: Ars Electronica 2001)**
Paul DeMarinis
www.well.com/~demarini/
Twenty water jets falling off a canopy, transport is not visible and with no audible sounds. Only if interrupted with an umbrella, which function as loudspeakers, do they become audible. So several persons together can contribute playfully with their umbrellas to a sound composition.

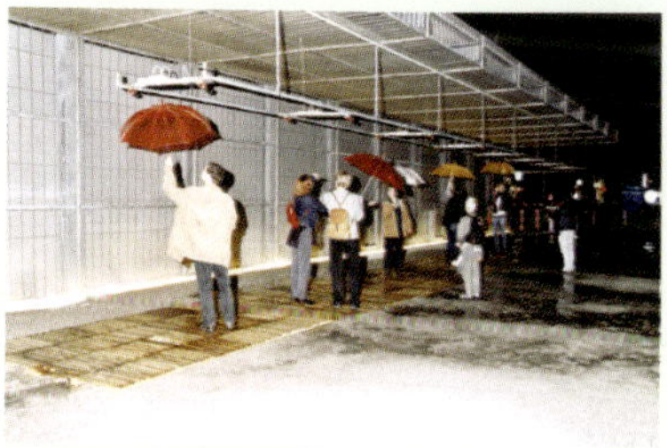

React **(Berlin 2005)**
Horst Konietzny
www.reframes.com/Projekte/english.htm
The project used the large screen at the Sony Center, Berlin, to engage four authors in a discourse with an urban audience. In a 3-hour performance, the writers commented on the local space and its people, connected in real time via a web interface to the large screen. The audience could reply to the observations of the hidden writers, who were sitting in the surrounding architecture, via SMS comments at the bottom of the screen.

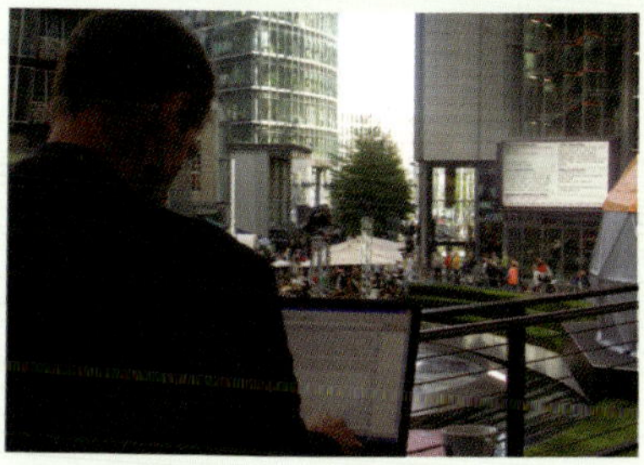

re:site projects **(Munich 2002–04)**
Felix S. Huber, Florian Wüst, Daniel Burckhardt
www.fshuber.net/projects/resite_web/info.en.html
A simulcast from video streams recorded in public space is matched up with suitable videos from local youngsters or feature cut-outs and text contributions from the interactive chat function on the Re:site homepage. Thus a collage from fleeting present and timeless past develops. The real-time pictures are recorded at clearly marked locations in the "Riem" neighbourhood so that inhabitants can co-design the image of their neighbourhood. They are shown on monitors in the street, on two screens at the Messestadt West subway station as well as on the Internet.

Richair 2030 **(2003–2004)**
TAKE2030
www.richair.waag.org
RICHAIR2030 imagines an "After the Net," "After the Crash" scenario and proposes shared public consumption of bandwidth and garlic rich air. The "Zone of Urgency" spills into Venice city limits as we seek patrons for wireless B-spot (B for bandwidth) and richair G-spot (G for garlic). Marking B and G with a stripped-down handmade lunchbox Chiputer, we measure the remaining network signal strength transmitted from its PoP (Point of Presence). The RGB coded strength is fed live onto the web – rich pumping air. RICHAIR2030 mobilises roaming nodes and calls for a trans-national virtual mesh network.

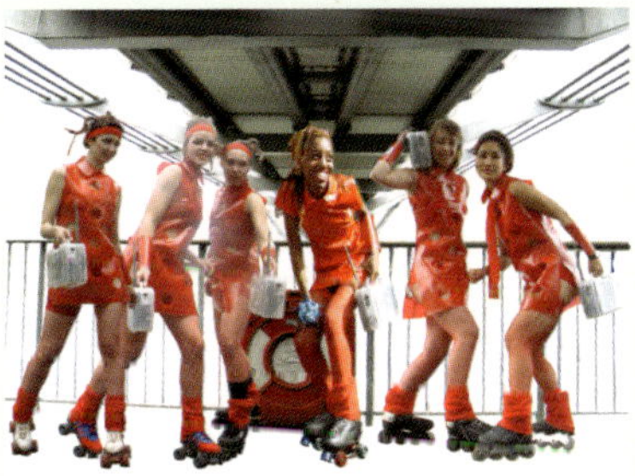

Sky Ear
Usman Haque
www.haque.co.uk/skyear.php
A one-night event in which a glowing "cloud" of mobile phones and helium balloons is released into the air so that people can dial into the cloud and listen to the sounds of the sky.

***StalkShow* (2003–2005)**
Karen Lancel
www.stalkshow.org
The StalkShow deals with the threat of insecurity and isolation. A backpack with laptop/touch screen is carried through public spaces. Being surrounded by the audience you are invited to touch the screen and to navigate through an archive of texts about threats of insecurity and isolation. The texts come from the Internet, written by people living in isolation, like a prisoner, a nun, a pilgrim, or a digipersona. By webcam and wireless Internet connection, your live video portrait appears together with the text on a large projection screen in the same public space. Your "watching" face watches the (watching) audience. The StalkShow makes connections between social experiences in virtual and physical spaces.

UMBRELLA.net
Katherine Moriwaki, Jonah Brucker-Cohen
www.undertheumbrella.net
UMBRELLA.net is a project exploring transitory or ad-hoc networks and their potential for causing sudden, striking, and unexpected connections between people in public and urban space. The project focuses on the theme of "networks of coincidence," or how shared, yet disconnected activities can be harnessed into collective experiences. UMBRELLA.net examines how the haphazard and unpredictable patterns of weather and crowd formation can act as an impetus to examine coincidence of need networks. In particular, when umbrellas are opened and closed in public space. The project will attempt to highlight these informal relationships by creating a system of ad-hoc network nodes that can spontaneously form and dissipate based on weather conditions.

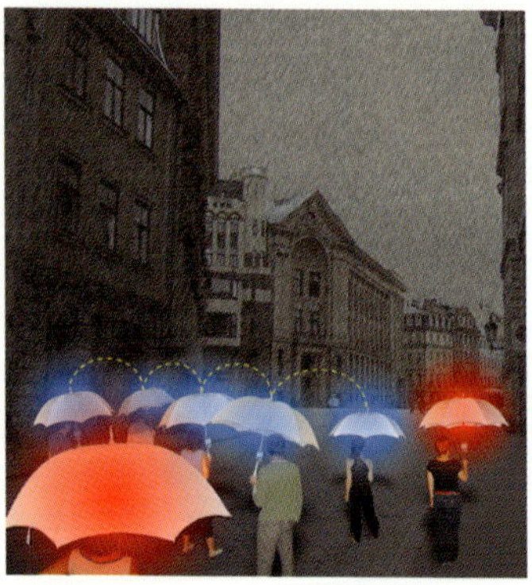

***World Bench* (2005)**
Greyworld
www.greyworld.org/artwork/worldbench/
Benches in school playgrounds in England, Germany and South Africa are linked up over the Internet. Each bench is in fact only a half-bench; at one end is a large display screen and a camera, connecting it to an identical bench somewhere else in the world. Pupils across the globe are put in touch with one another through the power of new media.

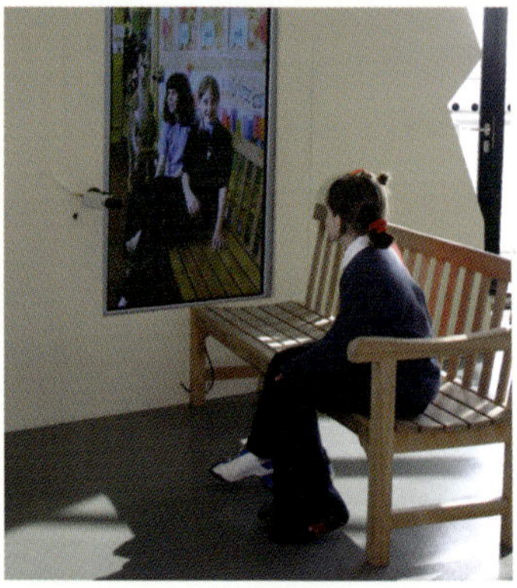

***Zhong Shuo—People say* (2005)**
ian Mott, Ding Jie
www.reverberant.com
This sound installation acts as a system for automated recording, collation and dissemination of stories. Inside the intimate hut questions concerning the rapid rate of change in China are posed and stories can be recorded via a simple phone interface. This is played back as interwoven narratives outside each installation and streamed to the Internet.

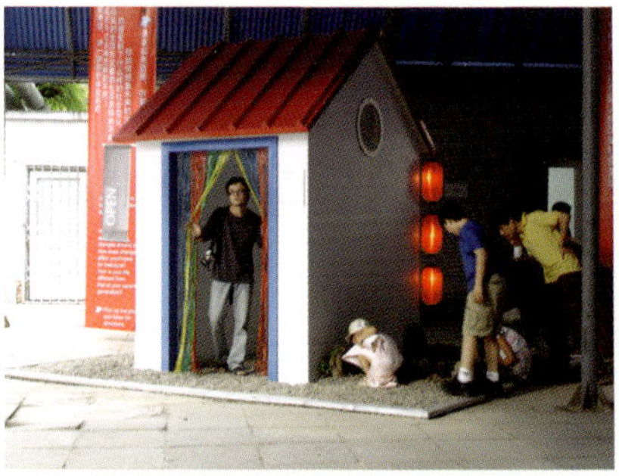

The Dark Side of Light: Ambivalent Interaction

Beryl Graham

Say the word "interactive" in the context of the art world, and it could mean disparate things. Unfortunately, it often means a desperate definition of "an interactive": some kind of device offering educational experience, which might vary wildly in interactional strategy from pressing a button and having a light come on, to a sit-at-a-computer-on-a-table and access the entire digitised documentation of an art collection. Similarly, mention the words "public art," and it could conjure up generals on horses, or home-made paper lantern processions, or complex long-term participative oral history projects. So, *Under Scan* could be said to sit (or lie) at the centre of a highly ambivalent crossroads.

What kind of interaction?

"Of course no interaction with a machine can currently approach the complexity of human interaction. Perry Hoberman's recent exhibits depend upon both interactions with the programme and interactions between other people using the exhibit." (Dave Franklin)[1]

"I'm standing on a bleak new University plaza on a freezing December night, but nevertheless, dozens of people have walked some distance from the bright lights of the shopping centre to spend some time with this... quietly moving around, falling into groups, gesturing to each other, wandering off for a more individual experience." (Beryl Graham, notes on Under Scan, 2 Dec 2005)

"This is the third time I've come over to see this, I've brought friends, and my sister and her kids. The kids think its fun, but I think it's quite serious really. I don't like it when the kids stand on the people." (Quote from an audience member at the Under Scan installation in Lincoln, 2 Dec 2005)

It has been artists rather than technologists who have avoided the hype about "interactives," and have been most wittily accurate about exactly what kinds of interaction work for their audiences. Perry Hoberman's artworks often satirise the deeply frustrating nature of much human-computer interaction: in *Workaholic* (2000) users must co-operate with old-tech hairdryers to get a madly swinging pendulum to read bar-codes; in *Cathartic User Interface* (1995/2000) the audience must throw koosh

1. Franklin , Dave (30 Nov 2001) "Re: Too Interactive: Nov theme of the month." *New-Media-Curating Discussion List.* [Online]. Available from www.jiscmail.ac.uk/lists/new-media-curating.html.

balls at keyboards on the wall to produce projected visual rewards—neatly frustrating the desire for intentionality and control that computers seem to promise. Along the way, the audience are united in shared suffering, or the need to collaborate, and who knows, this might even produce interaction between strangers in a British art gallery.

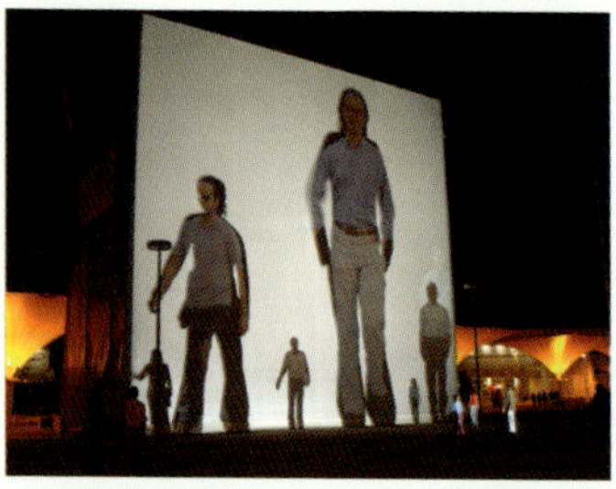

Rafael Lozano-Hemmer, *Body Movies* (2001-2006). Shown here outside the Atlántico Pavillion, Lisbon, Portugal.

Lozano-Hemmer's work is less straightforwardly satirical, but nevertheless has cleverly realised what many fail to learn: that interaction between human and programmed artwork provides an interesting but strictly limited range of interactional strategies—the full potential of artworks "depend upon both interactions with the programme and interactions between other people using the exhibit." *Body Movies, Relational Architecture No. 6* (2001) for example, works on at least three interactional levels: On the first level the audience must cover the projected photographs of people with their own bodies in order to perceive the images; the second level is to collaborate to cover all of the images, at which point the programme produces more images (this might involve non-verbal co-operation with strangers); an important third level is where the audience has full creative input to play with the shadows—running the full gamut of human power relationships—flirting, mock sex and violence, or more complex narrative improvisation. Lozano-Hemmer has observed carefully the patterns of interaction: If certain groups were thought to be going too far, then other groups could collaborate to stand in front of the spotlights and "censor" them. In Rotterdam, people came back and brought elaborate props with which to "perform" Certain Liverpool participants showed a marked fondness for stripping naked after a night in the pub. Such regional differences are a key: would the interaction be very different in the USA, where shared public spaces are rare, and fraught with issues of "danger?"

These complex interactions tend to go well beyond certain public art or regeneration agendas for a simplistic "wider audience" or "more involvement." Some attempts have been made to categorize kinds of computer-involved interaction,but there is the difficulty of crossing over between art and computer fields.[2] As *Under Scan* could be said to be not only interactive in product, but interactive in process (as all of the video "portraits" are of local people), does this then cross over into terms like "site specific," "activist art" or "community involvement" as well as "interactive" Interestingly, what these buzzwords have in common is a concern with power and control.

2. I summarised some categories of interaction in my doctoral research in 1997, using a metaphor of "conversation," and have more recently written: Graham, Beryl (forthcoming) "Snapshots from Curating Mobility (if you build it, they won't necessarily come)." In: Martin Rieser (ed.) *The Mobile Audience.* London: BFI.

Power and Control

"Instead of just reacting or responding to a changing perception of art, artists have started to interfere in the perception process itself by anticipating the audience's movement. The artist now uses or guides the audience's movements and is steering its perception and interpretation of the work. The best way to capture the attention of the audience is by showing hospitality, by creating playful and interesting spaces of engagement." (Josephine Bosma)[3]

"... we're producing Tim Etchell's 'Surrender Control' SMS project... (its a series of 75 instructions sent via text messages over 5 days. ...). It's exciting to be working in this medium, but we do feel a loss of control, as we have no real chance of getting feedback from the audience. In fact we deliberately decided not to include more obvious feedback mechanisms when we were developing the UI [User Interface] for the piece, as they stood out as being too obviously 'interactive' in relation to the curt, but thought-provoking messages that make up the project." (Matt Locke)[4]

"I saw pictures in the paper, but I'm a bit disappointed that the video isn't 3D, like those Peter Gabriel shows ..." (Quote from an audience member at the Under Scan installation in Lincoln, 2 Dec 2005)

Lozano-Hemmer is unusually aware of the history of the media he uses. The history of the "light show" has often been one of bombastic spectacle, from Nazi propaganda and "participative" torchlight event, to portentous Prog-Rock high-tech blow-out. The history of much new media, from the Internet to Virtual Reality, is one of military "command and control," with all the concomitant power relations.

So, how does an artist use these media without succumbing to the shock and awe of the "technologically correct?"[5] Either by satirising the control-freak tendency, as Tim Etchells does with *Surrender Control* (2001), or by "creating playful and interesting spaces of engagement" as Lozano-Hemmer has done. As he has said, "successful pieces that feature 'interactivity for groups' are usually out-of-control" and this demands trust from both the artist and the curator.[6] With *Under Scan,* the artist has been cognisant of the responsibility of "steering" the interaction and the perception; making the audience very aware of where they are standing, who they are standing on, and how they are moving. The nature of the positioning and the reverse spectatorship of "reverse puppetry"are very carefully considered.[7] The artwork has managed to harness the bodily play and spectacle,

3. Bosma, Josephine (2006) "Art as experience: meet the active audience." In: Tom Corby (ed.) *Network art: Practices and positions.* London: Routledge. p. 31.

4. Locke, Matt (19 Nov 2001) "Re: Too Interactive: Nov theme of the month." *New-Media-Curating Discussion List.* [Online]. Available from www.jiscmail.ac.uk/lists/new-media-curating.html.

5. Ranzenbacher, Heimo (2001) "Metaphors of Participation: Rafael Lozano-Hemmer interviewed by Heimo Ranzenbacher." *Ars Electronica Festival 2001.* Available from www.aec.at/festival2001/texte/lozano_e.html.

6. Lozano-Hemmer, Rafael (6 Dec 2001) "Too Interactive (belated)." *New-Media-Curating Discussion List.* [Online]. Available from www.jiscmail.ac.uk/lists/new-media-curating.html.

7. *Under Scan* publicity panels.

without losing the importantly dark side of the content.

Dark and Light

"Surrender Control explored the darker shadows of communication technologies, illustrating the umheimlich twin of the shiny, happy world of ubiquitous connectivity that we are always being promised ..." (Matt Locke on Tim Etchell's Surrender Control artwork)[8]

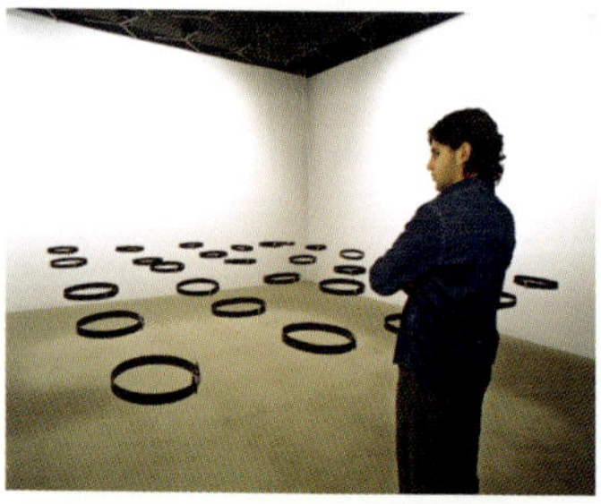

Rafael Lozano-Hemmer, *Standards and Double Standards* (2004). First shown at Art Basel Unlimited, Switzerland.

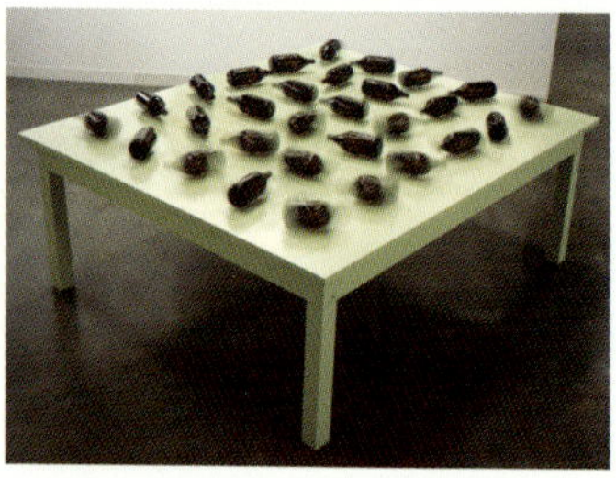

Rafael Lozano-Hemmer, *Synaptic Caguamas* (2004). First shown at OMR Gallery, Mexico City.

"I'm standing in a gallery in Geneva, and 40 or so black leather men's belts are suspended in ranks, at waist height. As I move around the room, they slowly rotate en masse so that the buckles face me wherever I go, with a noise like the sighing of a distant but powerful machine. In another corner, a table full of beer bottles lie on their sides, rotating violently but purposefully, placing their mouths close together as if in order to pass some Chinese whisper around the table, in a sinister screech of glass against metal." (Beryl Graham, notes on Lozano-Hemmer artworks Standards and Double Standards, and Synaptic Caguamas, Galerie Guy Bärtschi, 13th Jan 2006)

"... are those grids supposed to follow you? It's a bit scary... like The Matrix." (Quote from an audience member at the Under Scan installation in Lincoln, 2 Dec 2005)

Publicists often seem determined to represent all interactive work as "hands-on fun for kids," at the expense of any content. The content of *Under Scan* deals with our highly ambivalent relationship to public spaces—those huddled bodies in doorways, those young people who flirt with an Anti-Social Behaviour Order in order to be sociable on their terms, our discomfort in empty places, the visible yet invisible presences. Lozano-Hemmer's work has often dealt with dark content: the paranoia of domestic power relations, of public spaces, or of technological surveillance. Hands often appear in his work—hands that ambivalently stroke buildings, but are refused entrance, or cover surveillance cameras—hands that could caress, chop, swipe, or reach for a belt or a bottle. Sometimes an interaction is an offer that you'd like to refuse, a surveillance you'd like to hide from, a domestic response that you do not want.

Critical Interaction

"I entirely understand the effects of social interaction. I think people responded a great deal to each other, rather than to the objects, to their relationship to the latter or to the awareness of their own physical processes. That is, they made up group games, competed, acted out their aggressions, showed off, etc." (Letter from Tate curator Michael Compton to artist Robert Morris, 13 May 1971, quoted by Steve Dietz)[9]

8. Locke, Matt (2003) "Tim Etchells, Surrender Control." *Test*, July 14, 2003 11:42 AM . Available from www.test.org.uk/archives/000617.html.

9. Dietz, Steve (2004) "Was it all Robert Morris's fault?" *Yproductions: WebWalkAbout* (December 19). Available from www.yproductions.com/WebWalkAbout/archives/000612.html.

"Homi K. Bhabha, in an essay from the Conversations at the Castle project in Atlanta, writes of 'conversational art,' and Tom Finkelpearl refers to 'dialogue-based public art.'... The concept of a dialogical art practice is derived from the Russian literary theorist Mikhail Bakhtin, who argued that the work of art can be viewed as a kind of conversation—a locus of differing meanings, interpretations, and points of view." (Grant Kester)[10]

"The individual tendencies of participatory art—the playful and/or didactic, the 'pastoral' and the 'sociological'—have at least one thing in common: the background of institutional criticism, the criticism of the socially exclusionary character of the institution of art, which they counter with 'inclusionary' practices. For all of them, 'participation' means more than just expanding the circle of recipients. The form of participation and the participants themselves become constitutive factors of content, method and aesthetic aspects." (Christian Kravagna)[11]

Those who are thoughtfully critical about interaction also tend to be those who can see parallels with other kinds of interaction, beyond those facilitated by technology. Steve Dietz, a curator of new media art amongst others, quotes correspondence around the Robert Morris exhibition, which was closed down in 1971 when an audience member injured herself whilst interacting with the sculptural forms. It is also notable that the press responses to that show are characteristically categorising interaction as necessarily childish and shallow: "Visitors Play Role in Funfair Art" *The Daily Telegraph* comments waspishly. Other more recent critics have made parallels with the interactive strategies of conceptual artists including the Fluxus group, or with participative aspects of performance art.

In fine art circles, there have been a recent slew of artworks where the audience can contribute to a growing artwork, for example Antony Gormley's *Field for the British Isles* (1993). Nicolas Bourriaud of the Palais de Tokyo in Paris, coined the term "Relational Aesthetics" for certain artworks which attempt to encourage interaction (although interaction between who and what is not always clear, as he cites Félix González-Torres, and Vanessa Beecroft as examples).[12] He also quotes Rirkrit Tiravanija as an example, an artist who has cooked Thai food, or set up a replica of his hospitable apartment, and has thoughtfully explored participation and interaction within the chilly strictures of art venues. Those from a background in activist or socially-engaged art tend to be more accurate about interaction: Grant Kester (quoted above) usefully

10. Kester, Grant (2004) Conversation Pieces. Berkeley: University of California Press. p.10.

11. Kravagna, Christian (1998) "Working on the Community: Models of Participatory Practice." *republicart.* Available from www.republicart.net/disc/aap/kravagna01_en.html.

12. Bourriaud, Nicolas (2002) *Relational Aesthetics.* Paris: Les Presses du Reel.

uses metaphors of dialogue to gauge how truly participative the relationship between artist and audience can be, and Kravagna is also aware of skills and issues from activism, but what most critics omit from such consideration of interaction, is any awareness of examples of art using new media. Critics of video may be aware of issues of time and media distribution, but not necessarily of interaction. This leaves new media to the tender mercies of positivist HCI (Human Computer Interface) methodologies, which are equally unaware of art. As Jon Ippolito of the Guggenheim New York has pointed out, interaction is "medium-independent behaviour" and hence critics must be able to move across different media.[13]

Rafael Lozano-Hemmer, from a fluid position straddling a history in performance, a sceptical mastery of the technology, a thorough experience of collaborative work, and a huge curiosity about his audience, is in an excellent position to form his own "aesthetics of interaction. " He was using the term "relational architecture" some time ago, which seems an excellent metaphor for the complexities of making interactive artwork: Architects bear responsibility—they must beware of bombast, they may study their users, and plan how spaces may be used; they may plan to be a perfect "host," but they are ultimately not in control of how people use their works, and have to be able to deal with that loss of control. It's not about the bricks and mortar, it's about how people use it. To leave the last word to Rirkrit Tiravanija: "I'm not a machine. I'm not a mechanical thing. I'm not a hardware, I'm a software."[14]

13. Ippolito, Jon (2003) "Accommodating the Unpredictable: The Variable Media Questionnaire." In: Alain Depocas, Jon Ippolito, and Caitlin Jones (eds.) *Permanence Through Change: The Variable Media Approach.* New York: Guggenheim Museum. Also available from www.variablemedia.net/e/preserving/html/var_pub_index.html. 47–54.

14. Harkrader, Lauren (2003) "Interview with Rirkrit Tiravanija." In: Linda Weintraub *Making Contemporary Art: How Today's Artists Think and Work.* London: Thames and Hudson. p.109.

From Within Shadows
Cuauhtémoc Medina

"The statues are now only stones from which the living soul has flown ..."[1] Hegel´s formula to describe the disenchantment with the decadence of "religion in the form of art" of classical antiquity, can also be taken as a confession of a certain longing for "idolatry," which involves an unremitting nostalgia for animated images. Whereas ancient Greeks were so convinced of the identification of the god with its image as to frequently chain their statues to prevent them from leaving their temples or cities,[2] and contemporary Hindus conceive worshiping as the pursuit of the gaze *(darsán)*[3] of the living incarnations of their deities brought to life through a complex set of rituals that culminate in the opening of their eyes,[4] the West has sustained an extraordinarily ambivalent relationship with human representations, at the same time fearful and overwhelming, superstitious and moralistic. As several historians have pointed out, far from assuming that representations are inert and dead objects, Western iconoclasm (as in the English Reformation, the Mexican Revolution or the Spanish Civil War), which went as far as to publicly execute images as if they were common criminals, betrays the continuity of an "animist" mentality that "perceives, reveres and finally destroys" representations.[5] In its love-hate relationship with images, Western culture seems convinced (despite all kinds of theological and philosophical discourses) that the power of images depends on the suggestion of a certain fusion between the image and its referent, or better said, to quote David Freedberg, a "sacred contagion" involved in the duplication of the powers of the body on its icon.[6]

As one goes to encounter the over one thousand moving portraits of individuals that come to interact with us in the installation *Under Scan* by Rafael Lozano-Hemmer, understanding the work as an attempt to renegotiate (and reflect on) the powers of the image within Western society becomes unavoidable. For, beyond its technical and formal motives, *Under Scan* is an essay on the operation of animated images in the public space. This whole device—which involves an archive of footage of personal attitudes and gestures of over one thousand

1. G. W. F. Hegel, *Phenomenology of Spirit,* tr. By A. V. Miller, Oxford-New York-Toronto-Melbourne, Oxford University Press, 1977, p. 455.

2. Moshe Barasch, *Icon. Studies in the History of an Idea,* New York and London, New York University Press, 1994, p. 39.

3. Diana L. Eck, *Darsan. Seeing the Diving Image in India.* 2nd. Ed. Chambersburg, Pennsylvania, Anima Books, 1985.

4. Richard H. Davis, *Lives of Indian Images,* Princeton, New Jersey, Princeton University Press, 1997, p. 33–37.

5. Michele Camille, *El ídolo Gótico, Ideología y Creación de Imágenes en el Arte Meieval.* Trad. Juan José Usabiaba, Madrid, Akal Edicines, 2000, p. 243. (Eng. Edition: Michael Camille, The Gothic Idol, Chicago: Univ. of Chicago Press, 1989.)

6. David Freedberg, El Poder de las Imágenes. Estudios sobre la Historia y Teoría de la Repuesta. Madrid, Cátedra, 1992, p. 448. (English edition: David Freedberg, The Power of Images: Studies in the History and Theory of Response, Chicago and London: Chicago University Press, I989)

people and an interface by which those clips are presented to the bystander using digital surveillance technology—is in fact a heavily mediated means of intersubjective interaction, where a group of people remotely interpolates another group through a repertoire of body gestures, which although recorded and played back at random to casual passersby, manages to meet the eye of another subject. The central tenet of such an operation is, in fact, the active illusion of an apparition: one walks in a public square and, as if invoked by a spell, a character emerges before our eyes on the pavement, and addresses us as if materialized from a dream. The whole cybernetic operation of the installation is aimed at provoking a moment of telepresence, where someone's smile, obscene sign or gesture of begging finally meets another person's emotional state. It is as if the whole intention of the artist would have been to populate urban space with a flood of random love and hate messages, which are generously distributed amongst what one would normally describe, as if validating the state of social alienation we have learned to live with, *as total strangers*. For a moment, thanks to the fascination provoked by the fact that these effigies seemed to be awaiting us, we are induced to engage in what, otherwise, would be perceived as improper or, even, dangerous: an exchange of emotionally significant public appearances. It is the more symptomatic of our shared historical condition that, as is the case with the Internet, this modality of intimacy has to be achieved through a maximum of technical illusion and artificiality. This process of experimental communicability is, to be sure, one of the main impulses behind Lozano-Hemmer's work: either because a certain technological physical and temporal distancing makes it possible to communicate under conditions of surveillance and social control, as is suggested by *33 Questions Per Minute* (2000) produced for the Havana Biennale. Or simply because the obscenity of the mediation seems, paradoxically, to excite the process of messaging itself, as for instance in *Amodal Suspension*: *Relational Architecture 8* (2003) in Japan, where text messages sent from mobile phones defined the behaviour of large-scale searchlights, until somebody would decide to catch the message and have it projected on the walls of the museum. Lozano-Hemmer's production would seem to suggest that under the present social circumstances, communication is a byproduct of an excited and at times fetishistic engagement with media: as readers of gossip magazines well know, personal secrets are not truly private unless broadcast by mass media.

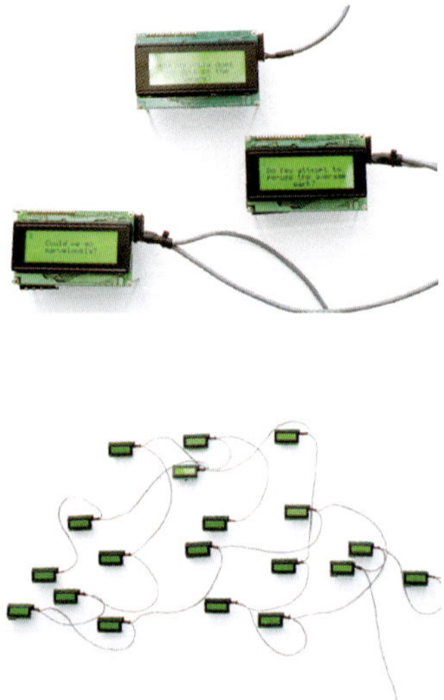

Rafael Lozano-Hemmer, *33 Questions per Minute* (2000). First shown at the Havana Biennale, collection MoMA, NYC

How can personal space be renegotiated in the public arena? It is not by chance that *Under Scan* has a certain gothic feeling: those images come to meet us very much as if they were the dead, emerging from inside the shadows on the pavement projected by the powerful beam necessary to the mechanism, in order to follow, describe and interact with our movement. As Ulysses, Aeneas or Dante, we have descended to communicate with dreams and phantoms, waking up their shadows in our quest to regain a certain form of community. It is this, in fact, which is at stake in the production of the public projects that Lozano-Hemmer has designated as "Relational Architecture," *i.e.* public works which transmogrify the experience of the city and its buildings by means of the ludic interaction of the audience with an apparently "false construct."[7] The intimacy with shadows proposed in *Under Scan,* involves an attempt to induce by means of the enactment of a public fantasy, a temporary alteration of our conventional social behaviour. Lozano-Hemmer's works induce their users to deviate the customary aims of contemporary public space (transit, trade and consumption, and advertisement) and instead promotes a form of spectral intersubjectivity, the meeting of visual fantasies in the guise of social illusions. This behaviour is akin to a form of collective hallucination, where a community of awe and entertainment is temporarily substituted for the structure of exchanges and powers of the current social fabric.

Thus he frequently operates by means of an inversion of the logic of the new means of electronic surveillance: instead of keeping the individuals under a permanent but secret structure of control and detection, he establishes a mirroring with the surveillance device that turns it into a mimetic device, where the subject observes his or her actions as effected on a visible mechanism. As a result of such alteration, means created by the technocratic state which normally induce in us the fantasy of trying to keep ourselves hidden from the eyes of Big Brother, individuals are stirred to self-representation and public appearance.

In writing and discussing artworks it is frequent that we overrate meaning, to the point of forgetting that images and works are, above all, tools, obstacles or recipients of our actions and messages. Public interfaces like Lozano-Hemmer's are not there to be interpreted but rather activated, or in any case described, later on, as the occasion of a certain interaction. They involve a re-distribution of powers; they provide the location of modified subjective interactions. The task of the artist in occasions like these

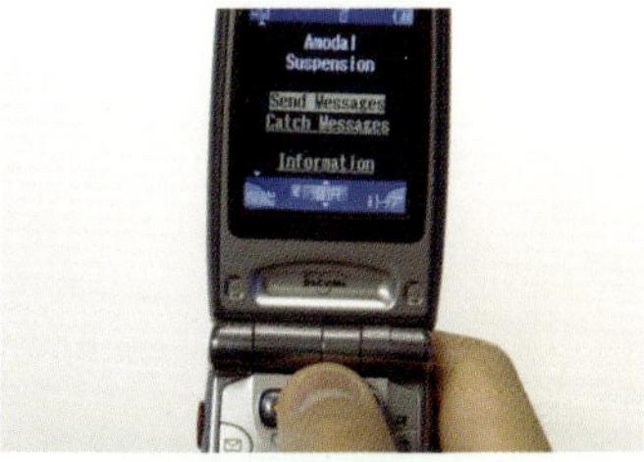

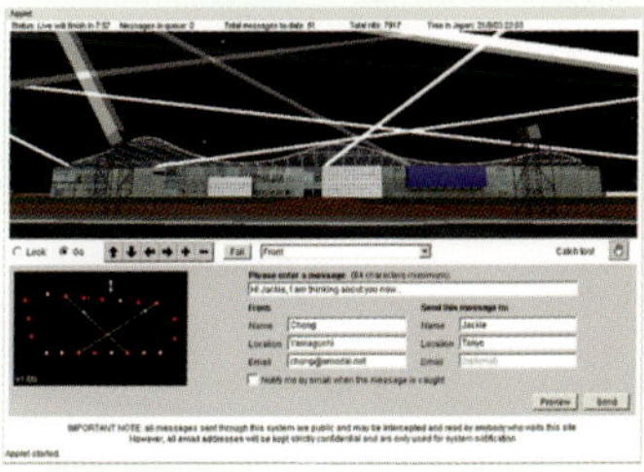

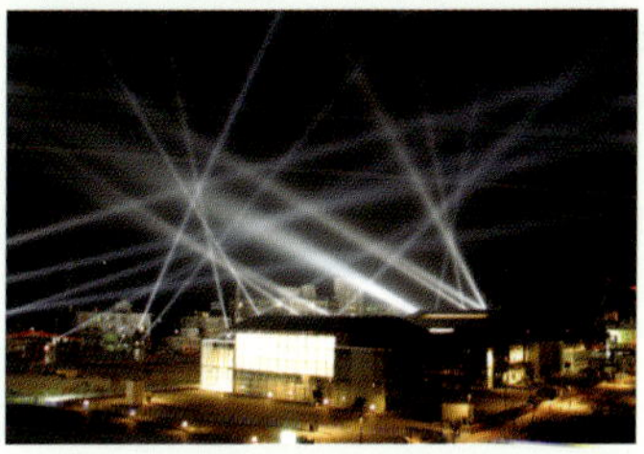

Rafael Lozano-Hemmer, *Amodal Suspension* (2003). Opening project for the Yamaguchi Center for Art and Media, Japan, www.amodal.net

7. See Lozano-Hemmer's original formulation of "Relational Architecture" as opposed to "vampire buildings" in: Geert Lovink, "Interview with Rafael Lozano-Hemmer, in: Rafael Lozano-Hemmer, *Alzado Vectorial: Arquitectura Relacional no. 4/ Vectorial Elevation: Relational Architecture no. 4,* México, CONACULTA, 2000, p. 55.

is to induce, to quote anthropologist Alfred Gell's words about the concept of art as agency, "social relations in the vicinity of objects mediating social agency."[8] *Under Scan* behaves, in that sense, as a modified *agora,* where individuals engage again in the game of interpellating each other, interrupting their business and monologues, and appearing for themselves and others; this is, the pleasure involved in their public existence.

Sure, this emergence is virtual or hallucinatory in part, and it requires that some of its "participants" (the images and the shadows) be reduced to a routine consisting in being activated by the steps of another person as they walk in the square, and then performing a pre-recorded action. But this remoteness, technically specified and randomly chosen, constrained and physically absent, is not any less poignant. For their actions, like all action (ours today, and even that of those that are dead) are aimed at another; and no matter how remote and delayed, they ought to reach their destiny.

8. Alfred Gell, *Art and Agency: An Anthropological Theory,* Oxford, Carendong Press, 1998, p. 7.

Local and Convivial
John Plowman

Being asked to write about *Under Scan* from a local perspective left me originally a bit perplexed and uncertain how to proceed. If local, as the dictionary states, relates or is restricted to a particular area or one's neighbourhood, my dilemma was what perspective should I use? But my uncertainty was clarified flying back recently at night from Aberdeen to East Midlands Airport. As my plane approached the airport in the dark, I looked through the window where I was able to have an overview of the East Midlands region, a particular area, the local. Looking down at the artificially lit clusters of habitation, the vista below me glittered like a treasure chest full to the brim of jewels. Surveying the local in this way it becomes immediately apparent that the urban is bright, visible 24 hours a day, whereas the surrounding area, the rural, is in darkness. It struck me that there were a lot more areas of darkness than brightness, like shadows cast by the urban areas, the rural forever in the shadow of the urban.

Taking the rural as local, what is happening in the shadow cast by *Under Scan* beyond its urban context, into the rural? It is significant that in this context the East Midlands region: *"The rural area, including the market towns, contains around 40% of the region's population compared to nearer 20% nationally."* [1]

Miwon Kwon, when writing about the siting of public art in an urban setting, has identified three paradigms: art-in-public-spaces, art-as-public-spaces and art-in-the-public-interest-mode. Although *Under Scan* as an art project positions itself firmly within an urban context I feel it doesn't sit easily within any of these paradigms and at best would seem to straddle the art-as-public-space and art-in-the-public-interest paradigms. It is this uncertainty of its taxonomic status that interests me, an uncertainty that is brought about by the project's engagement with issues pertaining to the relationships between art, site and audience,[2] aspects of contemporary art discourse that have been at the fore front in recent years, in particular the positioning of audience in relation to art and site.

1. East Midlands Development Agency website www.emda.org.uk

2. The word *viewer* could quite easily be substituted here but I feel that audience is a better word as it doesn't form such a closure on what the individual has to do, i.e. look. The word audience can be applied collectively or individually and refers/infers much more to the temporal experience of what ever is being witnessed.

A lot of things come together and conspire to make it easier to locate and communicate with an audience in an urban environment. Whereas, a rural landscape with its scattered population, necessitates the creation of different strategies in order to engage with such a dispersed audience. So, what is happening locally in the rural, at the present time in the shadow cast by *Under Scan,* and can such activity enrich and challenge urban centric experiences?

Beacon is a visual art project that is firmly rooted in the rural: it provides an opportunity for the audience to access relatively unknown heritage sites through innovative visual art activity in rural Lincolnshire.[3] By foregrounding the temporal relationship between audience, place and art *Beacon* creates an experience that offers a new model of how art can be perceived without relying on an urban model.

Beacon engages with issues pertinent to the rural, in particular that of isolation, both physical and cultural. There are residents in rural areas that do not have easy access to transport, private or public, limiting their opportunities to engage with cultural activities which usually take place in urban centres. I have written elsewhere that *"Urban cultural values are the paradigm used for any discussion, writing or reading of and about contemporary art. These values in turn determine the way the artist makes art and how we, the audience, look at art. In the same way the gallery and museum, as social and institutional place, are the norm for exhibiting and looking at art. Likewise the exhibition in a disused space such as a warehouse or empty shop has become ubiquitous in the urban cultural landscape. All these places have a cultural and social role within the local, regional and national community, becoming fixed points located in the urban landscape. For the artist such places provide a validation of their cultural identity, with each exhibition or project measuring up to the previous one in another city, town or country. The ramifications of the use of this urban paradigm by the institution, artist and critic is that the audience inevitably ends up using these same criteria to measure their own experience of engaging with and understanding of contemporary art. The audience, or more importantly their role within contemporary art practice is, I would suggest, worthy of reappraisal. One in which they cease to become a passive participant in the viewing experience and adopt a more proactive participatory role in the area of art production. The main protagonist, as I see it, in such a debate is place, as it is to (a) place that the artist and audience respond, although as I have stated above, the established hierarchy art, artist and*

3. Established in 2004 an archive of past and current projects can be found on www.beaconartproject.com

institution would indicate that the audience is almost conceived of as an afterthought, an inconvenience if you like. But it is to the audience that we must look to when considering these inescapable aspects of urban cultural values that are present when transposed to a rural context.”[4]

By not relying on an urban model *Beacon* offers an alternative to how art can be experienced, the *Beacon* coach excursion takes the audience to the art. Filling a void, allowing it to explore this potential of making contemporary art visible in the rural and by so doing the rural visible to the urban. Anne Douglas has noted that the *Beacon* audience is invited *“...to visit each site in sequence and to commit a period of three and half hours to making a journey that links the sites into one coherent, complex experience. The journey by coach is a pragmatic means of getting an audience around the six different sites. It is also an artistic device that acknowledges and builds on a challenge inherent to the rural—geographically dispersed living. Plowman has appropriated this challenge of everyday life to establish a journey in two senses, one functional and the other metaphorical, a journey of discovery.”*[5]

The act of travel, is a reassuringly familiar activity. The coach and the time taken to travel becomes the focus of attention for the audience. The journey creates a site of social interaction, enabling the audience to have a non-intimidating cultural encounter experience. During the course of the coach excursion the interior of the coach becomes a convivial environment, one in which Nicolas Bourriaud has said: *“...bring into play this great ‘What's it for? Which marks the true dividing line between entertainment and artistic praxis' he goes on to say that ‘ the use value of conviviality is combined with its exhibition value within the framework of an artistic project.”*[6]

I would go further and say that this line should also be seen as one which not only divides but also encircles. It becomes a process which assigns to each member of the audience the role of collaborator with the artist, art and site. Best described by Grant Kester: *“...as a process rooted in a discursively—mediated encounter in which the subject positions of artist and viewer or artist and subject are openly thematized and can potentially be challenged and transformed. I am particulary interested in a discursive aesthetic based on the possibility of a dialogical relationship that breaks down the conventional distinction between artist, art work and audience—a relationship that allows the viewer to ‘speak back' to the artist in certain ways, and in which the reply becomes in effect a part of the work itself.”*[7]

4. John Plowman “senseless and placeless” catalogue essay “sense of place:place of sense” 2005

5. Dr Anne Douglas, Senior Research Fellow, Gray's School of Art, The Robert Gordon University, Aberdeen. “A new curatorial practice” Essay in “sense of place : place of sense,” Beacon evaluation report 2005

6. Nicolas Bourriaud “Berlin Letter about Relational Aesthetics” in From Studio to Situation ed. C. Doherty 2004 Black Dog Publishing

7. Grant Kester “Dialogical Aesthetics: A Critical Framework for Littoral Art” www.variant.org.uk

What Kester is advocating here is a much more socially engaged practice, one in which the emphasis of the role of the artist is less as an expressive agent and more as collaborator in dialogue with the audience. Whilst *Beacon* is not an example of a socially engaged practice of the type Kester advocates it does create relationships that are played out in real time, forming a narrative that in turn creates meaning for the viewer as it unfolds. It really again comes back to this idea of participation, as Nicolas Bourriard notes, that *"Artists seek interlocutors."* and that *"The meaning of the work emerges from the movement linking the signs put out by the artist, but also from the collaboration of individuals within the exhibition space. As Karl Marx wrote 'reality is none other than the result of what we do.'"* The relational aesthetic integrates this reality. [8] Whilst both Kester and Bourriaud advocate participation they do so from different positions. It is this idea of a relational aesthetic, as propagated by Bourriard that I find interesting in relation to *Beacon* in particular and art practice in general. Taking the opposite viewpoint to Kester who advocates a socially engaged art practice, Bourriaud talks about: *"the formal construction of space-time entities that may be able to elude alienation, the division of labour, the commodification of space and the reification of life. We could thus say that the exhibition constitutes an interstice, which sometimes reproduces or uses the very forms of our alienation."* [9]

Visual art practice is pivotal in questioning how inhabiting, visiting and looking at art in both urban and rural places can inform and enrich our everyday experiences. By considering culture as intrinsic to everyday life *Beacon* (and *Under Scan*) place the audience at the centre of the whole artistic approach, creating a space in which the audience, individually and collectively, are able to establish meaningful relationships between art, artist and place. Although the dominant cultural paradigms and value systems are becoming increasingly urban in character, I would like to think that perhaps it is the urban that is in the shadow of the rural. I would like to offer up a new paradigm to be added to the list of Miwon Kwon: that of art-as-local-and-convivial.

8. Nicolas Bourriaud ibid.

9. Nicolas Bourriaud ibid

Section 3
Location Reports

Under Scan in Lincoln
25 November – 4 December 2005
Rotunda, Brayford Campus, University of Lincoln

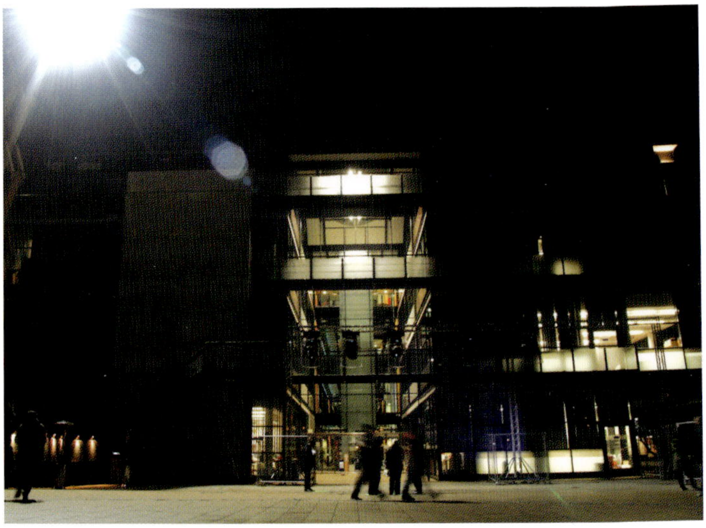

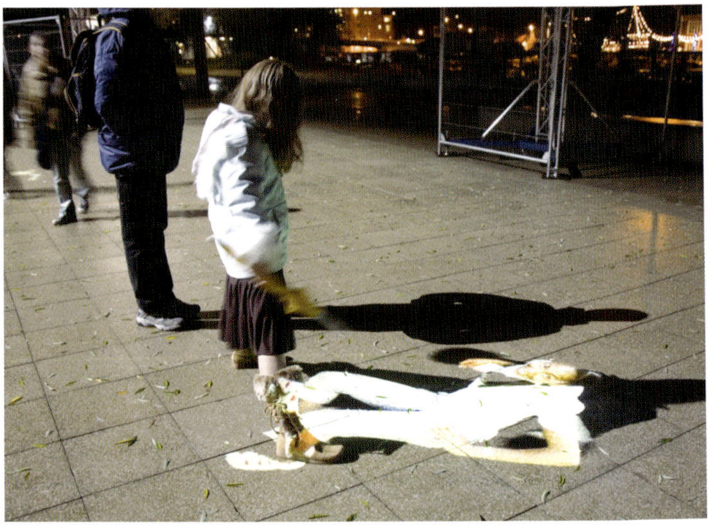

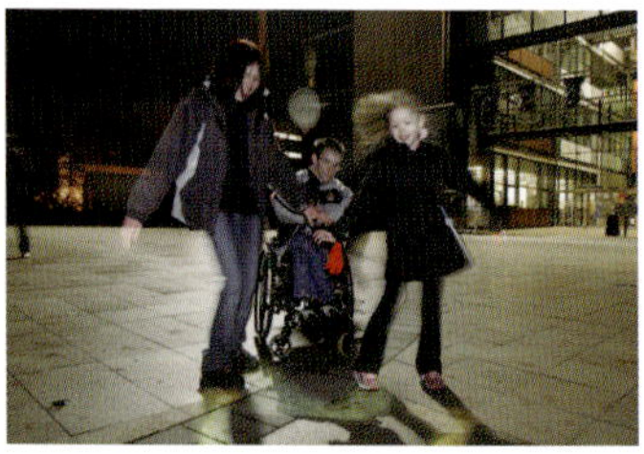

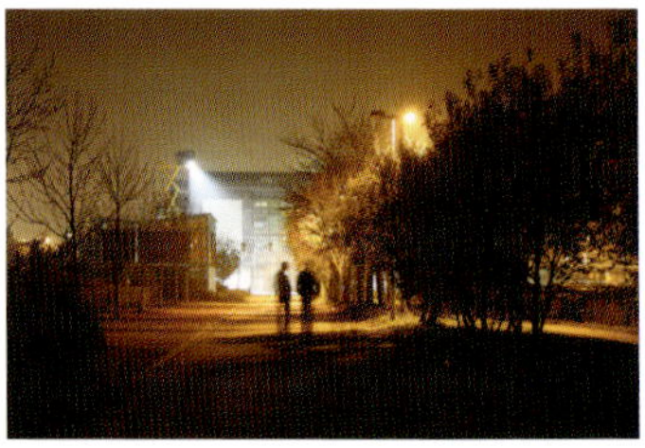

Silent Voices
Jayne Bingham

Head of Art University of Lincoln

The University of Lincoln was delighted to be the first regional host of *Under Scan* and therefore the venue for the world premiere of the work on the 25th November 2005. During its appearance in Lincoln, *Under Scan* attracted many groups and individuals to an environment used to quite different activities. Installed in the Rotunda at the Brayford, the university's main campus in the heart of Lincoln, it occupied an outdoor thoroughfare and meeting area, a location regularly accessed by city residents and visitors as well as those who work and study at the institution.

Each evening *Under Scan* transformed the space from the familiar to the extraordinary. New and unexpected spatial panoramas emerged effecting a disorientation and uncertainty in an environment of routine and daily business. Now there existed a constant invitation and challenge to interact with the art and inevitably with each other. The sociability of *Under Scan* removed barriers; became liberating. There was an infectious shared engagement, and many returned with others new to the experience of interactive art and video installation on an immense and public scale. It was the drama within the video portraits, however, that seemed to create the rapport, sustaining involvement through the various narratives, pleadings and confessions enacted by the performers. For those uncertain about their role within the work such confrontations were disconcerting, unsettling but nonetheless addictive.
The revelation of the "other community" became a darkly entertaining encounter.

Rafael Lozano-Hemmer first shared his ambitions for the project with the city through a public lecture, as an invited guest of the Lincoln Academy, the university's programme of cultural outreach activities. He charted the development of *Under Scan* from its infancy as a concept, through to realisation. The references to location specific work, as opposed to that produced within the traditions afforded by the gallery system, and collaboration or shared practice, highlighted issues that are very much part of a rich discourse, across a broad spectrum of current art practice. The lecture proved to be the start of a unique opportunity for students, who would be able to experience at first hand, work that reflects contemporary perspectives.

A significant element of the university's Fine Art degree programme profiles relationships between audience and art work and particularly a consideration of the mutually active exchange; creative partnerships that are interdependent. Students also generate work that should both respond to location and be seen in that venue as a means to begin to contextualise their art practice beyond the study environment. The presence of the *Under Scan* installation within the learning environment itself, and for students to be able to meet the artist and his team, and then participate in the work, enhanced a curriculum experience that seeks to champion many aspects of the project.

Under Scan is an artwork reliant on the participation of its own potential audience to exist. It is forever dependent on that continuing participation to remain visible. The essential dynamic of art, artist and audience that enables the creative cycle, is demonstrably evident here, though the audience enjoys an unusual authority in the work. It was invaluable for students to witness and contribute to these relationships as they were built, and then nurtured to the point where their own image investment was visibly tangible and attributable to the success of the project. It was a rare and welcome opportunity to see a work in progress, and to evidence the dual role of the artist as a project's creative energy and in this case, its art director as well.

The university's involvement in the *Under Scan* project though extends beyond the provision of a site for the work. It reflects the commitment it has to supporting cultural initiatives that provide for the regional audience as well as its own academic community. Projects such as *Under Scan* as well as the Lincoln Academy's series of public lectures, international concerts at the Drill Hall venue, drama productions and the university's new arts centre signify a progressive campaign to help shape the cultural landscape of the East Midlands.

The new Performing Arts Centre, scheduled for completion in 2007, will present quality productions, complemented by lectures, talks and creative workshops, an arena for national and international performers, film makers and musicians. The 450 seat theatre is to be a creative and vocational environment for the performing arts with a remit to enhance academic mission and generate opportunities for regional access to innovative, contemporary works.

Under Scan operates on a grand scale through an innovative use of new technologies and it has a substantial physical presence, though it sets out to disclose its secrets on a much more intimate human level. Ultimately it is the transience of the video portraits, the fleeting presence of us by virtue of our shadows, the catchers of those silent voices that made this public event an additionally private, contemplative experience.

The Wider Context
Lincoln's Cultural Quarter

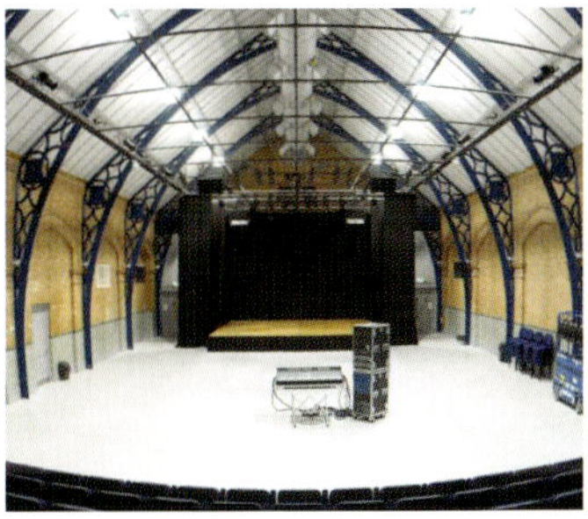

Lincoln's developing Cultural Quarter rests neatly in the heart of the Cathedral area of the city, creating a vibrant and strong cultural identity.

Lincoln City Council continues to work with partners through master-planning and public realm development to encourage investment in, and promotion of, a strong and cohesive mix of contemporary and historical facilities. The area of the Cultural Quarter has undergone recent renovation with a new signage and interpretation scheme in place.

The Cultural Quarter consists of:

The Collection-Art and Archaeology in Lincolnshire
The Collection is an exciting free-entry facility incorporating the Usher Gallery and a new state of the art museum. The buildings sit side by side in the city centre enjoying spectacular views of Lincoln and its magnificent Cathedral.

The art collection includes work from JMW Turner, Stubbs, LS Lowry, Grayson Perry, John Piper and Ivon Hitchens. The Gallery boasts the largest public collection of works by Peter DeWint.

The Collection includes a wealth of artefacts from the Iron Age, Roman, Saxon, Viking and Medieval eras as well as fine, decorative visual arts and a flourishing temporary exhibition programme.

Creative Industries Managed Workspace
Lincoln City Council, in collaboration with partners, has developed a state of the art new creative industries project (due to open March 2007) which will deliver forty-five leased spaces, ranging from independently accessed workshops at ground level to studio and office space with floor areas ranging from 150 to 900 sq.ft.

The central reception and management office is at the core of the development, which comprises three distinct blocks linked by glass sided bridges. Adjacent to the entrance area is a café/bar seating around forty people to provide a meeting place for occupiers and visitors. Facilities for meetings and conferencing will be available as well as a gallery/ exhibition space.

Lincoln Drill Hall
A key cultural venue for the city for over half a century, Lincoln Drill Hall underwent a £3m refurbishment and is now Lincoln's newest arts venue. On offer is an exiting programme of events including theatre, comedy, dance, classical music, jazz, rock and pop, as well as workshops for children and families.

Theatre Royal
Lincoln's Theatre Royal is an intimate late Victorian theatre hosting a variety of performances including opera, drama, comedy, musicals, concerts and pantomimes.

Lincoln Central Library
The County Council aim is to provide a library service that can be used by everyone regardless of age, state of health or where they live. Situated in the heart of the Cultural Quarter, Lincoln Central Library is a perfect example of this diversity.

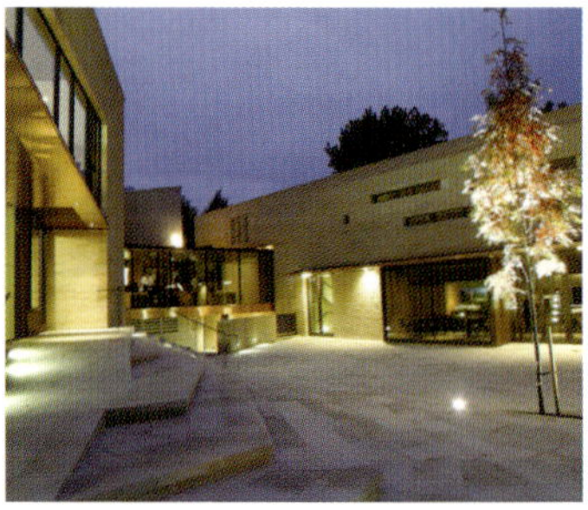

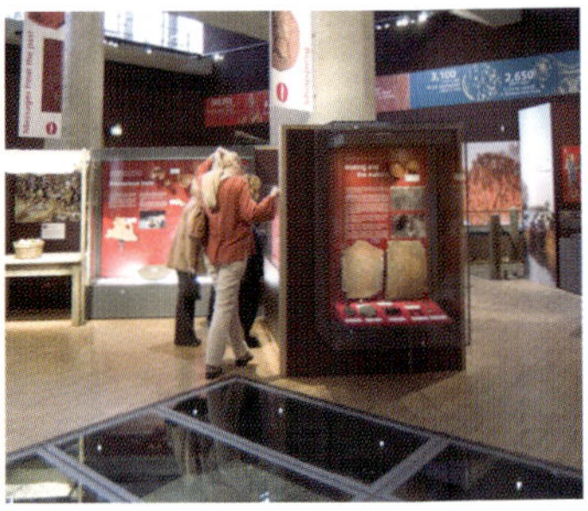

The Collection

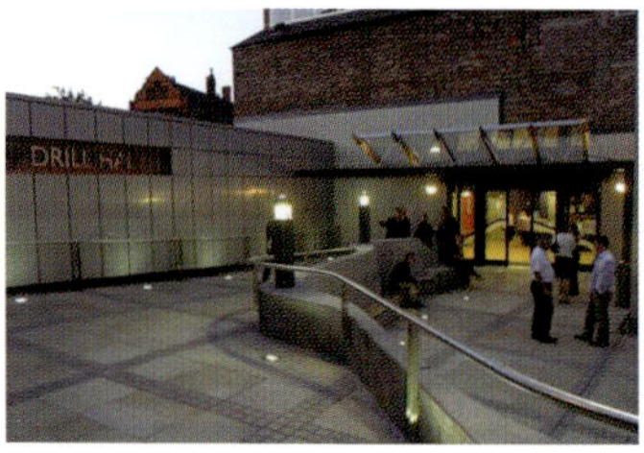

Lincoln Drill Hall

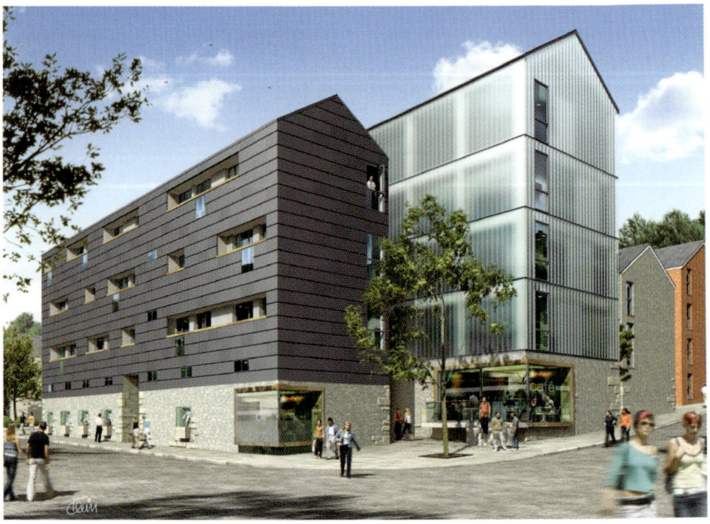

Creative Industries Managed Workspace

Under Scan in Leicester
12 – 22 January 2006
Humberstone Gate West

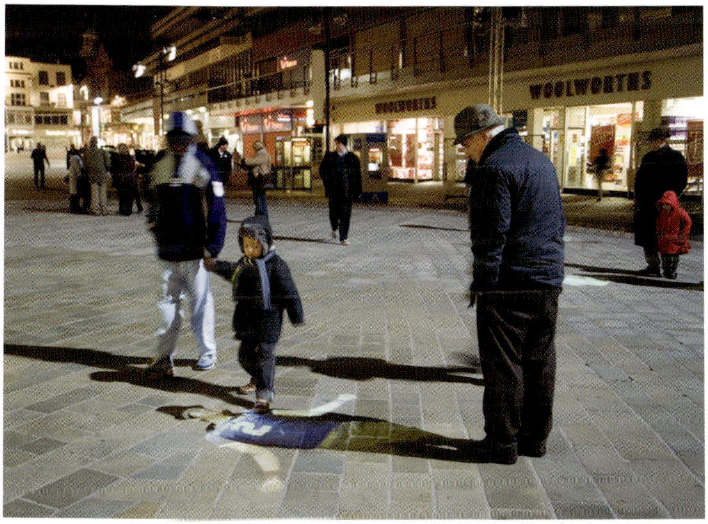

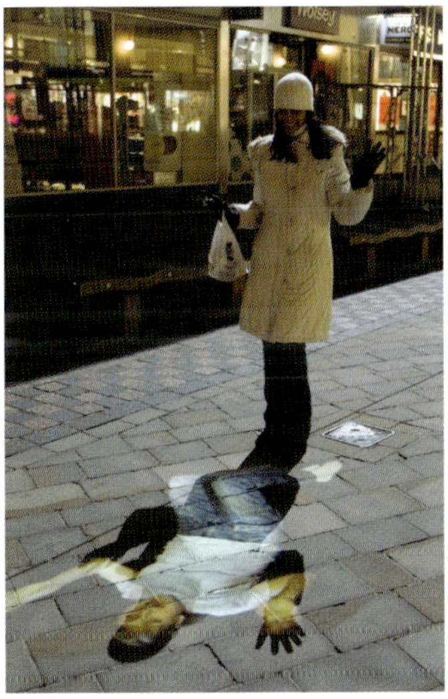

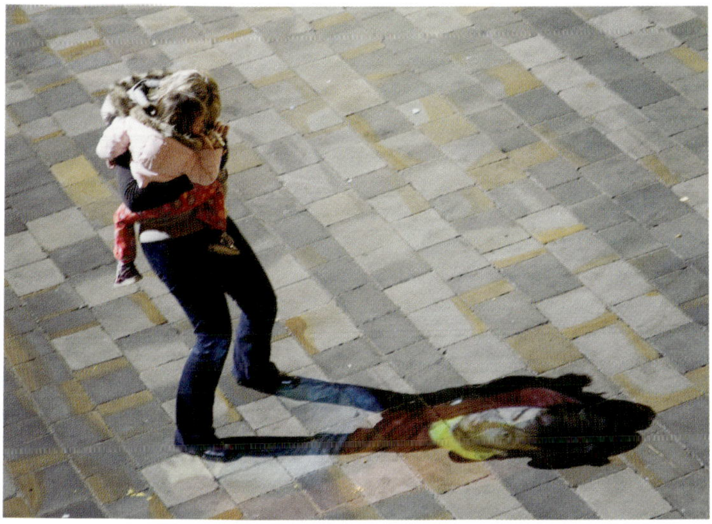

The Wider Context
Leicester's Cultural Quarter

Leicester City Council is working with a wide range of partners to develop and deliver an extraordinary new Cultural Quarter in the St George's South area of the city centre. The aim is to establish Leicester as a major regional centre for the creative industries.

The Cultural Quarter consists of:

1. Phase One
- Leicester Creative Business Depot (LCB Depot—completed June 2004)
- Performing Arts Centre (PAC)
- The Creative Industries Regeneration Team (CIRT)
- Public Realm & Infrastructure improvements

2. Phase Two
- Digital Media Centre (DMC)
- New Contemporary Visual Art Gallery (VAG)

Leicester Creative Business Depot
Refurbishment of the former Leicester City Bus Depot on Rutland Street has provided studios and workspace for a range of creative industry businesses. The building also provides three conference / meeting rooms, a gallery space and fully licensed café / bar.

The award winning building (RIBA Award and East Midlands Property Award for design excellence) was designed by Ash Sakula Architects.

Performing Arts Centre
The Performing Arts Centre (PAC) is the major development of the first phase of the Cultural Quarter programme. It is a significant flagship building, designed by Rafael Viñoly Architects (RVA) and is expected to open in 2008.

The PAC will contribute to the renaissance of the City as a whole by providing a replacement for the Haymarket Theatre and making a space where a special and new kind of theatre can be developed for Leicester and its people. The PAC is expected to deliver:

- 134 new jobs
- 20 new businesses
- 70 jobs safeguarded
- 200 – 300 trainees per year in cultural industry skills

Creative Industries Regeneration Team (CIRT)

CIRT was established in January 2005, in partnership with Business Link Leicestershire, to provide business support to the Creative Industry Sector in Leicester. It will drive forward the overall development of the creative industries and provide the promotion and support to encourage business start up, competitiveness, growth and innovation. CIRT will assist companies with relocation, training, financial support, technology, e-commerce, computer-aided design, and other identified needs.

Public Realm & Infrastructure improvements

A major programme will:

- Contribute to the wider (physical) regeneration of the St. George's area
- Improve the quality of the built environment and assist / encourage other developers to re-use / develop redundant buildings
- Improve the streetscape—pedestrian, cyclist and vehicular movement into and through the area
- Improve the environmental setting of the new cultural facilities
- Create new public space and public art
- Improve safety, taking into account the 24 hour economy
- Support the development of the Citywide Construction ILM

Digital Media Centre (DMC)

The DMC will be a key feature in the development of the Cultural Quarter and in due course will provide a new base for Leicester's Phoenix Arts Centre.

At the core of the facility there will be four cinema screens (capacities 300, 150, 75, 35) offering the highest quality audience experience, programmed with commercial, specialised and independent film, but with capacity and facilities for the screening of a wide range of other moving image products and to support seminars, education, participative arts practice and community events.

Visual Arts Gallery

It is intended that the brief for this project will include:

- Creating a new home for Leicester's City Gallery
- Providing a focus for visual arts provision within the Cultural Quarter
- Providing both workspace and demonstration space for artists in Leicester,
- Creating a new regionally significant tourism attraction.
- Containing units for visual artists and companies in order to incubate and develop this sector.

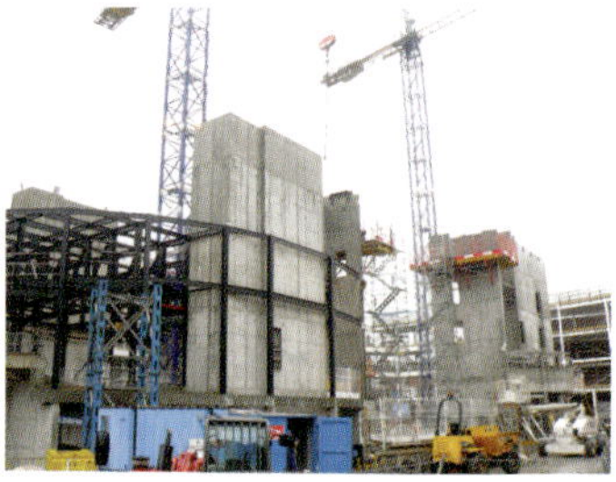

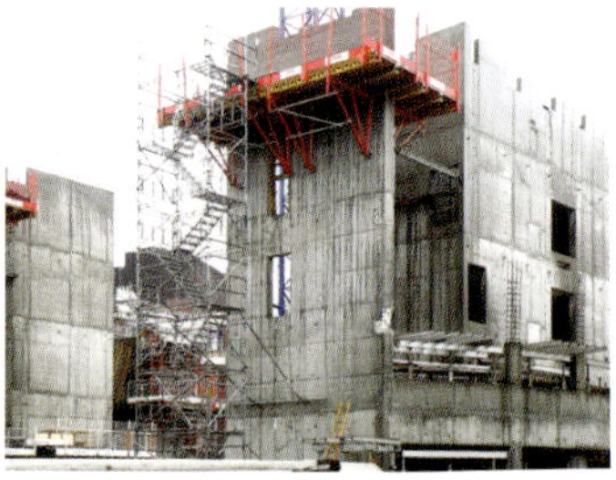

Leicester's new Performing Arts Centre

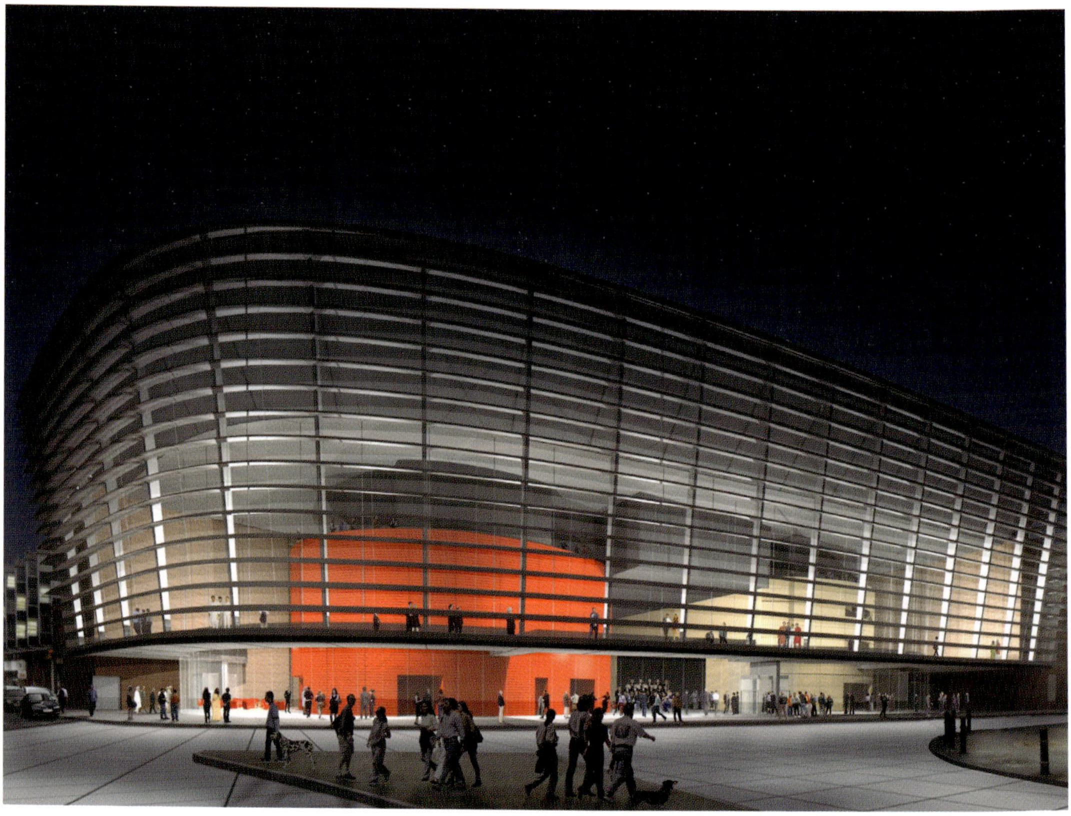

Under Scan in Northampton
3–12 February 2006
Northampton Market Square

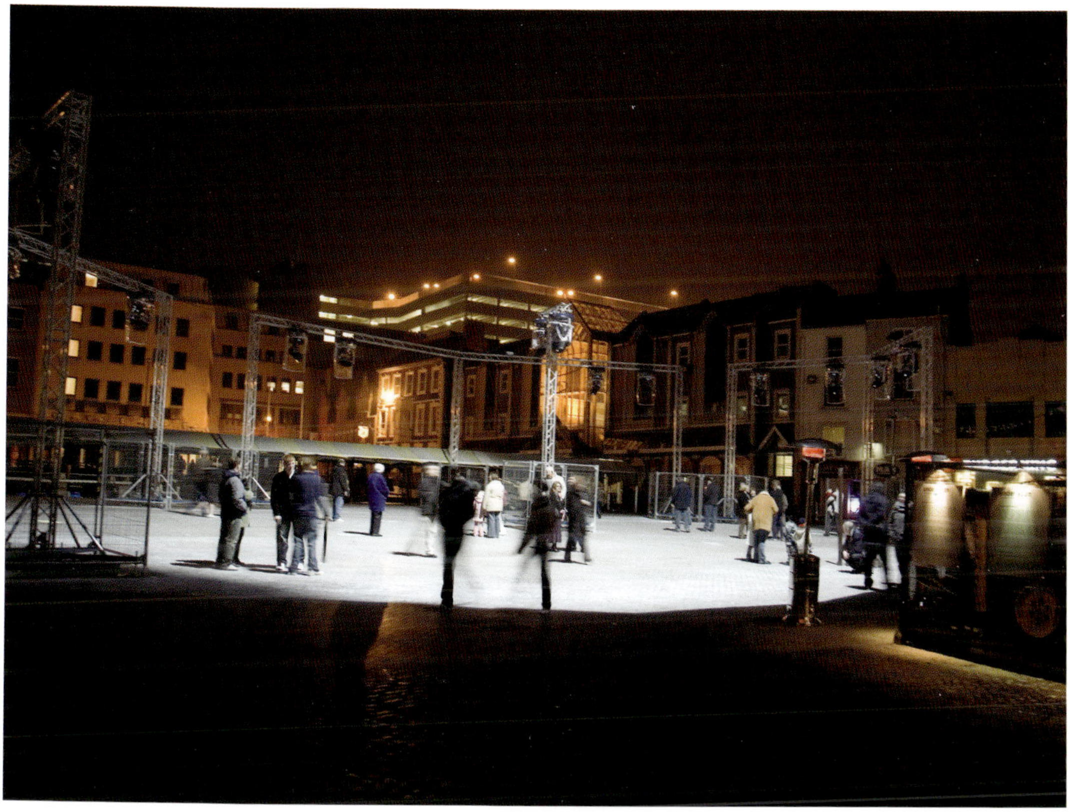

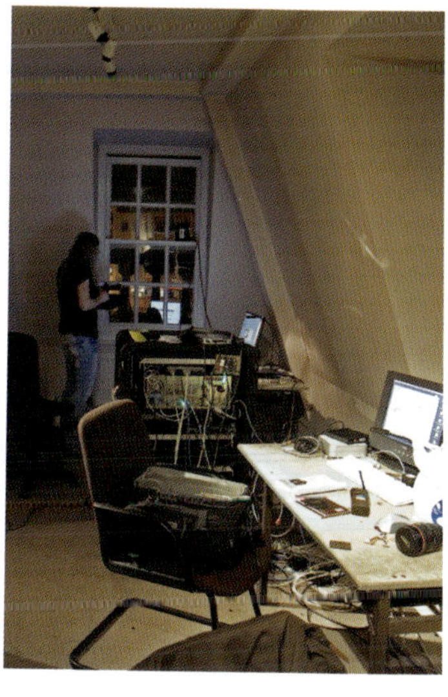

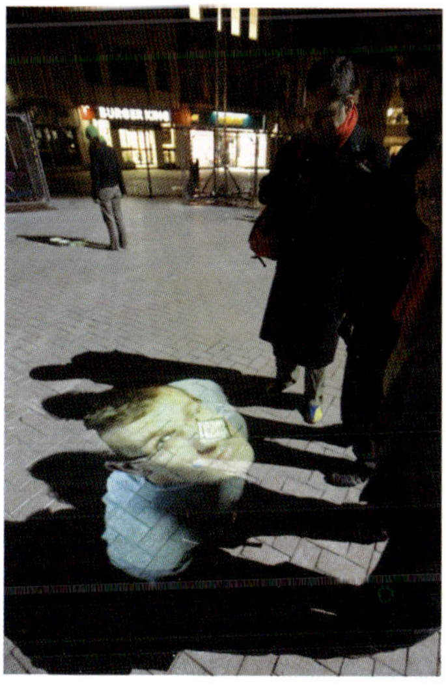

The Wider Context
Northampton's Cultural Offer

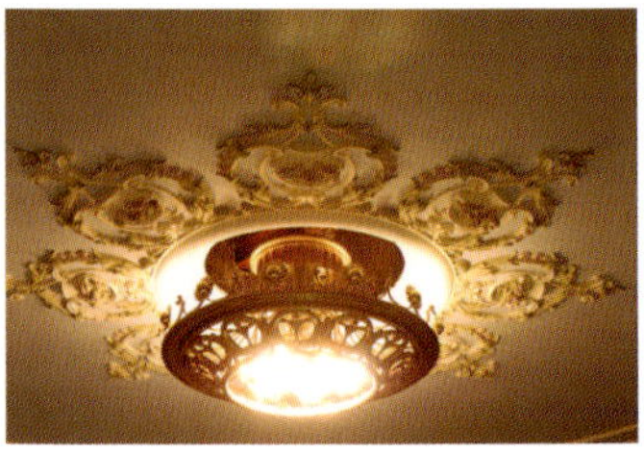

The Royal

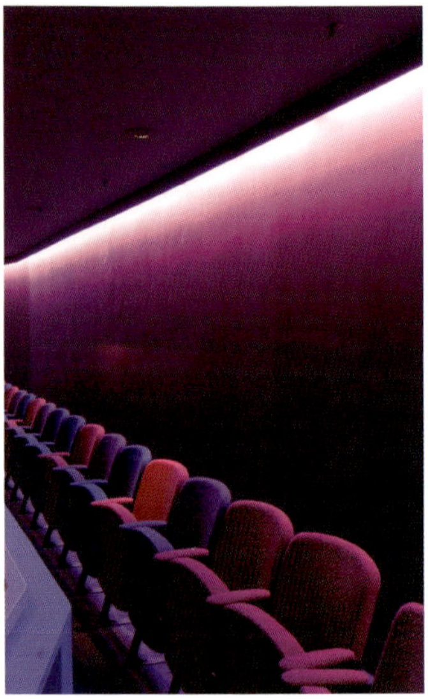

The Derngate auditorium

Northampton is at a key stage in its development, having been identified as a growth area by the Office of the Deputy Prime Minister. Northampton Borough Council is working closely with the West Northamptonshire Development Corporation (WNDC) to co-ordinate the wider development of the town. This offers real opportunities for regenerating the town centre, allowing it to develop and grow to meet the changing demands on Northampton.

Opposite the refurbished Museum and Art Gallery, the final stages of a major renovation of the Royal & Derngate theatre complex was completed in October 2006. Along with plans for the development of Northampton Market Square (including use of the Fish Market for arts events and activities), there is an opportunity to realise a long-term vision for a Northampton Cultural Mile. A Cultural Theme Group has been established to champion cultural issues and to work closely with a new Town Centre Commission providing a forum for consultation and debate.

Town Centre Commission

The Northampton Town Centre Commission (TCC) has been established to enable local people to have a voice on the issues affecting the long-term vision for the town centre. The Commission was set up by Northampton Borough Council in June 2005 to shape the future of the town centre. Involved in all aspects of the town centre, studies have been organised to look into shopping, tourism, culture, leisure, business and the environment. This work will lead to the creation of a Town Centre Action Plan that will guide the future development of the town centre.

Royal & Derngate

Royal & Derngate is a unique arts facility in the heart of Northampton. In autumn 2006, the venue re-opens following a major £15 million redevelopment which has completely transformed the building. The new complex is home to three performance spaces: the Royal auditorium, a beautiful CJ Phipps Victorian theatre; Derngate auditorium, a modern performance space offering a variety of seating configurations for up to 1500 people; and Underground, a new performance area that can be viewed from all over the foyer and workshop space. The transformation is remarkable, with old and new combined to spectacular effect. The Royal has been lovingly restored to its 1880s glory, whilst the Derngate has been redecorated using paint that will change colour under different light conditions, thereby changing the mood. Both auditoria will be more comfortable with new seating and air conditioning, and the building will now be open throughout the day with a new café bar serving light snacks and pre-theatre food.

Royal & Derngate offers a truly diverse programme of work. The in-house produced drama has attracted national critical acclaim, whilst the Royal Philharmonic Orchestra is resident and forms the centrepiece of a popular orchestral programme. The venue is a focus for cultural activity in the community and offers everything from comedy, dance, music, children's work, opera, ballet and creative projects.

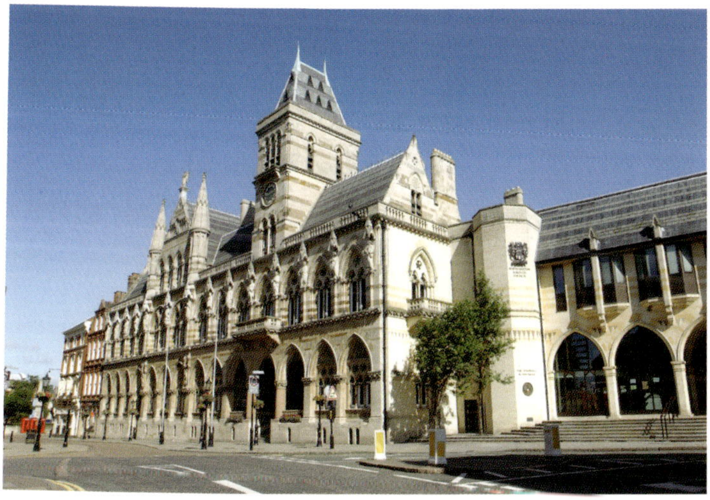

The Guildhall

Under Scan in Derby
24 February – 5 March 2006
Derby Market Place

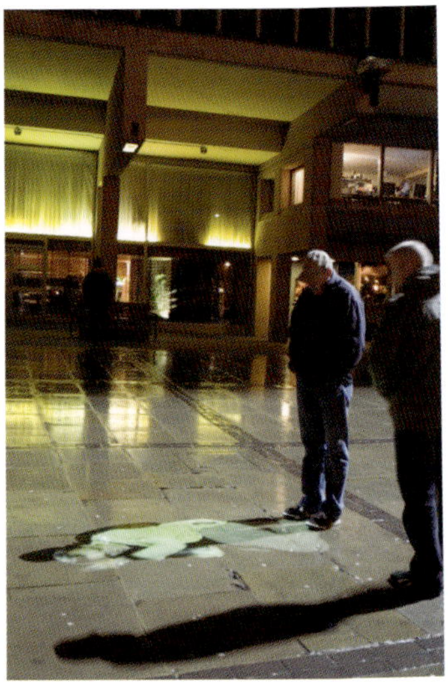

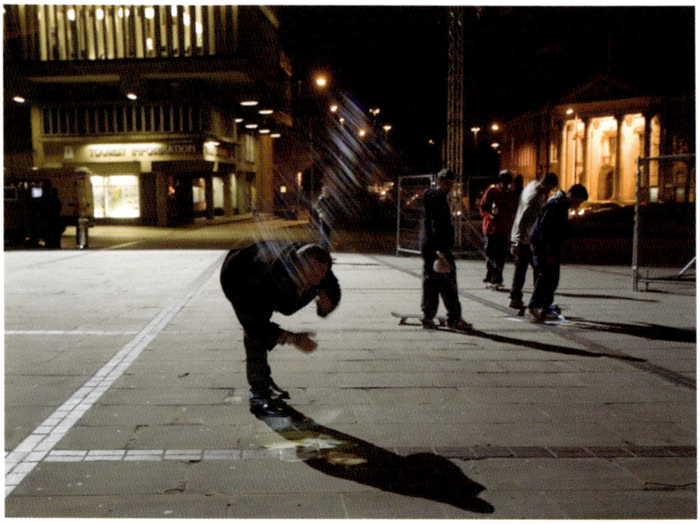

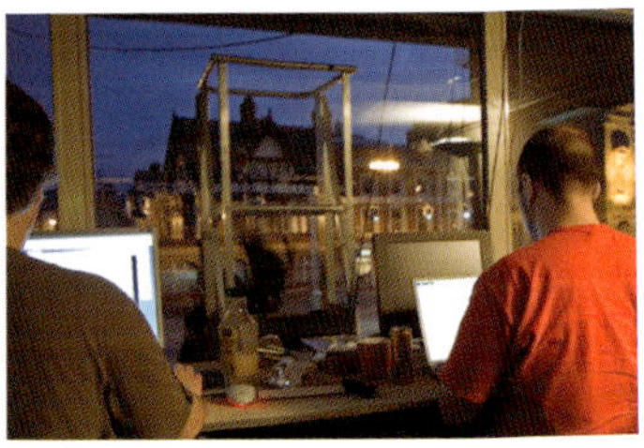

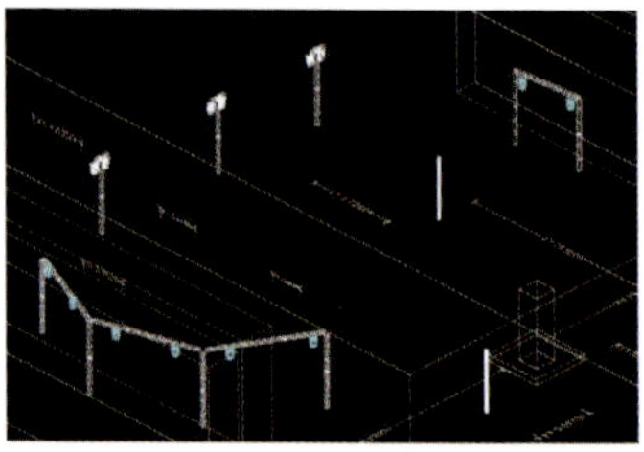

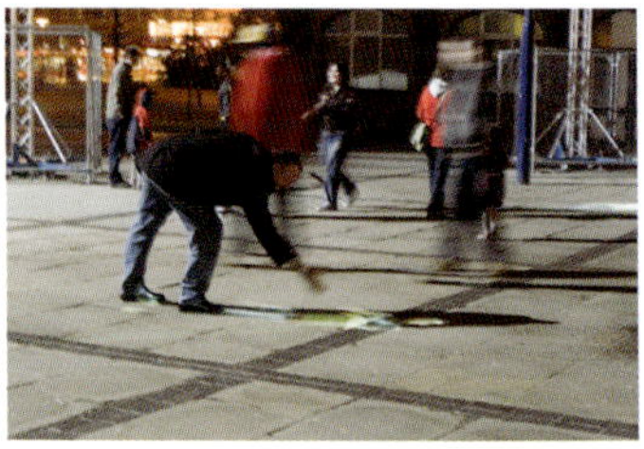

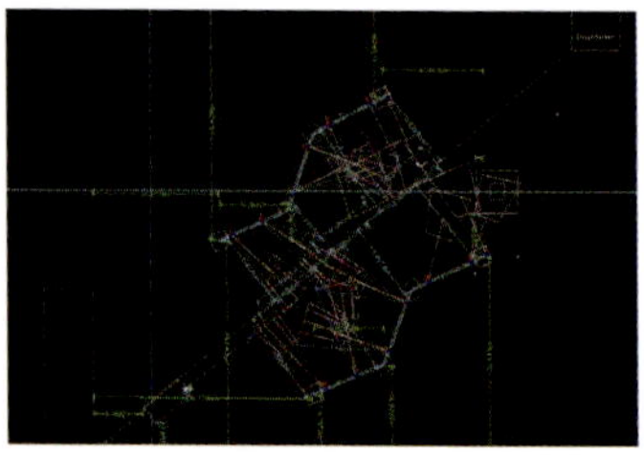

The Wider Context
Derby's Cultural Quarter

Derby is fortunate in being so relatively compact that its "cultural quarter" actually embraces the whole of the city centre. Culture in Derby is therefore both integrated and visible—a fundamental part of the life of the city.

The city is currently reinventing itself with major projects to renew its infrastructure in terms of roads, retail, learning and culture. In 2006 work commences on QUAD, Derby's new Visual Arts and Media Centre. Positioned in the very heart of the city next to the Assembly Rooms and the Guildhall Theatre, QUAD is a confident statement about the importance of culture to the future of the city. The people of Derby have a fascination with the uses of light and the possibilities of technology. These are the inspirations behind Joseph Wright's paintings and Rolls-Royce's world beating engineering. In QUAD those legacies are brought together in a new cultural agency which will demonstrate and stimulate the use of moving image and digital technology in the 21st century.

Coinciding with the emergence of QUAD and its stunning new building, Derby is re-discovering the cultural gems of its past and restating them in exciting new ways. After a lull of ten years the city has revived the tradition of photographic festival activity through its Format Photography Festival, taking place not in one venue for an elite audience, but as a distributed activity around dozens of venues across the city, including bars and public spaces as well as galleries and exhibition spaces. Derby's ambition is that the Format Photography Festival should become recognised nationally and ultimately internationally as the showplace of excellence and innovation in photographic work.

The democratization of cultural activity, reflected in the integrated cultural quarter, is illustrated with the ground-breaking approaches taken by Derby's performance venues—the Assembly Rooms, Derby Playhouse, Derby Dance Centre and the Guildhall Theatre. The Dance Centre has experienced a hectic period of expansion and diversification, raising it into the top rank of cultural agencies in the region.

Derby contains a unique asset as a city with the Derwent Valley Mills World Heritage site reaching right into the city centre to finish at Derby Silk Mill.

Ambitious plans are being devised to revamp the open space (Cathedral Green) in front of the Silk Mill so that it becomes a high value civic space and recreational area. The Silk Mill itself is being comprehensively redesigned so that it can tell the story of Derby's development as well as providing a gateway to the rest of the World Heritage Site in Derbyshire.

On the edge of the city centre but within walking distance stands the new Derby University Multi Faith Centre. This building in combination with QUAD speaks volumes about the new identity and the new confidence of this city. The confidence springs from a heritage of technology and innovation; and the ambition springs from new skills, new technologies and an openness to new cultural experiences.

Under Scan in Derby Market Place provided a means of expression for the city's new-found confidence and ambition. *Under Scan* was the biggest public art project undertaken in the city for a decade and it has triggered a new interest in public art in the context of a thriving, prosperous, diverse, urban community. Rafael Lozano-Hemmer's supporting lectures, as well as the installation itself, were pivotal in stimulating rigorous and informed debate around the concept of public art—its impact and its benefits.

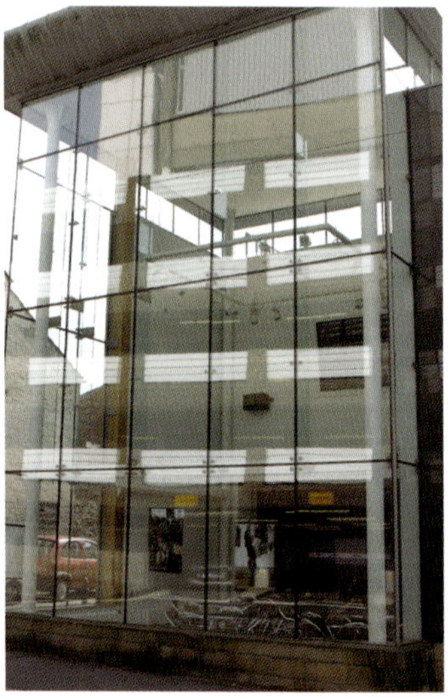

Derby Assembly Rooms

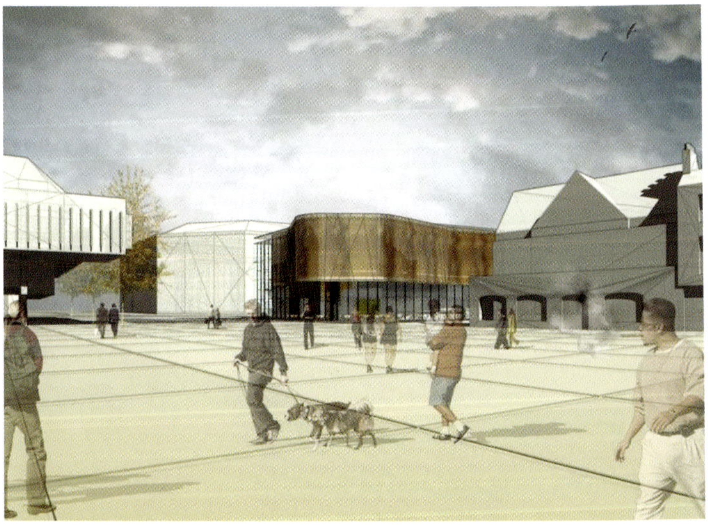

Derby Market Place

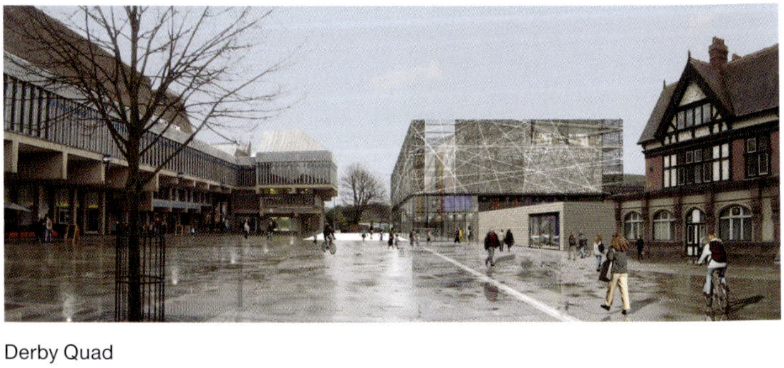

Derby Quad

Under Scan in Nottingham *16 – 26 March 2006*

Canal Side at Castle Wharf

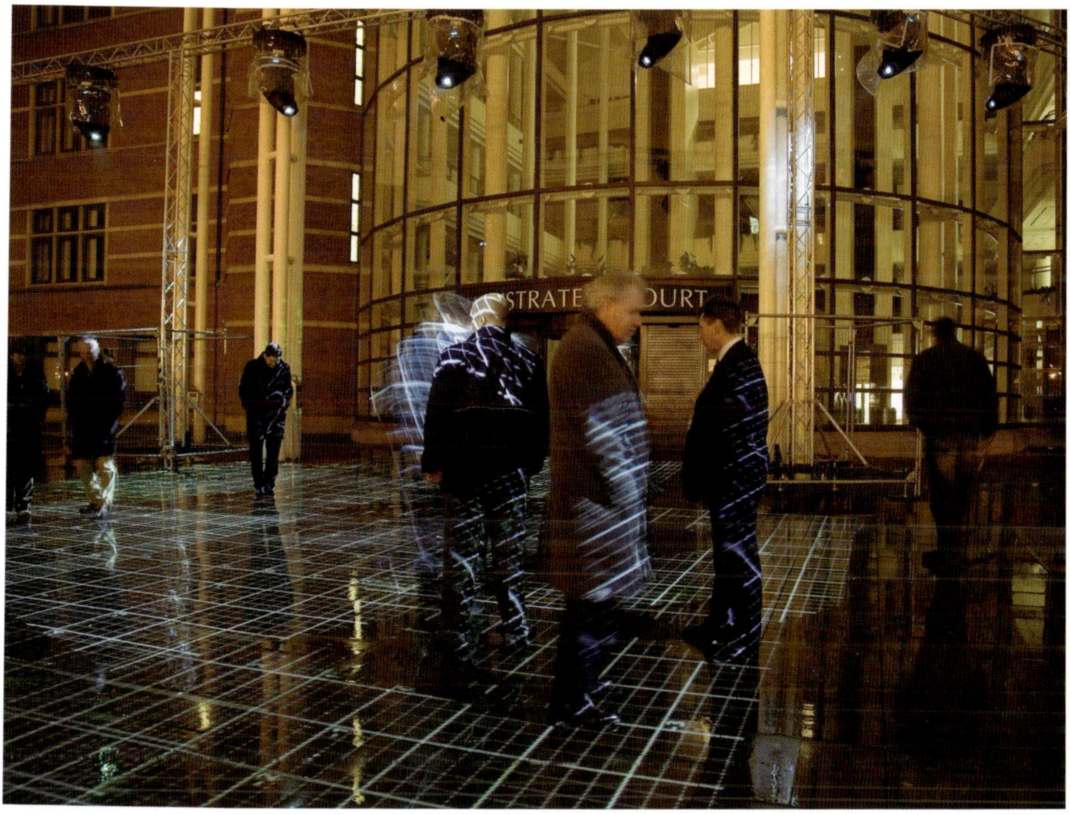

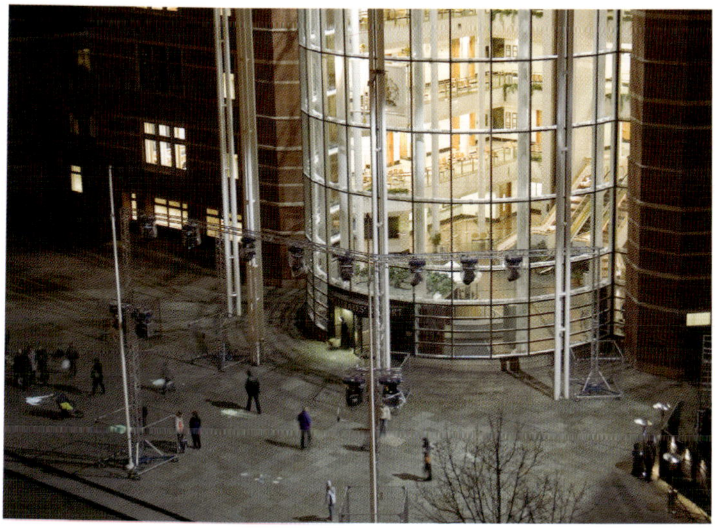

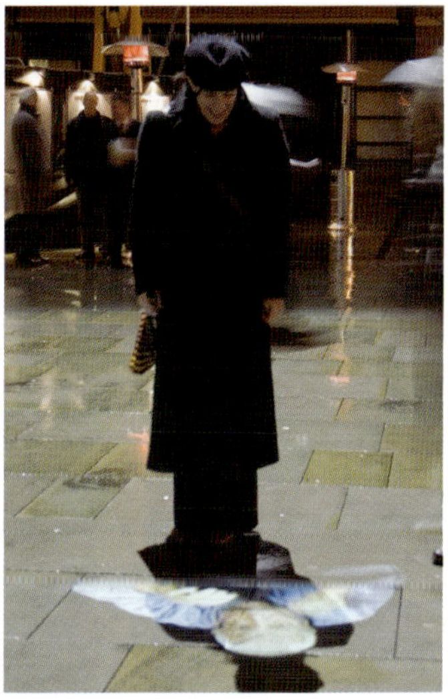

The Wider Context
Nottingham's Cultural Offer

Nottingham has linked its wide range of arts and leisure activities (a city-wide Cultural Quarter) into a "cultural offer" in keeping with its role as one of eight Core Cities designed to lead a renaissance of the UK regions.

From Nottingham Castle, the first municipal art gallery to open outside London in 1880, to two new purpose-built art centres now under development—the landmark Centre for Contemporary Art Nottingham (CCAN) and the New Art Exchange (the only centre outside London dedicated to Black and Asian artists), Nottingham has long recognised the value of culture in driving regeneration and boosting the economy.

Centres of excellence include The Theatre Royal and Royal Concert Hall, Nottingham Playhouse (with the Anish Kapoor Sky Mirror sculpture on the forecourt), the Broadway Media Centre and the Lakeside Centre incorporating the University of Nottingham's D.H. Lawrence collection. Broadway is currently completing a major refurbishment to ensure the venue provides state of the art facilities for artists and audiences alike.

The city centre is crucial to Nottingham's cultural life and offer with exciting plans for a re-modelling of Old Market Square in progress. The design is from award-winning team Gustafson Porter and the work will see the Square transformed into a vibrant new public space by mid 2007, providing a high calibre location for events and entertainment.

Within ten years there will be twelve new squares across Nottingham, all offering versatile spaces for the arts, and acting as catalysts to spread the city centre and help regenerate some of the poorer inner city areas.

New centres for further education, and media and creative industries rub shoulders with the clubs, bars, restaurants and apartments that have rejuvenated the Victorian lace and textile buildings. The ripple effect of the National Ice Centre on the edge of the revitalised Lace Market is helping expand city centre prosperity into Eastside where an innovative landscape design by rising star Thomas Heatherwick has been unveiled for the EastsideCity development. The Island, a high-quality, integrated and mixed-use space will be the first part of this masterplan.

Nottingham City Council received a major award from the English Sports Council towards the £36 million National Ice Centre. The twin-rinked complex doubles as the 10,000 capacity Nottingham Arena, providing a large-scale venue for pop and rock concerts, ice dance and entertainment spectaculars. Bolero Square in front of the complex is now the site of Axel, another piece of iconic public art from international sculptors Wolfgang and Heron.

Working collectively with agencies, artists, voluntary organisations and in a variety of partnerships the City Council is driving the cultural agenda ensuring the maximum is gained from the sum of the parts that make Nottingham a capital for culture.

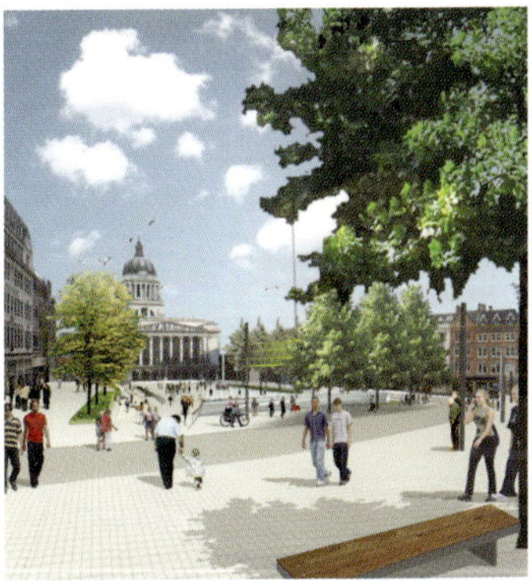

The Old Market Square

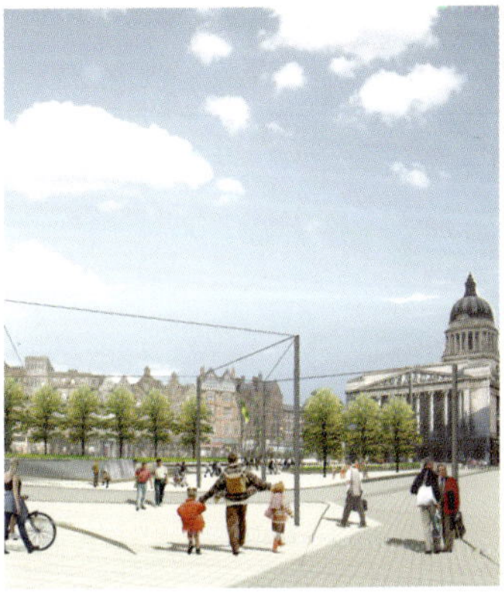

CCAN (Centre For Contemporary Art Nottingham)
Opening to the public in autumn 2008, the establishment of CCAN offers a major opportunity for the City of Nottingham to develop and enhance its cultural and creative industries infrastructure. The building will be an interdisciplinary arts space and regional gallery of international standing and provide a focus for, and access to, the creation and experience of contemporary visual and live arts in the city, region and beyond.

CCAN will be housed in a landmark building with an approach to construction and operation that is environmentally sustainable, and where the operation includes a high level of integrated information and communication technologies, along with an ambience that offers a warm welcome to all sections of the community.

CCAN will be one of the largest contemporary art galleries in England in terms of display area. Facilities include six galleries, a small performance space, café and bar, retail space, education and workshop areas, offices and supporting facilities. The new development is located on a key city centre site at Weekday Cross, in Nottingham's historic Lace Market quarter, an area that is itself a key base for the city's creative industries.

The development of CCAN is led by Nottingham City Council, with support from a range of stakeholders, including Nottingham Trent University and the University of Nottingham.

NAE (The New Art Exchange)
The New Art Exchange will be a state of the art centre for African, African Caribbean and South Asian arts in the East Midlands. The landmark building will establish the East Midlands as a cultural hub, benefit the local community and be an important development for multi-cultural arts nationally and internationally.

Building work begins in autumn 2006 with the completion scheduled for spring 2008. The facility will contain exhibition galleries, a performing arts space, digital media suite, education and workshop spaces, hot desk facilities and an attractive café.

The NAE programme of events, exhibitions and workshops will embrace the old Art Exchange's long history of work, maintaining a strong focus on African Caribbean and South Asian arts, whilst also reflecting the continuing changing face of British culture.

The NAE will project a positive image of the area and the city, helping to raise the profile and confidence of the local area and Nottingham, through improving the quality of local facilities and opportunities, supporting local regeneration and improving the environment with a beautifully designed environmentally friendly building.

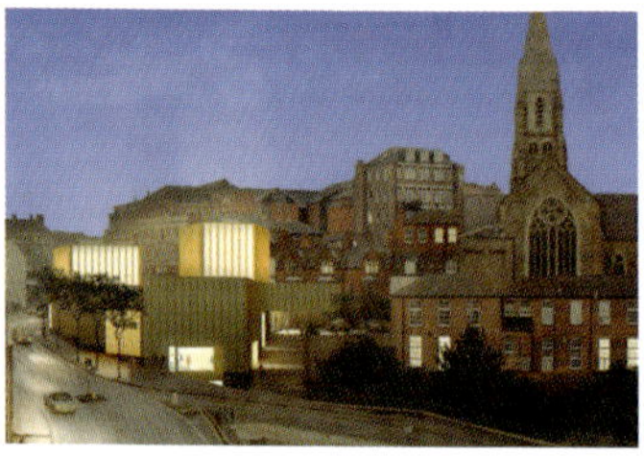

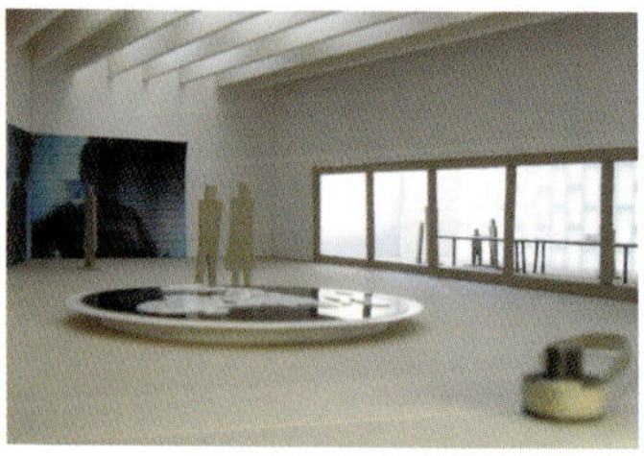

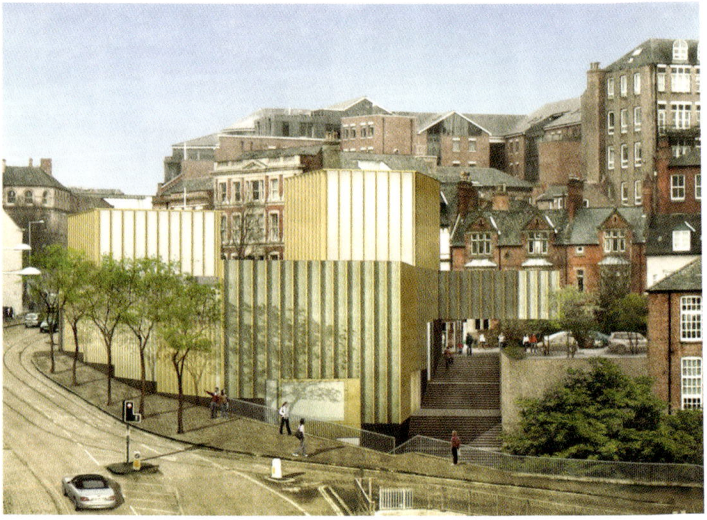

CCAN, a New Centre for Contemporary Art in the making

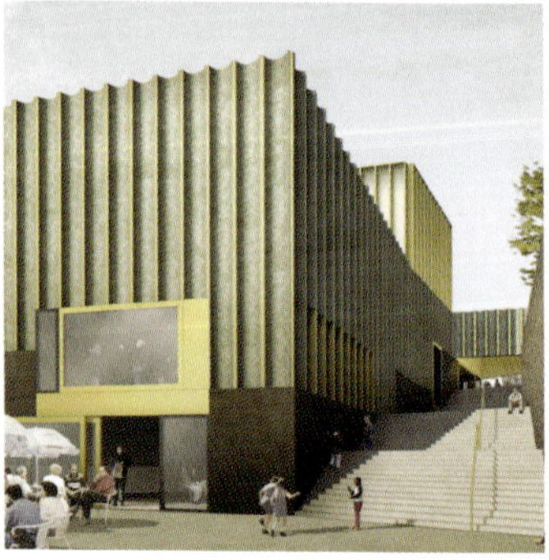

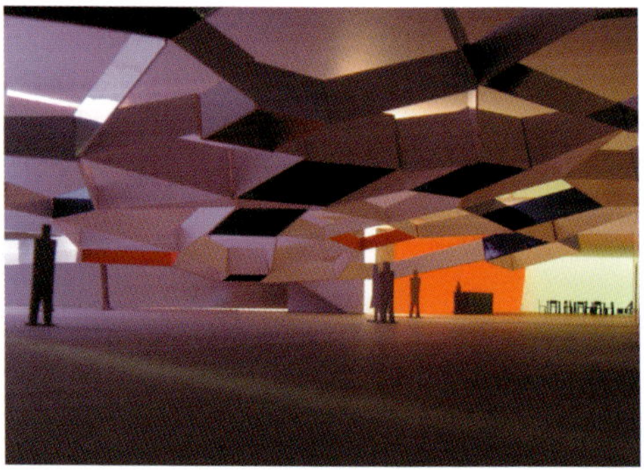

Interviews with the Public
Compiled by Nadja Mounajjed

Under Scan was exhibited in different spaces in the United Kingdom during a five-month period, in winter 2005–2006. At that time, I carried out a close investigation of the project. I followed the installation in different contexts and cities and interviewed participants from all ages and categories (children, students and adults; women and men). This article aims to qualify and classify aspects of peoples' experiences and practices in the space of *Under Scan*—as expressed by the users of the installation. Here I report findings which were collected during the interviewing process.

Sixty interviews were made differing in depth and length (from 3 to 30 minutes). I interrogated participants on their individual and collective experiences. I wanted to know how they responded, felt and interacted with *Under Scan.* More specifically, I was keen to know what they thought of the different virtual settings which were projected during the installation, and if this changed their perception of the original space. Questions were designed thematically and focused on the following issues: socio-spatial practices (interactivity, movement, and social integration), the virtual setting (video portraiture/interlude) as well as questions on memory and time—or the duration of engagement. Interviewing was very useful for gathering key data which conveyed the thoughts and feelings of people concerning the different aspects of the work. Feedback was generally constructive, and interviews were later transcribed and classified for further interpretation. The following discussion will illustrate people's views, interviews and expressions concerning the *Under Scan* project.

Public Space in *Under Scan*

In general, findings from the five cities confirmed that the *Under Scan* project improved the quality of spatial experience and the use of public space. People argued that the installation allowed the users to relate with public space by means of communication and digital technology as well as introducing interactivity and representation as part of our everyday spatial experiences. In this context, two young students commented:

> "Nowadays, people sort of use images to communicate through video conferencing, emails ...etc. What this artist is doing is that he is questioning how we interact with each other through the media. I think he is sort of playing with us. Instead of meeting up with people, we are meeting with images of people, they act, they move and they talk like real things. So maybe, it is like a parody of meeting a real person in a public square—even if it is not with a real person."

> "I think what is quite interesting is the self-representation of local people in a public space. This is something of an unusual/unexpected setting where it is not just any kind of projections but there is a reasoning behind these characters—of why they are there and what they are doing. But I am not sure people realise it. I think most public think that it is just fun!"

On the other hand, many users confirmed that the installation has changed their perception of the site; for these people, the space became "friendlier," "livelier," more intimate and inviting. One person in Leicester told me: *"I think it is much better now. I think it is lively; Leicester was not like this before! It was only for pubs and nightclubs but now it is ordinary public that are around. This was not the case before. So, I think it is good, good for the city!"* In Lincoln, the installation was set up on the threshold of one of the University buildings. I talked to a lady there who also confirmed that *Under Scan* changed the site. She said: *"It is obviously located in the entrance—which is an outside/inside space. Normally, this is just an empty space that people would walk through or sit in... But now, this installation is bridging this area. It has become busier. It brings people to the building in that respect."* Another participant from Leicester explained that she wouldn't normally come to the city centre by herself, but this was a good reason to walk to the square. She said:

> "If one doesn't want to come in by oneself then it would be nice to have things like that. But walking through it, I think it is very interesting, it is unusual, I never heard of or seen anything like it. And I think it would be interesting later in the evening when people are coming from clubs and pubs, how they would interact with it."

Under Scan brought to light a new public playful activity and a practice that falls between gaming, art and the media. Users describe how they play with the portraits: "*We were trying to move around, trying to make ourselves bigger to cover the image. It is like we have become actors in a way, as we wander around interacting with it!*" One participant explains why this kind of work can actually invite interactivity:

> "It is nice. You can play with it. I am sure kids will love it and when you have art works in which you can interact, not just like a static paintings in modern galleries—which is often cool but it can be also quite boring sometimes and in this kind of stuff outside, it is good, I think it is nice."

Also, the piece revealed a social dimension. Some regarded it as a conversational piece—bringing people together from different ethnic groups, ages and background, and giving them something to talk about and play with. As a result, *"It made the space more social and more intimate for people to integrate socially"* as one participant said. He continued: *"It is beautiful; the space has become more user friendly. Perhaps, if these things weren't here then we wouldn't come."* Another participant indicated:

> "I think it might have social dimensions because it is changing some aspects of the social engagement in public space. People would not be here if it wasn't for this. So it needs something else not just the space. It needs something to bring people to the space; to get kids out in the space. I don't know what this is doing but people are still coming. Certainly tonight it is working!"

Another woman expressed that the piece allowed for more intimacy in public space, which is not always available nowadays, she argued:

> "I found this really amazing because the interaction is very intimate. Suddenly, you are with a person who is looking at you, doing things to you or pointing at you. So, you feel really involved with it. I mean it is like an intimate moment. Not only that, but you feel complicity with the image because suddenly s/he is doing something at you and you are the only one who is really seeing it. It is demanding something from you. So, you feel involved really."

This moment of complicity, which the woman was describing, was clearly reflected in the behaviour, movements and activities of participants in response to *Under Scan.* The following section will discuss further the impact of *Under Scan* on socio-spatial practices.

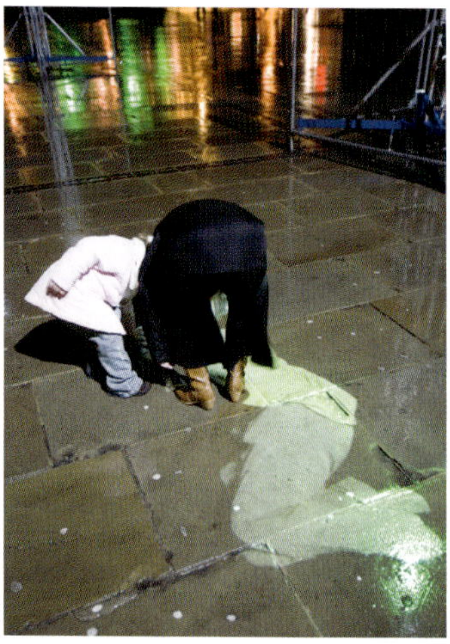

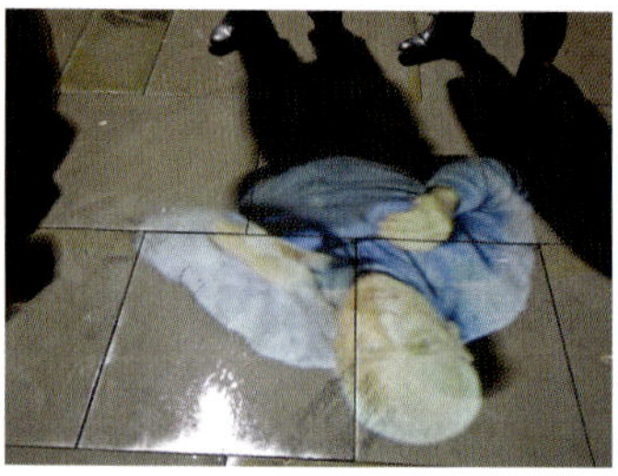

Mapping Spatial Practices in *Under Scan*

Findings showed that the way people moved during the projections were different from normal behaviour in public space. The fact that the whole concept was centred on the idea of the shadow (lighting up and inviting for interactivity) can be directly linked to body movement. One participant in Lincoln said: *"I saw many people behaving and interacting differently with the piece through their bodies."* In Derby one participant told me:

> "The space has obviously changed. Usually, it isn't used. I don't think there would normally be anybody here this time at night. The space has changed. Usually, we are down here without children. You wouldn't see children normally. But this gives them a reason to come. Doesn't it?... I am glad it is being used for some artwork. If this weren't here, I would just walk through. There is no reason to stand here unless there was a market. The market is also good. I don't know which is better: the market or this? I think if this piece was selling olives then I would stay even longer..."

Indeed, several interviewees confirmed that the projections changed the general behaviour of passers-by—particularly body movement. I met a lady in Lincoln who said:

> "Usually in concrete spaces like this one, you usually wander through. Normally you wouldn't walk through an area in Lincoln and do things that you do with your body generally. You wouldn't do that this time at night in a Saturday evening in Lincoln. Would you?"

Interactivity depended on a participant's age and on projection setting. Older people took a contemplative role (an observer role)—watching other people interacting—while younger adults and kids were more playful, engaged and curious about the piece. An old lady from Leicester explains this further: *"I did play a little bit and I probably would play with it a little bit more, but it is for younger people they would interact with it—not for an adult. I think the children are enjoying it... You see it is mainly children at the moment."* But even having a contemplative behaviour is also enjoyable for some participants: *"I think it is really interesting to see how people perform when they see the shadows or how they move or how they interact with the shadows."* On the other hand, peoples' behaviour also depended radically on the setting since the work included two settings: (1) the video portraiture and (2) the interlude.

Interactivity with the Video Portraiture

Interactivity with the portraits was the key issue behind the work. Most people interacted and played with the different characters in the portraits. During the projections of video portraiture, the act of mimicking the portrait and checking their response was the focus of their attention. One participant was explaining to me how the video portraiture stimulates interactivity:

> "I was copying one myself. They do seem to be asking you to do something, don't they? Most of them are trying to get you involved. The movement that they do is quite funny really because I don't know what they were asked to do when they were being filmed. I mean a lot of them seem to be sort of asking for things. Somebody down there was taking photographs. Nobody was trying to frighten you!"

People appreciated the intuitiveness and spontaneity of the piece, one man was telling me: *"I like the spontaneity of the piece, so that when you are walking around upon it then people would do these different things."* Other people thought that the filmed characters were quite interesting, yet intriguing at the same time. Like this young student who was expressing his reaction to the video portraits:

> "What I don't get is that they are all there. And you have to come to them, but if they appear in your shadow then that would be a lot more shocking. But I don't know if they have the telepathy to detect shadows. It is obviously detecting something because it is supposed to react when you move on them, I like that, and I just wonder if there is more than that! 'Hello is there anyone there?' I thought the whole point was like a ghost thing, and he is undisturbed and you disturb it and then it goes: 'Help me, hello…!' That doesn't seem to be what is going on. It just seems completely random."

Actually, many people were wanting to communicate with the character in the video portraits, as one girl told me: *"I want the images to talk: 'Hello!' One should have a conversation with it! I want it to do some good things but that would be too hard, I think."* Moreover, the video portraiture stimulated contemplation, awareness and curiosity for the people: one lady was telling me:

> "You felt that they were seeing you as you were seeing them! That was quite strange really! Because we know that they are not, but we thought that."

In the interviews, each participant was telling me about the characters they met in *Under Scan.* For example: *"There was a woman who was trying to get up and there was another one who was shouting"* or *"that girl is crazy with the hair"* or *"There was a man rubbing his back, He looked like he was dancing on the floor, and weaving; it was a bit of a Michael Jackson thing'*. One lady described the video portraits, which she saw:

> "I haven't picked that one, I picked the one over there that did the tongue out at you. As you stand in front of them and cover with your shadow, then they kind of do things and then you should go."

Other people expressed their feelings when they saw the different characters. In Nottingham, one man told me: *"We had one that scared us because it stood up really suddenly. We had one that flashed at us. And there was a track with three. Some people didn't seem to do much."* Another one said:

> "There is one that was feeding something in her mouth, I didn't know what. At first I was quite shocked to find it was people. And it is quite real as well if you are standing over them, it is like they are there! And this portrait: he is angry—about what, I don't know! But it is cool."

However, the majority of people enjoyed the variety of the characters and tried to imitate them as one explained: *"we have done the rowing with one of the portraits over there! The guy was rowing and I rowed."* Another participant explained her movement in response to the portrait: *"when you are playing with them then you would automatically move your head closer. I was behaving stupidly because I wanted to stand on them. I don't know why but when you see them it just brings out this feeling inside that you want to jump on them I don't know why."*

Generally, observation and interviewing revealed a certain pattern of movement or behaviour as users approached the space. First, the participant would start looking; then shuffling; stopping; staring; standing on the portrait; mimicking the portrait's movements, talking to others and looking at it—at this point s/he was clearly engaged and became part of the installation. The portraits initiated conversations between participants; some were talking with the portrait or about it with others while interacting with it. The following is an extract of conversation between three young girls (*P1, P2* and *P3*) while playing with the portraits in Northampton:

> "P1: These are fantastic. But there was this girl in the portrait; she wouldn't play with us anymore; she just went back to sleep again!
> P3: This one is our favourite. He is quite cute!
> P2: They are really good. But I thought it was going to be us!
> P3: He switched off and went back to sleep again for a little while, but we only played with him a bit… Oh, here he is back again!
> P1: She is really looking at us!
> P3: That is a man. He is cute…
> P1: No, it is a woman. I don't know what is going on, it is a girl!
> P3: But I think it is a pretty boy…"

However, many users thought, at the start, that their images would be projected among the portraits. They expected a camera to film them and constantly project the images in real time. As one participant explained:

> "Some people thought they might see themselves, which is again fun. Everybody is having fun with it and it is light-hearted... people would like it if it could transmit their image. If the camera was there and they transmitted your image, then that would be really good! But we don't know if it could work like that. That would be really good."

At the same time, the people who participated in the production were looking for themselves or for people they knew: *"I definitely haven't seen any one that we know yet. It might be a bit scary to see someone you know in the portraits. I think it can be disconcerting"* one man said. Another was looking for his own portrait because he was filmed previously for the projections:

> "I am hunting to find me. It is taking ages. How long do people spend here looking for themselves? ... I would like to see myself in the floor. I have been filmed for this, and I have been waiting for being projected on the floor—thinking that I will be the lucky one. I need to go around and keep going round to find it. But, that is interesting!"

Yet, the most interesting interactions came from children. Kids would shout, jump and stamp on portraits as one boy told me: *"I like to jump on their heads; I go around and jump on all their heads!"* I talked to other children and got their views on the portraits. One child answered:

> "It is nice. I am watching the spirits! I like the spirits. I think they should do some Christmassy ones... How do they do these movements?... How do they make humans on there... Do they go to bed and then they come on in the morning?"

However, many kids found their shadows to be smaller than the actual size of the portraits. The issue of size was twice noted in the interviews by parents, one woman told me: *"I have got my kids with me and their shadows aren't big enough so we had to stand with them to get the interaction. So, on little people it is not working."* But even so, this did not affect the interactivity of the children. They still expressed as much interest and fascination with the video portraits. One girl told me:

> "That one scared me. But I am not scared now... but it is strange! You look at them and, in one way, they look like they are real people and then they disappear or

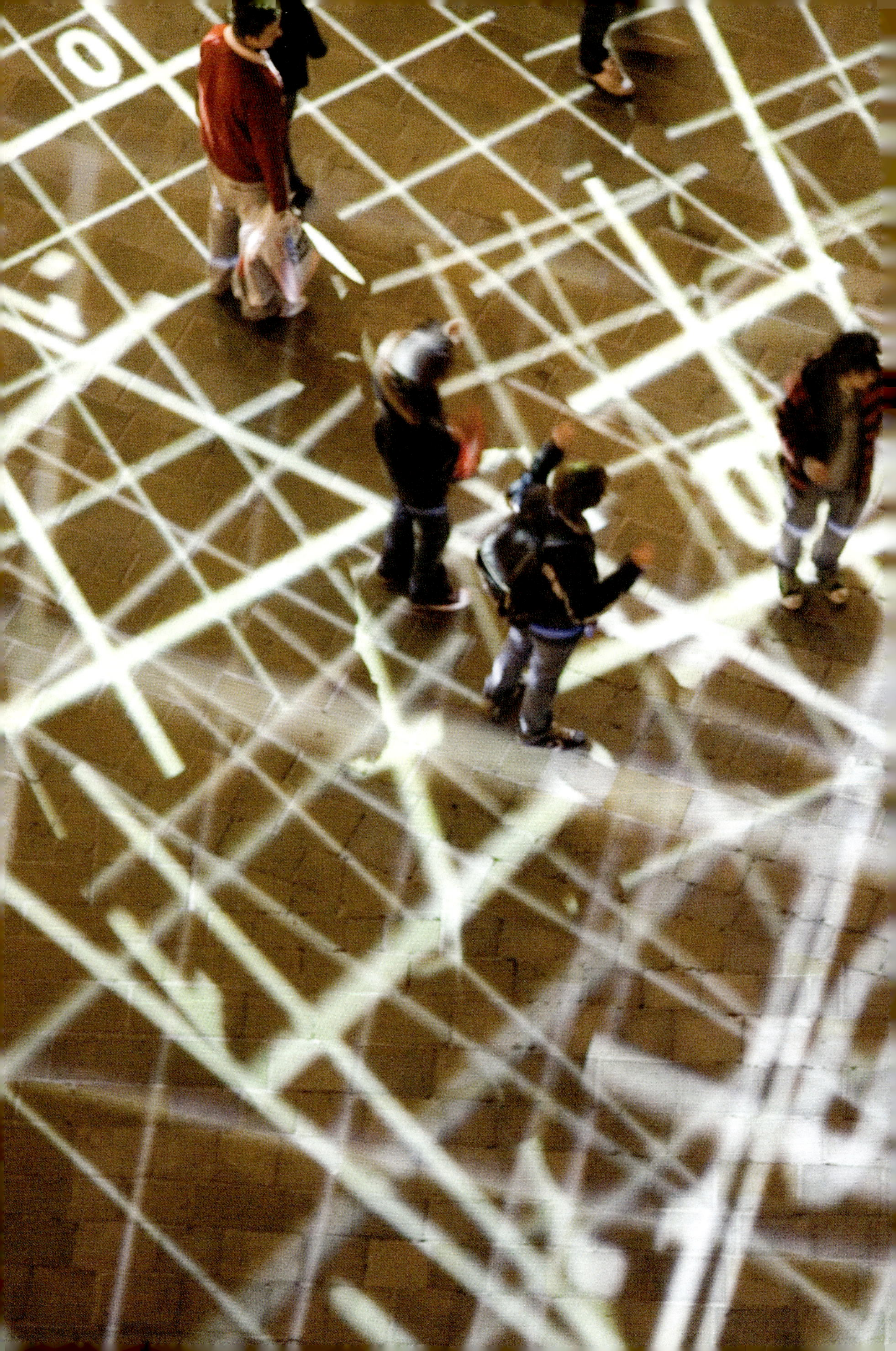

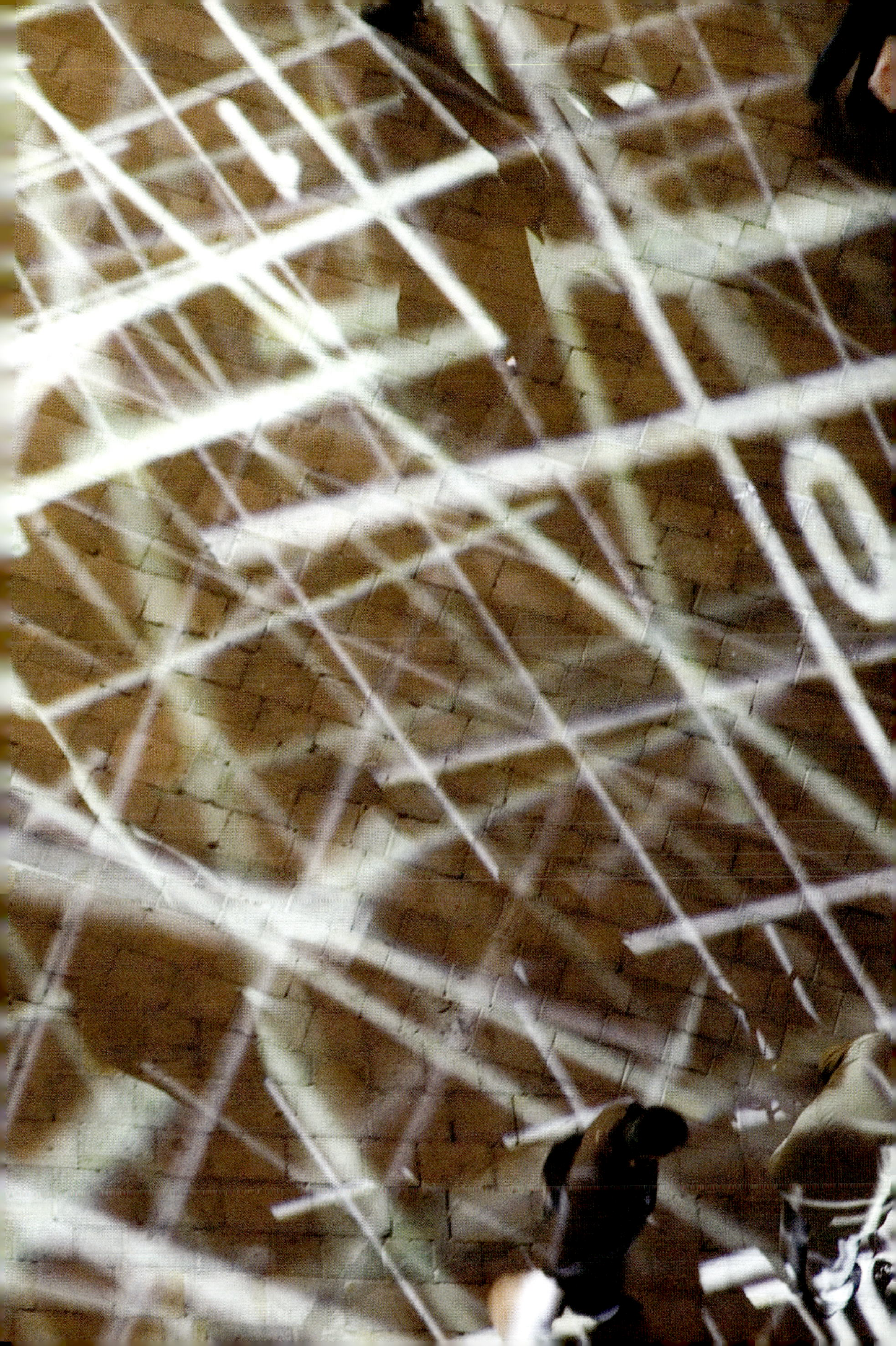

> they move or something and then they kind of pop up again. They look like they are real, and they see you doing that. It just feels like they are seeing me when they wake up and they suddenly start moving. They are real people! But they are not actually there but it is like they are. It is strange!"

Interactivity within the Interlude
In order to highlight the tracking system, the system was programmed to periodically stop the projections for a couple of minutes. During this period, the lights were shut down and a moving grid appeared on the floor: this in-between time is called "the interlude." Initially, the projection of portraits was intended to be the dominant part of the interaction, yet surprisingly, the interlude proved to be highly popular and enjoyable amongst the users, which was a surprising result. The artist relates this to the fact that the interlude allowed a breather or *a moment when participants could suspend their engagement.*

In the interlude, the participants' behaviour switched from a calm/contemplative attitude to a more active and intuitive way of behaving. Users were running with the moving projection and the space suddenly came to life. People would give different names to this setting: they call it "scanning" or "grid." Someone else called it the *"check board,"* he told me: "*I like when it all gets dark and all the check board comes around and moves!"* Nonetheless, feedbacks reported that the interlude provided a more intimate and immersive experience for the users than the video portraiture setting. One participant argues:

> "... All these grids become your reference of movement, so even if you are standing still you feel like swimming in the space and these grids dance around you. You feel like you are moving through the darkness. I don't know what he is trying to achieve with that but it is a very interesting approach."

This engagement with the interlude was intriguing to many. People compared it with the experience that was provided by the video portraiture setting, as one participant told me:

> "I like the interlude bit; it is like the best bit, it is a really cool! I did find this bit when you suddenly go: 'Ooh!' This is interesting! And when it is like that and it is all around you, you do feel immersed. But with the little pockets [portraits] you don't."

This was an even more interesting point for people who knew that the interlude was just an added part to the *Under Scan* setting.

> "Just a video projection of a computer screen can have all that effect... It is frightening that most people like the

interlude better! Because we don't have a history of video installation, we are behind Germany, we are behind North America in video installation and video work; we just don't get it, do we? You know that is why. Just put shining patterns of colours and things just like in traditional video projections style. Or projection of moving image on the floor with lots of patterns then people would like that. This installation is trying to say something more than that!"

It seems that the interlude provided an unusual experience for the people in public space, more than the video portraits. And perhaps this is the reason why most participants really liked it. The following quote is from another participant describing the interlude:

> "I think actually the most exciting moment that people seem to be enjoying is when it shuts down, and the grid appears, and the cameras relocate to the next set of portraits and then fill up the centre because that is like an activity; there is an impact, or an event, or something, and people go: 'Ooh!'. That is interesting!"

I heard different people explaining their experience of the Interlude: *"I quite like the grid thing that comes zipping around!" One participant said, and he continued: "I like it when it all sorts of goes off and they have the lights where; the way that makes you feel, because it is very strange feeling. All I can say is that it is strange and weird. I think I will remember this feeling."* The following quotes are few feedbacks on the interlude from Lincoln and Leicester:

> "It was really good, pretty fun with all the lights and stuff… and then they had all the squares and stuff. That felt really wicked because they were moving but you were not and it makes you sense that you should move but you are not actually moving. So, it is really exciting; you should come and try it!"

> "…As soon as that light went out you get the whole effect! So you see it comes to life then. You see this bit. Wait… stand… Stay in one old place! Oh, there it is! Oh wait it comes back! You see that square, let's go!"

> "That was pretty impressive! I think the interlude gets your attention then you kind of notice the rest of it as well. Because if you don't know that it is here, then you could just easily walk past it without noticing, and there were no signs directing people here, so…"

Also the interlude stimulated interesting conversation with people, I was talking to a little girl with her mother and the conversation conveyed the kid's fascination with the interlude:

"Child: Oh...This is the scanning it is scanning!

Mother: My daughter has got a fascination with the grids when they happen. The video screen also intrigued us and we were trying to figure out where the images are going to appear. But this grid... the kids like it, they run with the lines.

Child: "I like the way it moved around! Well, it is confusing; I try to run with the lines but it is too quick!"

Again, the children seemed to be the most involved in the interlude, a girl was telling me that the interlude was such an unusual experience, for her this was fascinating but also scary, she said:

"... And it is dead freaky, you know, when the squares start and it makes you dead dizzy when the squares comes and then if you follow the squares, it is like you just go round and round and this is strange. I like it so much, I wish I could be here all the time because this is really, really cool, and I wish to have it everywhere and things like that"

Generally, people enjoyed the two experiences offered by the video portraiture and the interlude. The video portraiture offered a more sophisticated experience for the users whilst the interlude was found to be more fascinating to people.

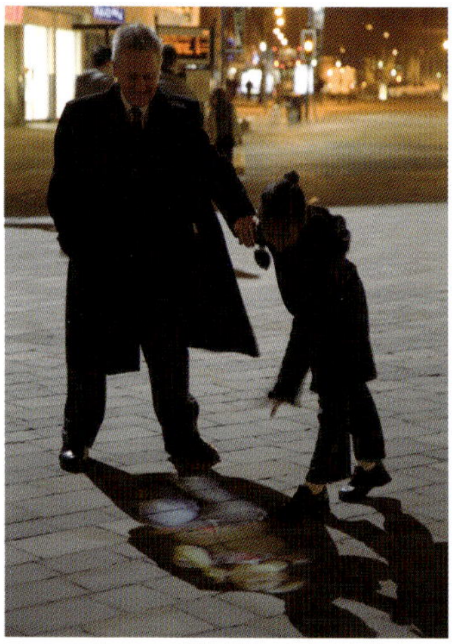

Memory in *Under Scan*
Like many other works by Lozano-Hemmer, *Under Scan* carried some references to memory. Although the artist himself noted, in our interview, that this is not particularly a mnemonic piece. However, the piece may be interpreted as a reflection on the anonymity, ephemerality and immateriality of the encounters in public spaces or *"rencontres"*—if we use Henri Lefebvre terminology. *Under Scan* became a representation of the memory of such encounters. A lady was arguing that "*Instead of meeting up with people we are meeting with images of people: they act, they move and they talk like real people, so maybe it is like a parody of meeting a real person in a public square*." The installation could be retained as a "moment" in time to be recalled or re-presented, as one participant suggested: "*I am a painter and I have taken some really fantastic pictures of my children with lights and patterns in the back. Now, I have got that on my camera. So, I might be able to use this in my paintings...*"

Most users expressed that they would remember some aspects of the installation—particularly in relation to the characters filmed in the video portraiture: "*I will remember the concept of it and the portraits,*" one participant said. Another lady explained:

"It is quite an intimate sort of experience. These persons,

whatever they are giving you, it is not conditioned by anything material, you just have a little bit of them. It has no beginning and no end. It is a representation of the ephemeral process in the memory—something like that I don't know how to explain it..."

Another participant interpreted the piece differently; his reading was that *Under Scan* symbolically made use of video portraiture to provide an interpretation of the nature of our existence. Through video representation of different human characters in public space, Rafael Lozano-Hemmer succeeded in representing aspects of human life, and thus, contributed to collective memory:

"For me, this installation is a kind of representation of the memory. It is a kind of representation of how we remember things and how things are inside us. You know how memory works... when you found each person... all this kind of iceberg theory; of a lot of people behind the square or whatever place that they were."

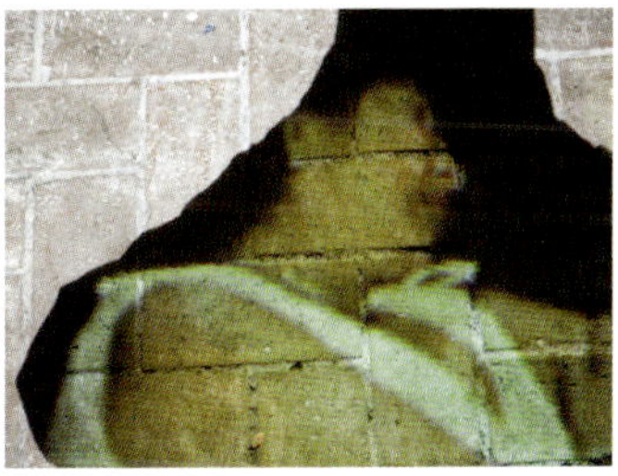

Time in *Under Scan*
The installation had a temporality of its own in relation to the interlude. The interface was set up to switch to the interlude every 7 minutes. And I observed that some users developed a certain "sense of time" in relation to this timeframe. What was particularly interesting, in this context, is that few people started thinking about time relatively, linking it to the interlude. For instance, when they were asked how they would estimate the time they spent, some participants answered: *"well, it reset twice since we arrived" or "is it on a timer?."*

Additionally, time was considered as a measure of the involvement and engagement of users in *Under Scan*. I asked twenty people about the approximate duration of their experience and tried to evaluate how long people spent in the space of installation. Findings showed that the average duration that participants spent in *Under Scan* was around 21 minutes. As a result, I suggest the duration of experience to be around 25 minutes. Whilst the maximum time spent was 40 minutes from personal observation. But this does not mean that participants were all the time interacting with the piece, many were just standing or chatting to others. Also, one has to take into account the conditions of the space. The installation was set up outdoors and the weather at this time of year is very cold. In Derby, for example, everyone was associating leaving with being cold. Perhaps, if it were warmer they would stay longer. Also the time people spend depended on the fact that they are alone or accompanied—generally, they would stay longer to chat with others if they are coming in groups. One more issue is related to the day (mid week, or weekend).

Under Scan is an evening event. So, during the weekends people are more relaxed and would stay longer. This is further evidence of their concentration and engagement in the work.

Concluding Notes

Generally, findings showed that most users expressed approval and enthusiasm for the work. However, it must be noted that I also had some critical feedback. A few responses were based on traditionalist preconceptions against digital artworks in public spaces as well as cost issues. More relevant to the topic of this discussion are the constructive comments, which were related to the design of the video portraiture as well as views on the interface and interactivity within *Under Scan.* I shall note some of these comments briefly as they may be considered for future developments of the piece or even in other similar interactive projects.

For instance, I talked to a few people who complained about the quality of projection. They wanted them to be clearer and described the video portraits as *"too dark so you don't have any sense of engaging with the people; they are like 'ghostly' presence, not real people at all; they are too pale; in some of them, you can barely see the people.*" I believe that this may be due to the nature of the site floor as the artist suggested in our interview. However, this point is particularly important as it a poses broader question on the design of projections in relation to the architectural configurations of the site, and on the dual coexistence of the virtual versus the physical/real.

Furthermore, some participants thought that the video portraits were too short or too few. This uncovered a certain misunderstanding of the piece because *Under Scan* had a big archive of videos and was constantly changing the set of portraits. Indeed, a number of participants expressed their misunderstanding of the interactive aspect of *Under Scan.* Sometimes, one would not see many people overlaying their shadows over the portraits. This was partly because they did not realise how they should interact with the piece—as one woman indicated: "*...we didn't realise at first that the people in the portraits were sensitive to our presence. So, we were kind of hoping that they would do something and wake up but then the artist said that if you cover it with your shadow then it would work."* I had a number of similar comments, like:

> "Now I got more of the concept of what you need to do. Initially, I was just wandering around a little bit and a bit aimless and a little bit lost but I think that was part of the discovery as well that made it interesting than if it worked straight away. Perhaps you can put effort in to find what can work and how it can work."

A frequent feedback from participants asked for the video portraits to be more stimulating, particularly when compared with the interlude. Whilst a few others expressed that the work is better when it is delicately overlaid in public space. However, this is a significant point, which is worth consideration if the project hopes to create a more stimulating environment for the users in public space.

To conclude, this article examined how *Under Scan* enhanced public space. The work transformed the socio-spatial use of some places into sites for exchange, dialogue and intimate experiences. The installation provided created lively "moments" in the space of the city where the body would get engaged in new site narratives and unique experience. Users acted and interacted with each other and with the environment in enjoyable and playful encounters.

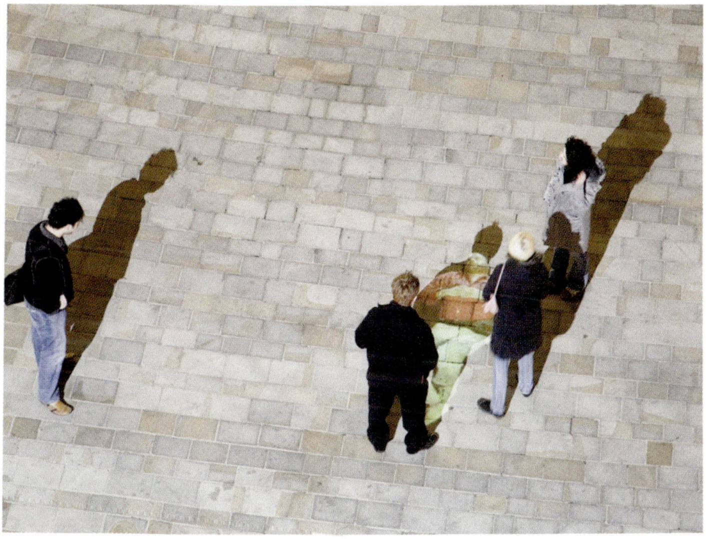

Acknowledgement
The study reported in this paper is supported by a research grant from the University Project Studentships 2003/04 at the University of Sheffield. The project is supervised by Dr. Chengzhi Peng and Stephen Walker.

ART

ANOTHER ME AND MY SHADOW

BLUEPRINT

Imagine those first tottering steps on an ice rink, people bunching and giggling. Only here no one is skating – they're shadow-shuffling, searching for 'video portraits' that loom beneath their feet like mirror images of somebody else.

It's the first night of Under Scan, a £1m public art installation funded by EMDA, the East Midlands Regional Development Agency, which combines the age-old amateur dramatics of shadow-play with high-tech street surveillance. It works by turning up to 2,000 sq m into an ad-hoc amphitheatre of light, using a powerful 12kW projector. Then, a computer tracks people's movement, and triggers 14 smaller projectors to throw the video portraits (short film loops of another person) into their path: they pop up within the shape of their shadows.

'If you pay no attention to it, the portrait is also not interested and disappears,' says Under Scan's creator, Rafael Lozano-Hemmer. 'If you engage, it'll come alive and look up at you, maybe send kisses or make questionable proposals, whatever. It's completely uncensored – people were invited to do what they liked.'

From its opening in Lincoln, it's now in Leicester (until 22 January), and then heads to Northampton, Derby and Nottingham, finishing 22 March. Local interest compares to that generated wherever Spencer Tunick shoots his mass nudity photographs. More than 1,000 volunteers were filmed last summer for the video portraits, except – this time – they kept their clothes on.

As you might expect, the man behind the scenes is a bright spark. A 37-year-old Mexican-Canadian artist, Lozano-Hemmer has staged similar events around the world. Most involve mischievous interplay between the built environment, clever software and some great lights. The East Midlands should feel pleased to have him: he's a multimedia magician with a beef about urban design, a digital sculptor of the radio spectrum, a lord of misrule for the iMac generation.

Under Scan is number 11 in a series called Relational Architecture, each one a temporary technological takeover of public space, exploring the artist's ideas about the civic realm. 'Design in public space today is all about getting us from work to home as quickly as possible,' he maintains. 'Or else being exposed to the largest advertising displays, but I'm interested in designing the social sphere so that, all of a sudden, you're invited to relate to people in a different way. It's really important to give agency to people in public space, and think of ways to occupy it other than shopping. Projects like these are eccentric experiences.'

His most stunning piece, Vectorial Elevation, played in Lyon for a UN summit, in Mexico City during its millennium celebrations, and in Dublin to mark the EU expansion. Yet Lozano-Hemmer was hardly pandering to officialdom. Vectorial Elevation enabled anyone, via a website, to design skyscraping patterns by controlling 18 robotic searchlights, visible from 15km away. In total, around 1.5 million people took part, with the results archived on personalised webpages.

Searchlights, as Lozano-Hemmer points out, have associations with Albert Speer's 'fascist spectacles of power' and authoritarianism generally. 'I tried to introduce interactivity to transform intimidation into intimacy,' he explains. If his theories sound didactic, in practice his work is good fun. Another project gives people the chance to scan shortwave frequencies, using their bodies as antennae, so that they eavesdrop on mobile chatter, air-traffic signals and, police bands. It's hacker art, and his democratic instinct draws him to Buckminster Fuller, too.

'He did many things,' Lozano-Hemmer enthuses. 'But what I'm really excited about is that he was the pioneer of networked architecture. You know, no central point – the centre being the romantic view, or the modern 'centre/suburbs' view – his was a true network, a mesh of interconnected nodes. To us in the internet age, it's completely logical, but he came up with this long before anyone else.'

Back with Under Scan, I see what Lozano-Hemmer means when he declares 'locality, like identity, is a performance'. Waving at the camera is nothing new, and the eagerness with which people look for their portraits reminds me of those observational films by Mitchell & Kenyon in the early 1900s, and how folk queued to watch themselves, and their towns, on screen. That's why 'people think twice about being too moronic' in the videos, he suggests: unconsciously, it becomes a source of civic pride how they behave.

Perhaps the later venues, where Under Scan is more covert, will be different; at the 'petri-dish' in Lincoln, however, a traditional culture was revived. Technology made its observers take their time, talk, linger – without having to be somewhere else. Like leisurely Edwardians, they were promenading, surely?

'Yes,' Lozano-Hemmer says, gleefully. 'That's such a good word. I've been saying "meandering", but rivers meander, people promenade!' *Richard Clayton*

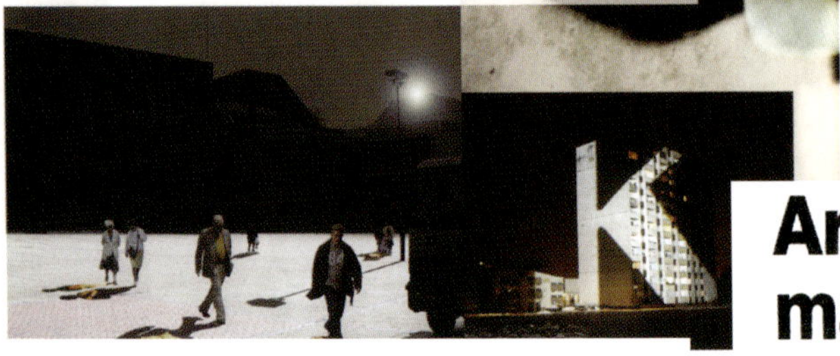

NORTHAMPTON Chronicle & ECHO
FRIDAY, FEBRUARY 3, 2006 www.NorthamptonToday.co.uk Northampton 467000

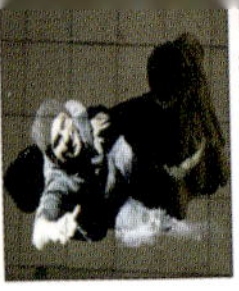

Northampton unde[r] surveillance

It's not everyday that Northampton can boast a [...] largest' something. But th[...] world's largest interactive [...] art installation: titled Und[...] is on its way to light up y[...]

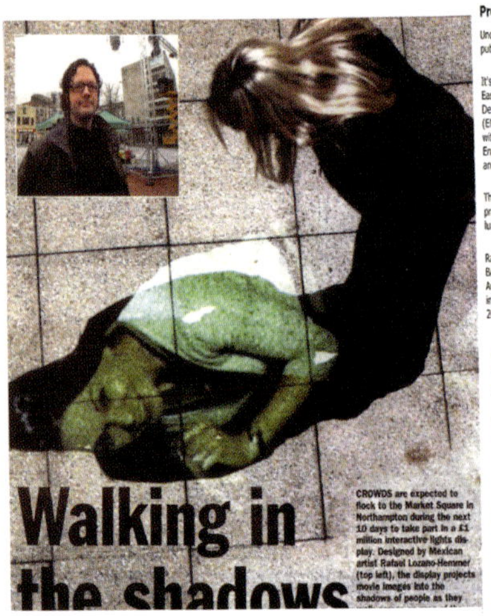

CROWDS are expected to flock to the Market Square in Northampton during the next 10 days to take part in a £1 million interactive lights display. Designed by Mexican artist Rafael Lozano-Hemmer (top left), the display projects movie images into the shadows of people as they

Walking in the shadows

Project Facts:

Under Scan is a free public art installation

It's commissioned by The East Midlands Development Agency (EMDA) in association with Arts Council England, East Midlands and local authorities.

The world's brightest projector emits 110,000 lumens of intensity.

Rafael has won two BAFTA British Academy Awards in Interactive Art in London in 2002 and 2005.

Such is the scale of this project (both i[...] and imagination) it's going to take a bi[...] explaining.

So, imagine yourself walking through t[...] Market Square one evening between 7[...] midnight (2am on Fridays and Saturda[...]

Overhead is the world's biggest project[...] flooding the Market Square with light, [...] casting your shadow on the floor. A su[...] camera 'whurrs' in to action; it spots y[...] fires a shaft of light into your shadow [...] video portrait appears and introduces themselves....ladies and gentlemen, the[...] here!

1000 interactive video portraits of mem[...] the public from the East Midlands (including 200 people fro[...] Northampton) have been made and are ready to pounce in [...] shadow! Who you get, is randomly selected by the projector[...]

Local filmmakers are behind these short films, but who is th[...] behind the entire project?

The man behind it all

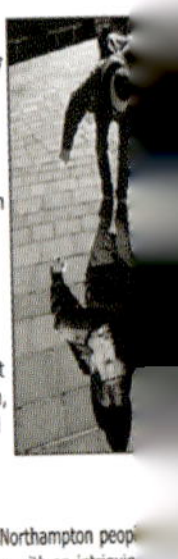

Rafael Lozano-Hemmer is the highly decorated Mexican-Canadian contemporary artist behind Under Scan.

His work in kinetic sculpture, responsive environments, video installation and photography has been shown in two dozen countries, including Switzerland, China, Brazil and Cuba to name a few.

Speaking about the installation, Lozano-Hemmer said: "The unveiling of Under Scan represents the culmination of almost a year's work including intensive research, technical and artistic development behind this, my latest and most ambitious installation.

"I hope it will bring a new experience to Northampton peop[...] visitors to the town, and will provide them with an intriguin[...] play where members of the public become actors."

Artist is going to make you a star

A WORLD-renowned visual artist who will be putting a major work in Northampton's Market Square next year is in town this week to reveal all.

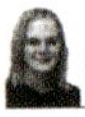

by Jodie Parsons

Rafael Lozano-Hemmer's huge interactive video installation Under Scan was commissioned by emda (East Midlands Development Agency) and will appear in the town in February 2006.

It will use a bright projector to cast shadows of passers-by on the ground and using the latest technology thousands of video portraits of local people will be projected inside the shadows.

Tomorrow, Friday, October 7, he will present the work in progress and host a question and answer session as part of the Under Scan lecture tour.

The free event will be held at the University of Northampton in the main hall at Avenue Campus on St George's Avenue between 11am and 1pm.

Although places are free numbers are limited so to book or for further information contact (0116) 261 6882 or email lecture@artreach.biz.

His work, Under Scan will be unveiled in Lincoln city centre in November before being installed in Leicester, Derby and Nottingham as well as Northampton.

The project will occupy more than 1,500sq m of busy pedestrianised areas and will be active for ten nights in each of the five locations.

Mr Lozano[...] a number of [...] including t[...] interactive [...] 2005.

He said: "I am interested [...] use their public spaces and each other in them. Under S[...] interactive shadow play where the normal routines associated with urban space are interrupted and members of the public become actors."

More information on his work can be found at www.lozano-hemmer.com

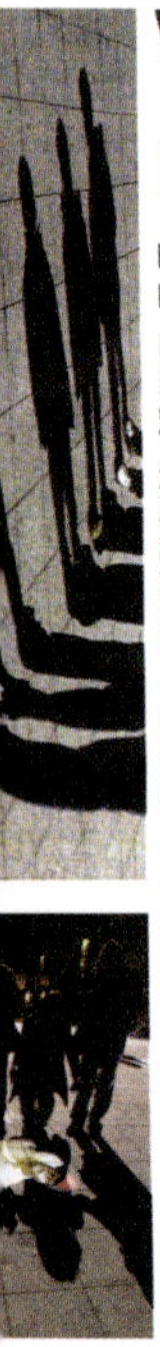

Walking with my shadows

Imagine standing in a brightly lit street and someone else's body appearing in your shadow. **Mark Irving** explains all

If you were in charge of "the world's largest interactive video project", where would you put it? An airy gallery space? A museum foyer? How about a regional British city centre?

Over the coming weeks, *Under Scan*, masterminded by the 38-year-old Mexican-Canadian artist Rafael Lozano-Hemmer, will take up more than 1,500sq metres of pedestrianised areas in Leicester, Northampton, Derby and Nottingham. Starting at dusk, the world's most powerful projector (110,000 lumens of intensity) will flood a vast area with bright light, casting strong shadows off the people walking through it.

Now for the science bit. A sophisticated camera and sensor system will track these passers-by, and a video portrait of a stranger will appear in their shadows. Using the latest technology, about a thousand video portraits of local people — filmed by a regional team of videographers — will be projected and activated. The portraits are shown in these areas of shadow without distortion and in scale through the use of a robotic device in the projector that tilts the image according to computer guidance. This means that your progress across the city centre is watched in detail and your encounters with your fellow citizens, albeit represented in images, are made as dynamic as possible.

If this makes you think of what CCTV hell might be like, then you are probably thinking along the same lines as Lozano-Hemmer. "I'm very concerned with surveillance as an issue, in what you might call the technologies of suspicion. Today it has become so ominous, with cameras being used to make judgments about ethnic traits and human behaviour. But instead of creating a project where the camera takes images, I want to see what would happen if we turned this around and they gave us images instead."

As you walk through this lit-up area, then, you'll experience a number of very different encounters as your shadow passes over certain surfaces: people smiling at you, beckoning to you, shouting, screaming, looking sad, swearing — the great range of human emotion on display. I feel twinges of Hogarth, the great 18th-century artist who held a vivid mirror up to English society.

But what about the problems? Wasn't Lozano-Hemmer worried about the Friday-night syndrome, with pub-crawlers delivering their stomach contents to camera?

"I'm obviously aware of the potential for moronic behaviour but I wanted to demonstrate something else, how people go about their own business. It's a way of taking over public space. I want to remind people of their sense of promenading, that there's a public notion of performance that we're all involved in, that being out in public isn't just about shopping."

"As you walk across the area, you'll experience people smiling at you, beckoning, shouting"

This is where I fear the cultural difference between the artist, a cultivated Latin, and most people in England might be rather telling. Lozano-Hemmer, 38, comes from a society, one nurtured under the softening southern sun, where people go out to enjoy themselves by showing how smart and prosperous they are. In his society, polite behaviour — indeed, over-polite, one might say — is the filter through which all sorts of messages are conveyed.

This is not, sadly, the English way, even if the expanse of flesh on display on an average midwinter's night in our city centres might seem more suitable to balmy evenings in Seville, Mexico City or Buenos Aires. Don't get me wrong, I love the notion of public performance that Lozano Hemmer's getting at, but it's just that we're going to need a crash course in the art of public courtesy to make the best of it.

The project marks a "massive programme of cultural activity" that "will support the creation of vibrant cultural quarters and will encourage innovative approaches to public space by linking the region's scientific and technological achievements to the flourishing arts scene", or so states the East Midlands Development Agency which, with Arts Council England, commissioned the project.

But aside from the debate about whether art can actually regenerate inner cities, what is interesting about Lozano-Hemmer's project, with its interaction between live and "fictive" people, is how it manages to reflect an interest in the magic realist encounters found in so much Latin-American literature.

Lozano-Hammer says: "You can't grow up in Latin America without knowing about the magic realism of García Márquez and Borges." He also cites the playwright Bertholt Brecht as an inspiration: "He wanted to show his audience where the deceit of the performance actually stops. He wanted people to understand that reality is separate from the work. That's why I wanted people walking through these spaces to be able to see also one large screen where the mechanics of the tracking process that makes these portraits appear will be visible."

Magic or no magic, the citizens of Leicester, Northampton, Derby and Nottingham will find themselves part of something bigger than their shopping list. ■

Under Scan is showing at Humberstone Gate, Leicester, until Jan 22; Market Square, Northampton, Feb 3-12; Market Place, Derby, Feb 24-Mar 5; and Canal Side at Castle Wharf, Nottingham, Mar 17-26 (www.threecitiescreate.org.uk/_EMDA_Cultural_Quarters/)

Under Scan projects human images on to people's shadows. Photographs by Richard Cannon

Mark, "Walking with my shadows", *The Times (UK)*, Saturday, January 14 2006, no. 68597, The Knowledge - Cultural Guide, p.33.

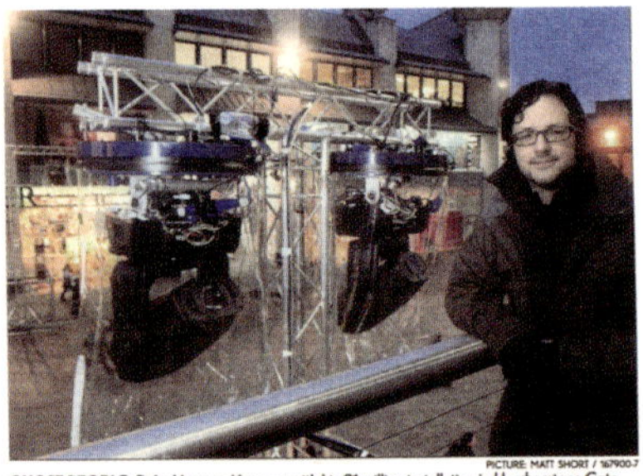

PICTURE: MATT SHORT / 167900-7

GHOST PEOPLE: Rafael Lozano-Hemmer with his £1 million installation in Humberstone Gate

Shadow magic will give 'ownership' of city

THE mastermind behind one of the biggest and most expensive artworks ever seen in Leicester says the exhibition will give people "ownership" of the city.

Bafta award-winner Rafael Lozano-Hemmer is behind Under Scan, the £1 million spectacle on show in Leicester for 11 nights from Thursday.

The project features 1,000 moving portraits of people from across the region, including 200 from Leicester, and is billed as the world's largest interactive video installation.

Pedestrians walking in Humberstone Gate from dusk until midnight will be able to watch ghost-like figures dancing, laughing and larking about in their shadows.

Among the floodlights and film projectors is a hi-tech tracking system that brings the spooky apparitions to life only when someone walks by.

Mr Lozano-Hemmer, who has spent years perfecting the art of shadow magic, said Under Scan would make people feel like they "own" a part of their city.

He said: "I think it will serve as an example of how we can make cities progress.

"I have been to cities all over the world where politicians seem to think the only way to regenerate a city is to stick up some 19th century lampposts.

"Here, we are actually giving people ownership of their city because it is a phenomenon that makes citizens feel connected to their surroundings.

"It is a very intimate experience because the figures only react when you are there to look at them. They seek your attention."

The 38-year-old Mexican-Canadian was picked out of nearly 100 applicants.

This is the first time he has worked with moving images and is his most expensive project to date.

The display will run from 6.30pm until midnight, and 2am on Friday and Saturday nights.

THE TIMES
No 68597 • SATURDAY JANUARY 14 2006 •

The Knowledge

SIGHTS

Museums
Galleries
Events
Kids
Eating out

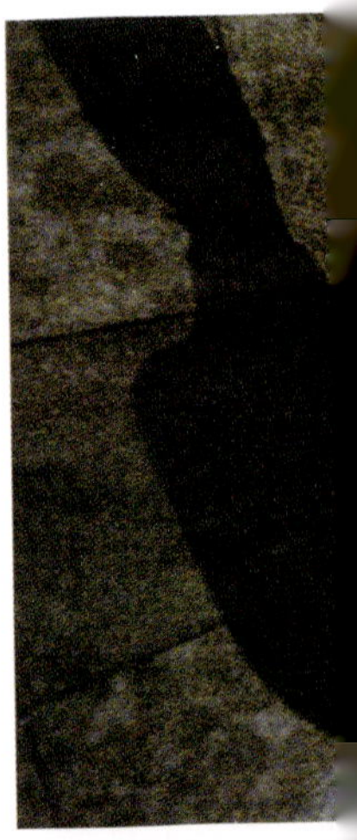

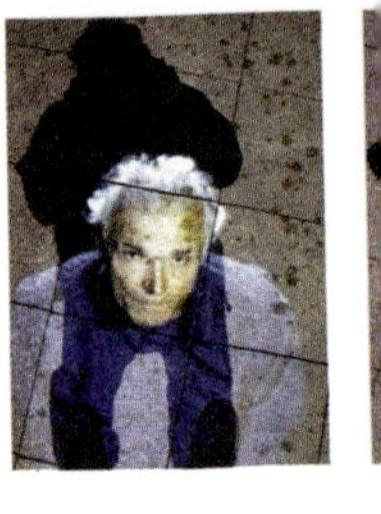

Saturday, June 18, 2005 Lincolnshire Echo

Interactive display is part of £1m project

Mexican to put his art in city

A MEXICAN artist is to create an interactive art installation in Lincoln as part of a £1 million project.

Rafael Lozano-Hemmer has set up huge visual sculptures, which often include light beams, for cities around the world – winning numerous awards in the process.

Now funding from the East Midlands Development Agency will bring the 37-year-old and his unique interactive installations to public spaces in the region.

Dave Rose (35), spokesman for Leicester-based ArtReach, which is managing the project, said: "This is a special one-off interactive installation which will be placed in the city.

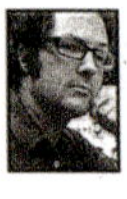

TALENTED: Rafael Lozano-Hemmer is to create an interactive art installation in Lincoln.

by Henry Killworth

Mr Lozano-Hemmer said: "I am delighted to have been chosen to work in the region, and with its

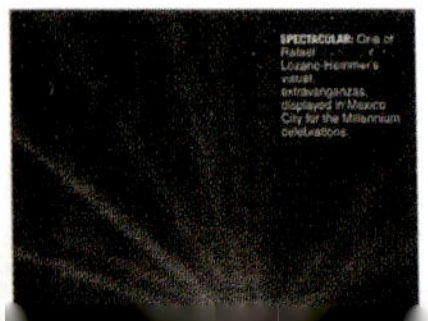

SPECTACULAR: One of Rafael Lozano-Hemmer's visual extravaganzas, displayed in Mexico City for the Millennium celebrations.

FRIDAY, JANUARY 13, 2006

BREAKING NEWS

SWITCH-ON: HOW PASSERS-BY LAUNCHED [...]

Lighting up ou[...]

bbc.co.uk

BRITAIN'S LOCAL NEWSPAPER OF THE YEAR

Lincolnshire Echo

Thursday, November 24, 2005 ESTABLISHED 1893 CITY & COUNTY EDITION www.thisislincolnshire.co.uk

INSIDE YOUR FREE going OUT MAGAZINE

Exhibition

Underscan
Outside University of Lincoln, Brayford Wharf area, Lincoln

A GIANT piece of video artwork featuring the faces of more than 200 Lincoln people is set to wow the crowds at the city's university.

The world premiere of Mexican-Candian artist Rafael Lozano-Hemmer's £1 million art project Underscan is launched tomorrow.

A team is already hard at work installing a 20m-tall light tower and 14 video cameras around the university plaza on the Brayford.

The team, made up of British, Canadian and American workmen, is also installing a 20m-tall scissor lift with a 110,000 lumen light to cast shadows of passers-by.

Lozano-Hemmer (37) said: "The idea is that the very bright light will cast shadows and the video cameras will track the shadows and in to the shadow will be projected short silent videos of people."

There are 1,000 video clips, which were filmed in Lincoln and other East Midlands cities.

They will stay with the art work when it travels to festivals in Sydney, Switzerland and South America.

"Wherever this goes it will have the videos of people from the East Midlands, so I think it will show the world that the region is really advanced and interesting," said Lozano-Hemmer.

"It will be an ambassador for the East Midlands.

"The video clips are really interesting.

"We told people to do whatever they wanted.

"The majority waved and smiled but we got people dancing, praying, shouting, screaming and some who were being very serious.

"I hope people will come and look for their own clip – it will be like the world's biggest Advent Calendar."

Underscan opens tomorrow and will be in Lincoln until Sunday, December 4.

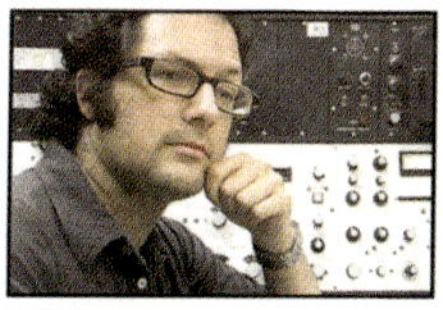

BRIGHT LIGHT: Artist Rafael Lozano-Hemmer's work is in Lincoln.

At a glance

What: Underscan
When: Launched tomorrow and runs daily from 6pm to midnight until Sunday, December 4
Where: Brayford Wharf
Tickets: Free

...ment:

...d out the 'Underscan' installation on the Market Square ...an 'intresting' expierence, it certainly is 'different'... but im ...orthampton is ready for 'Art' the amnunt of people I saw ...sparse (very) I got the impression people where ...med' by Underscan. The most enjoyment seemed to be ...youngsters, it's The Market Square, not the Tate. I think ...would work well in a large indoor set-up the images were ... plus the lack of an kind of audio made it a bit of a ...urtunity, imo. Well at least yes we can boast 'the biggest ...or other', briefly... L Jennings comments regarding the ...r does raise the question... another missed oppurtunity, a ...d facility the Town needs resurecting.

...nings
...s will be an amazing event, andd I am look forward to ...m just scared that money being payed into short lived ...his, and misplaced things like the new sculpture in ...eet is taking money away from projects that need it such ...ojects and the roadmender.

...n't wait to have a look tonight!

... this a few weekends back when I was visiting mates in ...'s engaging, fun, and brought a spark of local life into a ...ess corporate shops. And, over a few pints whilst we ...afterwards, it inspired a long discussion about serious ...CCTV surveillance and the stuffiness of art galleries. I'm ...ard to seeing how it changes the Market Square - and I'll ... bringing a few friends along.

...forward to seeing the work tonight and I hope that it will ...nore people to see the potential the town has for ...world-class art work. Congratulations to all involved in ...project up and running. The work involves/ employs a ...eople in it's construction and operation and the people ...velling miles to see it will benefit the local economy. The ...y trained in science and has applied some of that ...nd understanding to produce his work across the globe.

...lley
..., that something is being created to make the winter ...inspiring!

...to
...enough to be in Leicester when Under Scan was there, i ...npressed. It really engaged the people walking by. I am ...k comes to Northampton it will do just the same. ...orth a look.

LIGHT SHOW: PAVEMENT PORTRAITS WILL BRING STREET TO LIFE

Moving pictures

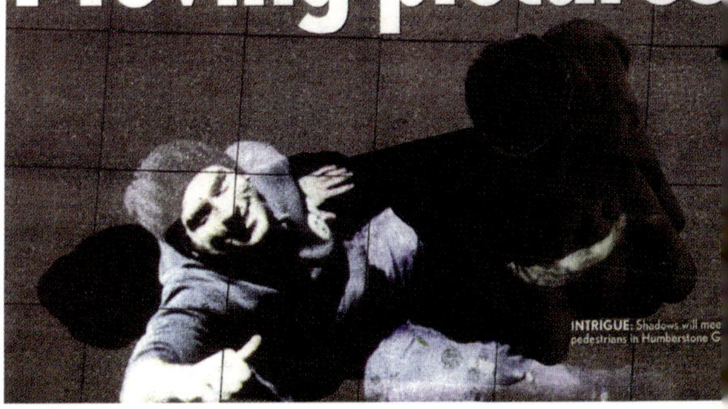

INTRIGUE: Shadows will mee... pedestrians in Humberstone G...

...y **LIZ CROWSON** ...nd **TOM PEGDEN**

...host-like figures will ...ise up from the pavement ...nd follow walkers across ... city square when an ambitious art installation gets under way.

The remarkable sight will meet pedestrians in Humberstone Gate and will be one of the biggest – and most expensive – works of its kind.

From Thursday, the stretch of pavement between Gap, Marks & Spencers and Woolworth's will host the world's largest interactive video artwork, featuring 1,000 portraits of people from across the region.

The moving figures, including 200 people from Leicester, will be beamed on to the ground for 11 nights and will come alive whenever people walk by.

The project is called Under Scan and has been designed by Mexican-Canadian artist and Bafta award winner Rafael Lozano-Hemmer.

In the coming months, it will tour five cities and towns in the East Midlands, and could go on to tour to cities worldwide.

Members of the international media have been invited to Leicester to see its official switch-on.

In all, it will cover 1,500 square metres, making it the largest installation of its kind ever created.

Using the world's brightest light projector, which will be mounted at the top of a tower, white light will flood the square.

The portraits will only appear on the ground when a computerised tracking system senses someone moving by. As the person's shadow covers the projection, it will come alive.

Rafael – who has created similar projects in Japan, France and Mexico – will be flying in on Monday to get his most ambitious installation to date running.

He said: "The unveiling of Under Scan represents the culmination of almost a year's work.

"I hope it will bring a new experience to Leicester people and visi... to the city, and will provide th... with an intriguing shadow-p... where members of the public ... come actors."

The project is costing £1 millio... stage and has been commissione... celebrate the £140 million that ... Midlands Development Age... (Emda) is spending on cult... quarters in cities such as Leices... The artist's fee is £25,000.

City council leisure spokesm... John Mugglestone said: "Leice... is continuing to provide and ... new arts experiences.

"Under Scan represents a uni... opportunity for local people to ... perience a very special video ins... ation on their doorstep.

"It is fitting that Under Scan ... helping celebrate cultural regen... tion as our own cultural quarte... being transformed."

Emda board member and councillor Ross Willmott said: "... stead of just doing a marketing ... chure of how good cultural rege... ation is, we are actually doing so... thing."

The display will be in the city fo... nights from Thursday betw... 6.30pm and midnight.

On Friday and Saturday night... will be switched on until 2am.

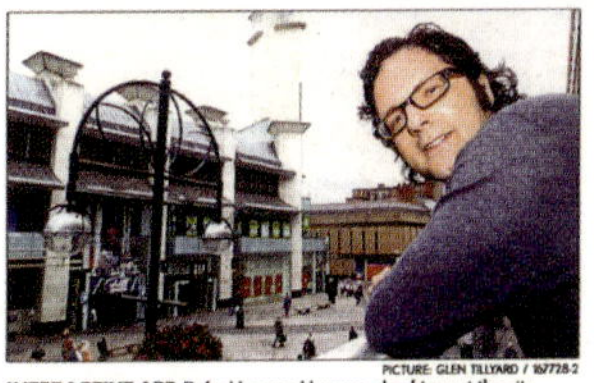

PICTURE: GLEN TILLYARD / 167728-2

INTERACTIVE ART: Rafael Lozano-Hemmer checking out the city centre last year. His latest installation, Under Scan, will cost £1 million

---

£1m LIGHT SHOW TO LURE TOURISTS

Temporary show visits five cities

DERBY'S Market Place will be transformed by a £1m light show for 10 days next year.

East Midlands Development Agency (Emda) is funding the extravagant exhibition at a cost of £20,000 per day.

The organisers hope the show will bring tourists flocking to the city.

Emda has spent £200,000 on the equipment needed for the display, which will see the shadows of people walking through Derby's Market Place projected onto a giant screen containing colour images of 1,000 people from across the region.

A further £285,000 will be spent on transport and staging for the show and an undisclosed fee has been paid to the Mexican artist who came up with the idea.

Derby is one of five towns and cities in the region which will host the exhibition.

Some critics have branded the exhibition a waste of money but Emda claimed it would "greatly enrich our cultural quarters" and attract tourists and investment.

● Full story Page three.

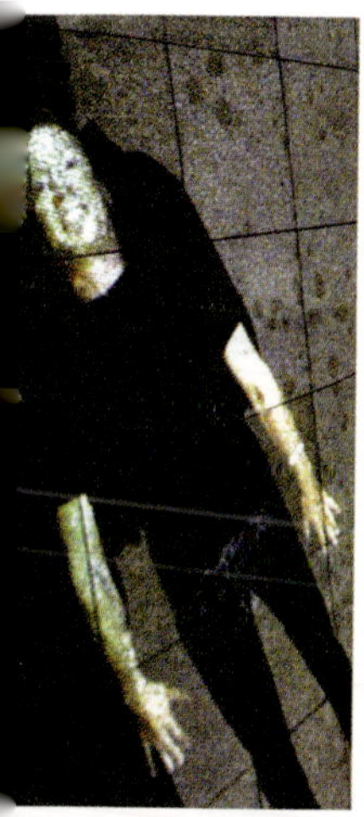

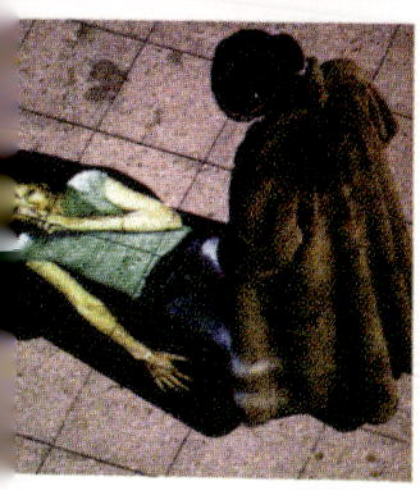

Rafael Lozano-Hemmer's interactive installations, using light and shadows, are designed to engage the public intimately. Richard Clayton talks to him about his plans to illuminate the East Midlands

It's a long way from Mexico City's Millennium celebrations to the campus of Northampton University, yet Rafael Lozano-Hemmer's energy and enthusiasm remain as sharp and luminous as the searchlights he deploys in his installations.

On the final day of a five-date public lecture tour to explain his latest work, Under Scan, the artist has only just 'finished arriving' (a Spanish interpretation, he implies, of 'settled in'), and is already due to leave – but not before he's delivered his talk with the aplomb of a motivation guru. A confused body clock must be the price of true global citizenship.

Born in Mexico, and now a Canadian national residing in Madrid, Lozano-Hemmer lives 'between' places. His ambitious, site-specific pieces grace cities such as Dublin, Lyon, Miami, Rotterdam and Valencia. So what is he doing in the East Midlands, then?

Playing with shadows is the short answer. Why? Because the East Midland Development Agency asked him to. Under Scan is a £1m public art commission that is due to appear in five local towns over the next few months, beginning in Lincoln on 25 November.

Active at night, a huge projector – 110 000 lumens making it the world's brightest, according to Lozano-Hemmer – will cast pedestrians' shadows in public squares. Into these shadows, a computer tracking system will project video portraits of different people, as though revealing alternative selves or rival presences. Spooky, eh?

'Your shadow activates these portraits and they interact with you,' Lozano-Hemmer explains. 'They look back at you, and stick around. Some dance, some send you kisses, some ignore you. It's a very simple, but effective, animation, with a little moment of complicity when you sense that you're being observed too.'

The people in the videos, including many students, were filmed over the summer. Everyone who took part (numbering more than 1000) was free to behave as they wished. 'The only thing we asked of them was to start by looking away from the camera, then to look directly at it, and then look away again.'

Like his projects in Mexico City (which, by the end, had seen 800 000 people 'sculpt' immense patterns with skyward light-beams) and Rotterdam (where a building became a vast screen for the public to play with silhouettes), Under Scan is part of a series called 'Relational Architecture', albeit on a more intimate scale. Only 14 shadows in total can trigger the video portraits at any one time, though, of course, passers-by can still watch.

Collaborating with a team of technicians, which he likens to a film crew, Lozano-Hemmer wants people to re-engage with public spaces, in ways that urban design can't imagine or consciously disavows. Tellingly, his formal training was in physical chemistry, rather than design.

'A lot of the work we're doing is design, to the degree that we're developing a platform,' he says. 'I'm not interested in big, capital 'H' history questions, but in creating platforms which people take over. I call Under Scan an anti-monument, because it's not about having one story reflected, as happens when you build a statue, but the myriad of relationships that emerge in this kind of eccentric environment.'

Citing influences as diverse as Buckminster Fuller, Dan Graham, and Samuel von Hoogstraten's 17th century engravings, the well-travelled 37-year-old has as many notions as passport stamps, and he's happy to cede control of his work to the user.

'Many times, my preconceived ideas of what will happen are wrong, and I really like that,' he says. 'One of the things about shadows that's cool is that – unlike most new media works, including my own – there's no need for explanations, manuals or buttons. People already have a sophisticated vocabulary of what they can do with their shadow. We're all familiar with playing by candlelight and every culture has a tradition of shadow-play.'

His complicated shadows might not bring the East Midlands its Bilbao effect, but they'll certainly take the shine off the Blackpool illuminations, and plenty of London shows besides.

Under Scan will be installed as follows: 25 November to 4 December 2005, Brayford Campus, Lincoln University, followed by installations in Leicester, Northampton, Derby and Nottingham

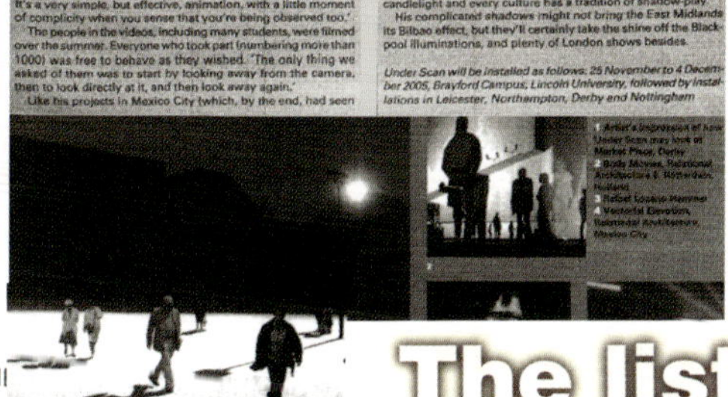

Evening Telegraph FIRST EDITION

It's behind you...and it's someone else's shadow
The weird world coming soon to Derby city centre: Page 12

See who's coming out of the city's shadow...

Market Place prepares to trip the light fantastic with £1m attraction

BY DAVID WALSH

A £1m public light show opens in the centre of Derby on Friday.

East Midlands Development Agency's Under Scan project will see the city's Market Place transformed by a futuristic network of light sensors and projectors for 10 days.

The system will pick out the shadows of pedestrians and project still colour images of people from Derby on to the ground in their place.

Once a person's shadow reaches the projection, the image will come alive and continue moving until the pedestrian is no longer in the system's sights.

The images were filmed at Derby Dance Centre, in Chapel Street.

EMDA hopes the project will attract tourists to the East Midlands. The system has already been used in Lincoln, Leicester and Northampton.

Agencies in New York and Sydney are interested in hiring the system.

Board member Ross Willmott said: "We want to draw attention to the arts across the region.

"This scheme is innovative and interactive. It will fill a public space and attract a lot of attention."

Construction of the light rigs, sensors and projectors began last week.

The project is the idea of Mexican artist Rafael Lozano-Hemmer. EMDA spent £225,000 on his fee and the system's software.

A further £465,000 was spent on the projectors, sensors and staging. The rest of the money goes on costs such as staff and transport.

The organisation receives about £150m in funding from the Government each year.

It is thought that about 5,000 people had a go in Lincoln and 10,000 in Leicester.

Becky Dunning (28), of Uttoxeter New Road, Derby, is among those whose image will be projected.

She said: "It was great to be involved. It will be excellent if it is used in New York and Sydney.

"It's great that something so high-profile has been produced in the East Midlands."

But some people are less happy with the project.

Chris Woodward (61), of Crompton Street, Derby, said: "It's an awful lot of money to spend.

"I know it's come fr... different pot but, ... you think that St He... House needs saving ... the situation that the... station is in, it seems... deserving."

Under Scan will ope... 7pm on Friday and e... night until Sunday, M... 5.

It will operate until ... at weekends and until ... night on weekdays.

dwalsh@derbytelegraph...

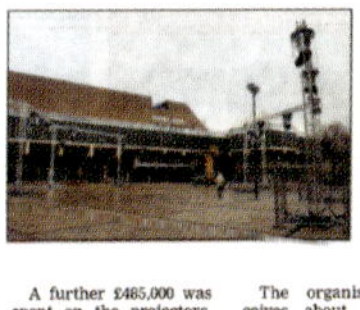

LET THERE BE LIGHT: The gantries for the lights and projectors are erected in Derby's Market Place ahead of the start of the Under Scan project tomorrow. Picture: Maria Marshall MM220206B-1

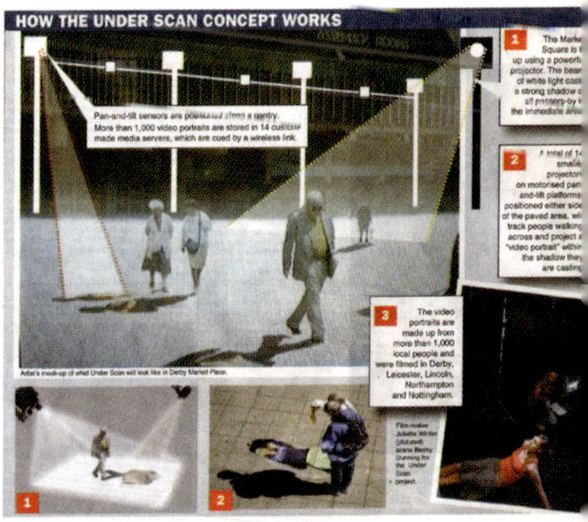

...ION ART SHOW

...ives

The list

Your guide to what's happening this week

Be a part of video art show

IF you're out and about near Northampton's Market Square tonight, you might want to check out a new art installation. Public artwork Under Scan, the ...

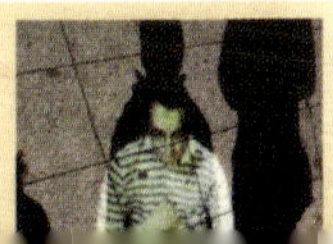

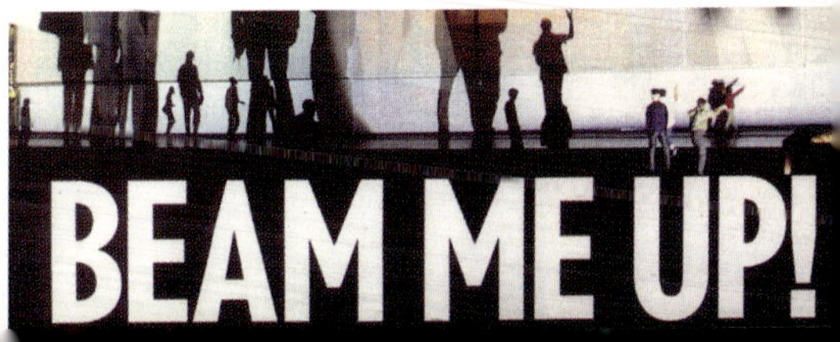

The Legacy
David Hill

Under Scan was a major investment by *emda*, demanding a legacy impact in addition to active engagement with and enjoyment of the work itself. The *Under Scan* legacy is significant and encompasses:

- *Inspiration*: provided in large measure to artists, Local Authorities, arts organisations, communities and people
- *Skill, ideas and new experience*: influencing people in the region and beyond
- *The Work itself*: it's ongoing impact (including through this publication) and it's availability for presentation on a global basis
- *New work*: originating as a direct result of *Under Scan* and incorporating use of the *Under Scan* equipment

The inspiration provided by *Under Scan* was focused through the accessibility and availability of Rafael Lozano-Hemmer. Rafael delivered visionary lectures in each city and town that was to host *Under Scan,* and subsequently delivered master classes, training sessions and shadowing opportunities for twenty-five practising regional artists. Lectures were attended by many under graduates studying visual arts programmes. Twelve months later student requests continue to be relayed to the artists for interviews, advice and comment on work. Many artists who engaged with Lozano-Hemmer remain in e-mail contact experiencing an invaluable form of electronic mentoring and support.

Inspiration is hard to measure, but there is no doubt that developments taking place, and that are planned, for spaces like Northampton Market Square, have been influenced by the inspiration provided by *Under Scan.* Arts organisations refer to *Under Scan* in funding bids and commission proposals, and people in local communities refer back to that "exciting and different event" that enriched their lives in autumn 2005 and winter 2006.

The skills, ideas and new experience gathered from the project have enhanced the work of artists, individual practitioners, arts organisations, Local Authorities, Festivals and other creative industry businesses.

The challenges of producing and staging the work have informed the ongoing development and project portfolio of ArtReach, Stage Right Productions and others.

Under Scan did not conclude with its last East Midlands installation in Nottingham (March 2006). Interest in staging the work has resulted in presentations to New Zealand International Festival, Biennale of Sydney, Québec Festival, Newcastle/Gateshead Winter Festival, Oxford Inspires, GLA (for Trafalgar Square) and the Venice Biennale. *Under Scan* will be installed at other locations across the globe, reinforcing the vision of *emda*, Arts Council England East Midlands and the Local Authorities concerned in commissioning and staging the work, and providing subtle, ongoing promotion of the East Midlands region.

This publication in itself will ensure that *Under Scan* is shared with many more people (including curators and artists) across the world. During the run of the project in the East Midlands, *Under Scan* attracted twelve separate TV news pieces, eighteen radio features and at least fifty three newspaper articles (international, national, regional and local). Regional newspaper coverage reached an estimated circulation figure of 5,632,000.

Sixty Years Celebrating the Arts, the Arts Council England Annual Review 2006 features *Under Scan* as its front cover image providing a timely reminder of the impact of the work.

Finally, a powerful and tangible legacy has been built into the project with the decision taken by *emda* to purchase and retain the equipment used for *Under Scan*. This equipment is available for artists, arts organisations, Festivals and Local Authorities to access and use, with the specific priority that it is provided to facilitate the creation of new work. This opportunity continues to be exploited, ensuring the best possible legacy from *Under Scan*, combining the inspiration, skill sharing and ideas generation that emerged from this important and ambitious project.

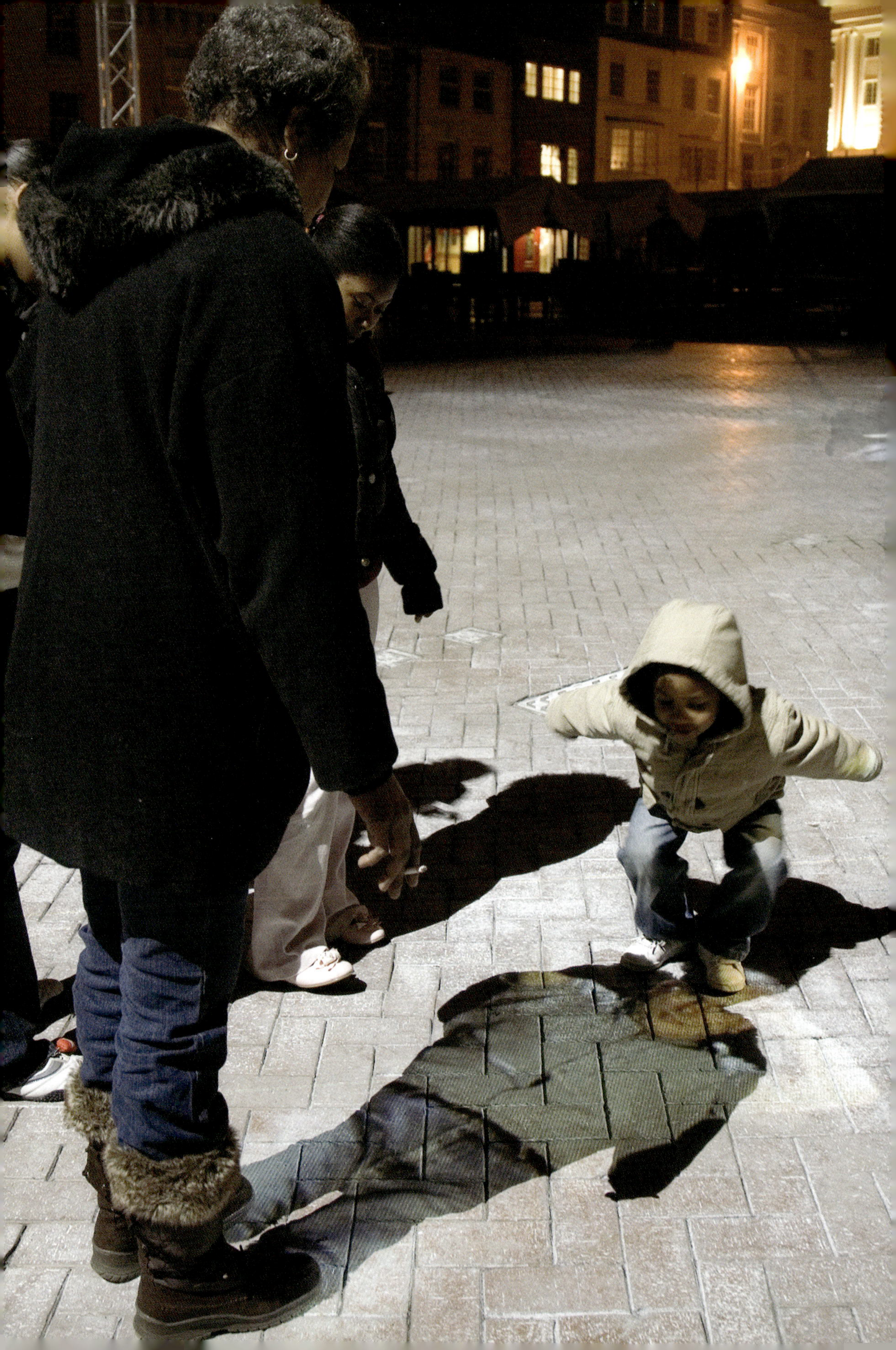

Section 4
Biographies, Credits and Acknowledgements

Rafael Lozano-Hemmer
Biography

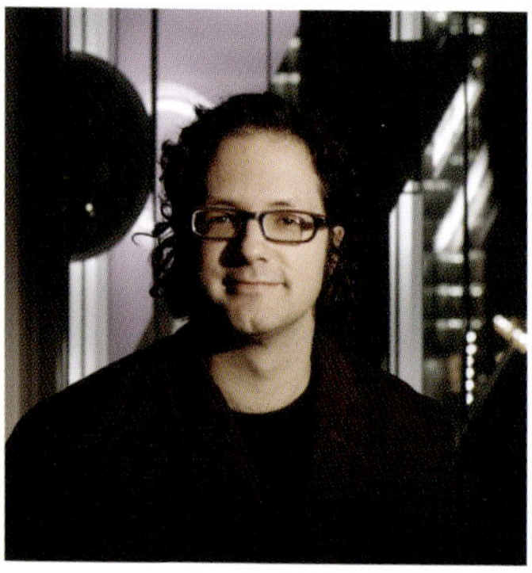

Photo by Bernd Hiepe

Rafael Lozano-Hemmer was born in Mexico City in 1967. In 1989 he received a B.Sc. in Physical Chemistry from Concordia University in Montréal, Canada.

An electronic artist, he develops interactive installations that are at the intersection of architecture and performance art. His main interest is in creating platforms for public participation, by perverting technologies such as robotics, computerized surveillance or telematic networks. Inspired by phantasmagoria, carnival and animatronics, his huge light and shadow works are "antimonuments for alien agency."

His work has been commissioned for events such as the Millennium Celebrations in Mexico City (1999), the Cultural Capital of Europe in Rotterdam (2001), the opening of the Basque Museum of Contemporary Arts Artium (2002) the United Nations' World Summit of Cities in Lyon (2003), the opening of the Yamaguchi Centre for Art and Media in Japan (2003), the Expansion of the European Union in Dublin (2004) and the Asian Cultural Co-operation Forum (2006).

His work in kinetic sculpture, responsive environments, video installation and photography has been shown in two dozen countries, including Art Basel Unlimited (Switzerland), the Sydney Biennale (Australia), the Liverpool Biennial (UK), the Shanghai Biennial (China), the Itaú Cultural (Brazil), the Istanbul Biennial (Turkey), the ARCO art fair (Spain), Bienal de la Habana (Cuba), Architecture and Media Biennale (Austria), Laboratorio Arte Alameda (Mexico), the Musée des Beaux Arts (Canada), European Media Art Festival (Germany) and others. His work is in private and public contemporary art collections such as the Museum of Modern Art in New York, the Jumex collection in Mexico, the MUSAC Museum in Spain, the Cisneros Fontanals Foundation in Miami and the Daros Foundation in Zürich. Lozano-Hemmer will represent Mexico in the 52nd Venice Biennale in 2007.

At the Prix Ars Electronica in Austria, his pieces have received a Golden Nica, a distinction and two honourable mentions. He also won two BAFTA British Academy Awards for Interactive Art in London, "Best Installation" at the IDMA awards in Toronto, a "Design Review Gold Award" given by I.D. Magazine, a Cyberstar award in Cologne, a distinction at the SFMOMA Webby Awards in San Francisco, "Artist/performer of the year" at Wired Magazine's Rave Awards, an Excellence Prize at the CG Arts Media Art Festival in Tokyo, WTN award in the Arts Category, a Rockefeller fellowship, a Langlois Grant, the Trophée des Lumières in Lyon, HorizonZero best interactive installation and an International Bauhaus Award in Dessau, Germany.

He has given many workshops and conferences, most recently at Goldsmiths College and The Bartlett School of Architecture in London, ICC in Tokyo, Loopholes Symposium at Harvard, at the MIT MediaLab in Cambridge, the Guggenheim Museum in NYC, IDCA in Aspen, LA MOCA, Netherlands Architecture Institute, UC Berkeley, Berlin Transmediale, British National Museum of Photography and the Art Institute of Chicago.

His writing has been published in Kunstforum (Germany), Leonardo (USA), Performance Research (UK), Telepolis (Germany), Movimiento Actual (Mexico), Archis (Netherlands), Aztlán (USA) and other art and media publications. He has been in several international juries and committees, including the Fondation Daniel Langlois, ISEA, Hexagram, Prix Milia d'Or in Cannes, GMD in Bonn, the International Art and A-life award and Cyberconf in Madrid. He has been a resident artist twice at the Banff Centre for the Arts in Canada.

www.lozano-hemmer.com
www.alzado.net
www.amodal.net
www.sitestepper.net
www.rhizome.org/artbase/2398/fear/

Contributor Biographies

Jayne Bingham

Jayne Bingham was born in Douglas, the Isle of Man. She studied at Gloucestershire College of Art and Design, the University of London Institute of Education and the Slade School of Fine Art (where she won the Steer Prize in Painting, and the drawing prize in the Harrison McCann exhibition of graduate work). She has subsequently shown work at venues in the UK, and most recently had solo shows of small-scale paintings and drawings in the USA and Chile. This new work considers rituals associated with collecting and keeping objects, and then encounters between the collected and a drawing process. She is currently touring work in a *Drawing as Reflective Practice* exhibition that has visited the Air Gallery in London and the Glasgow School of Art. A one-person show of drawings is scheduled for February 2007 in Philadelphia. She is a trustee of the Heslam Trust in Lincolnshire, which makes recommendations on the purchase of sculpture, and a member of the Arts Special Interest Group that advises on the exhibition programme at the Usher Gallery in Lincoln. She was also a member of the planning team for the exhibition of Michael Kenny's sculpture at Lincoln Cathedral and De Montfort University in the late 90's. Jayne Bingham is a Senior Academic in the Faculty of Art, Architecture and Design at the University of Lincoln, and a Fellow of the Royal Society of the Arts.

Timothy Druckrey

Timothy Druckrey is Director of the Graduate Photography and Digital Imaging program at the Maryland Institute. He also works as a curator, writer, and editor living in New York City. He lectures internationally about the social impact of electronic media, the transformation of representation, and communication in interactive and networked environments. He co-organized the international symposium Ideologies of Technology at the Dia Center of the Arts and co-edited the book *Culture on the Brink: Ideologies of Technology* (Bay Press). He also co-curated the exhibition *Iterations: The New Image* at the International Center of Photography and edited the book by the same name published by MIT Press. He recently edited *Electronic Culture: Technology and Visual Representation* and is Series Editor for *Electronic Culture:*

History, Theory, Practice published by MIT Press. This series now includes Ars Electronica: Facing the Future, net_condition: art and global media, Geert Lovink's, *Dark Fiber, and Future Cinema: The Cinematic Imaginary After Film* (edited by Jeffrey Shaw and Peter Weibel), Stelarc: *The Monograph* (edited by Marquard Smith), and (forthcoming) *Deep Time of the Media: Toward an Archaeology of Hearing and Seeing by Technical Means* (Siegfried Zielinski). Recent exhibitions he has curated include *Bits and Pieces* and *Critical Conditions*. He was Guest Professor at the University of Applied Art, Vienna (2004) and Richard Koopman Distinguished Chair for the Visual Arts at the University of Hartford (2005).

Beryl Graham

Beryl Graham is Professor of New Media Art at the School of Arts, Design, Media and Culture, University of Sunderland, and co-editor of the CRUMB web site resource for curators of new media art www.crumbweb.org/. She is a writer, curator and educator with many years of professional experience as a media arts organiser, and was head of the photography department at Projects UK, Newcastle, for six years. She curated the international exhibition *Serious Games* for the Laing and Barbican art galleries, and has also worked with The Exploratorium, San Francisco, and *San Francisco Camerawork*. Her Ph.D. concerned audience relationships with interactive art in gallery settings, and she has written widely on the subject for books and periodicals including *Leonardo, Convergence, and Switch*. Her book *Digital Media Art* was published by Heinemann in 2003, and she is co-authoring with Sarah Cook a book on curating new media art for MIT (Cambridge, Mass.). She has chapters in the books *New media art: Practice and context in the UK 1994 – 2004* (Arts Council of England), and *The Photographic Image In Digital Culture* (Routledge). Dr. Graham has presented papers at conferences including *Navigating Intelligence (*Banff*), Museums and the Web* (Seattle and Vancouver), and *Caught in the Act* (Tate Liverpool).

David Hill

David has many years experience in arts management and creative practice, combining theatre directing, senior management and chief executive roles through commercial, subsidised and community arts sectors. He established ArtReach as a specialist arts events agency and consultancy in 1996. ArtReach specialises in capital project development, business planning, fundraising, organisational development with artists and arts organisations, and event direction/delivery (performing and visual arts). With a portfolio of over one hundred clients ArtReach has been responsible for supporting key new venues such as The Peepul Centre (Leicester) and the New Art Exchange (Nottingham) and has supported the development of

Kinetika Art Links International as a global street arts and carnival company. As a successful theatre practitioner and director David's roles have included Associate Director, Everyman Theatre Cheltenham and Artistic Director Theatre Station Blyth, Northumberland. As the first Marketing Director at the 2,000 seat Birmingham Hippodrome in the 1980's, he established the marketing and publicity department during two major capital refurbishments of the venue. He has been an adviser to West Midlands Arts, Northern Arts and South West Arts and an assessor for the Regional Arts Lottery Programme, Capital Arts Lottery and Arts for Everyone programmes. www.artreach.biz

Cuauhtémoc Medina
An art critic, curator and historian, he lives and works in Mexico City. He has a PhD in Art History and Theory from the University of Essex, UK. He is Researcher at the Instituto de Investigaciones Estéticas and at the National University of Mexico, and Associate Curator of Latin American Art Collections at Tate Gallery in London. He is also member of *Teratoma*, a group of curators, critics and anthropologists based in Mexico City. He has published extensively on contemporary art and curating, including the book *When faith moves mountains* (Madrid, Turner, 2005) coauthored with artist Francis Alÿs, a book that documents an action produced in Lima in 2002, and essays such as "High Curios" (in: Diana Augatis et. al. *Brian Jungen,* Vancouver Art Gallery, 2005), "Una ética obtenida por su suspensión/An Ethics achieved through its suspension" (in: *Situaciones artísticas latinoamericanas*. San José, Costa Rica: TEOR/ética, 2005) and "The 'Kurturbolscheviken' I. Fluxus, the abolition of Art, the Soviet Union, and 'pure amusement'." (*Res. Anthropology and Aesthetics*. Vol. 48, Autumn 2005). Among his recent curatorial projects are: *20 million Mexicans can't be wrong* (South London Gallery, 2002), Francis Alÿs: *Diez cuadras alrededor del estudio* (Museo del Antiguo Colegio de San Ildefonso, Mexico, 2006) and *Melanie Smith: Spiral city and beyond* (MUCA-Campus, Mexico 2006).

Nadja Mounajjed
Nadja Mounajjed was born in France in 1976. She did her BSc and trained as an architect in Damascus, Syria. In 2001, she moved to London where she did her Master degree (MArch) at the Bartlett School of Architecture, University College London under the supervision of Prof. Peter Cook and Yael Reisner. She is currently a full time PhD candidate at the School of Architecture, University of Sheffield, working in an interdisciplinary capacity under the supervision of Dr. Chengzhi Peng and Stephen Walker. Her research investigates users' experience of digital interactive interventions, particularly

soundscapes and interactive imagery, in urban and architectural spaces. She combines installation with ethnographic tactics in her work to map socio-spatial practices and interactivity. Nadja Mounajjed is part of the Leonardo-Net: an interdisciplinary collaboration of researchers, artists and designers in the field of people and technology in the UK. She has a Postgraduate Degree in Higher Education (PCHE) and has been teaching in different courses at the School of Architecture, University of Sheffield.

John Plowman

John Plowman graduated from Leicester Polytechnic in 1980 with a 1st class honours degree in Fine Art and from Goldsmiths College London with a MA Fine Art in 1987. Since 1980 he has exhibited on a regular basis in this country and abroad. His most recent exhibition was *Twilight Shift* at Shillam and Smith 3 London in December 2005, and he has in the last three years contributed essays to four exhibition catalogues. His current practice encompasses two strands. The first is *The Labour of Art*, an enquiry into strategies foregrounding the temporal aspect of making art; the time spent becomes the product rather than the finished object. Such an enquiry at this point in time is timely as the traditional site of this labour, the artist's studio, has been shifting through the late 20th Century to include the gallery and other non-art sites both real and virtual. The second strand, *Beacon*, is a curatorial project whose mission is arttravelsite and whose aim is to establish new art and new artists in the rural. It is a project in which the audience are seen as active collaborators and participants with the artist, art, site and curator. This project has, since its inception in 2004, attracted substantial funding from Arts Council England East Midlands, County and District councils and other funding bodies. *no place, like home* the next *Beacon* project will launch in September 2006. John Plowman was appointed Reader in Fine Art at the University of Lincoln in February 2006, where he had previously been Senior Lecturer since 2002

Mirjam Struppek

Mirjam Struppek works as an urban planner in Berlin. Since 2002 she has been developing the online-platform interactionfield.de about interactive projects in urban public space. After she had worked for one year at PLAY_Gallery for Still and Motion Pictures, Berlin, she founded in 2004 Urban Research, with a special focus on the liveability of urban space, public sphere and its transformation and acquisition through new media. Since 2005 she has organised the monthly lecture and discussion evening "Urban Media Salon." The Institute of Network Cultures and the Department of Art in Public Space, Amsterdam, currently commissioned her to develop the conference "Urban Screens 05-discovering the potential of outdoor screens for urban society," being followed by "Urban Screens 06" the following year. She holds a degree with distinction in Urban and Environmental Planning from University of Kaiserslautern, where she also was assistant teacher in Geometry for Architects and Planners and worked as a research assistant in the Institute for Mobility and Transport during her studies. In 1999 she spent two research semesters with a DAAD scholarship at the Graduate School of Environmental Studies at Nagoya University, Japan.

Credits

Production Team

Antimodular Research (Montréal, Canada)
Matthew Biederman
Natalie Bouchard
Matthew Marino
Susie Ramsay

APR (Edmonton, Canada)
Conroy Badger
Will Bauer

ArtReach (Leicester and Maidenhead, UK)
David Hill (Director)
Emma Jones (Project Manager)
David Rose (Marketing & PR)
Aoife Daniels (Marketing Coordinator)
Carol Sutherland (Administrator

Stage Right Productions (Northampton, UK)
Kevin Roach (Director)
Eamonn Byrne (Technician)
Gerry Coles (Technician)
Ian Brame (Technician)

Video Artists
Juliette Winter (Derby)
Lesley Stableford (Lincoln)
Matthew Humphreys (Northampton)
Steve Friendship (Leicester)
Jim Boxall (Nottingham)

Facilitators
Sam Lindley
Juliet Preston
Aoife Daniels
Rachel Jacobs

Commissioning Panel

Ross Willmott (Chair), Sophie Fletcher (*emda*), Samson Kambalu (artist), Dr Beryl Graham, Deborah Dean (Angel Row Gallery, Nottingham), Alison Lloyd (Arts Council England, East Midlands), Mike Roberts (Lincoln City Council), Mike Candler (Leicester City Council), Mike Brown (Derby City Council), Gerry Arterton (Northampton Borough Council).

For *emda*:
David Wallace (International Director), Chris Ward Brown (Construction Policy Adviser), Caroline Shutter (Head of Communications). Sophie Fletcher (Economic Policy Adviser for Culture and Sport).

Acknowledgements

Many thanks to the following organisations and individuals:

Derby

Assembly Rooms
City Centre Management
City Centre Police Office
Derby City Council
Derby Dance Centre
Guildhall Theatre
Metro Cinema
Q Arts
St Benedict's School
University of Derby

Melanie Allen, Andy Falconer, Sally Griffith, Peter Ireson, Professor David Manley, Peter Meakin, Andrew McIntyre, Ray Rippingale, Jessamie Self, Rab Singh, Harriet Spalding, Sergeant Paul Tatlow and Barbara Wheildon.

Leicester

Clerical Medical
City Gallery
GAP Clothing Store
Gateway College
Haymarket Shopping Centre
LCB Depot
Leicester City Council
Leicestershire Constabulary
Leicestershire Fire and Rescue
Leicestershire Promotions
Phoenix Arts

Sarah Baxendale, David Best, Kathy Fawcett, Edward Fenwick-Moore, Tiz Gibson, Lorna Hamilton-Brown, Terry Hammond, Jenny Higgs, Gareth Hughes, Ed Kocik, Jasia McArdle, Jo-Anne Marlow, Barry Page, Clive Roberts and Phil Toyne.

Lincoln

Brayford Trust
Cathedral City Cruises
Lincoln City Council
The Collection
University of Lincoln

David Mullaney, Jayne Bingham, John Handley, Keith James, Phil North, Jonathan Platt, Professor Vincent Shacklock, Toby Stableford, Jeremy Webster and Professor Brian Winston.

Northampton

Market Traders
Millets
Northampton Arts Collective
Northampton Borough Council
Northamptonshire County Council
Northampton Museum and Art Gallery
Royal and Derngate
Threshold Studios
University of Northampton
Working Links

Lorraine Austin, Jacqui Cabey, Steve Candlish, Peter Field, Cavan Kelly, Andrew Langford, Cllr Phil Larrat, Cllr Tim Hadland and Davin Madhavji.

Nottingham

Angel Row Gallery
British Waterways
Broadway Media Centre
BT
Castle Wharf Management
Hyson Green Youth Centre
Nottingham City Council
Nottingham Magistrate's Court
Nottingham Trent University
Powerhouse
Radiator Festival

Frank Abbott, Lou Butler, Michaela Butter, Bob Chaffin, Clarissa Corfe, Gerry Garrard, Paul Hough, Joanne Lee, Victor McClymont, Peter Milton, James McVeigh, Mick Ryan and Sharon Scaniglia.

Additional footage shot by Wellington Films, Nottingham

International

Apple Computer (Cupertino)
Brunswick Group (London)
Graphic Thought Facility (London)
High End Systems (Austin)
Imaging Source (Bremen)
Pani Austria (Vienna)
Solotech (Montréal)

Sandra Badger, Richard Belliveau, Cyril Bême, Rebecca Blackwood, Fred Brookes, Craig Burross, Daniel Canogar, Grace Chapman, Luc Courchesne, Bernhard Hoefert, Richard Lachance, David Lemieux, Robbie Mahoney, Susie Ramsay, Jill Roach, Michael Regan, Alexandra Robat, Markus Sautter, Paul Sermon, Rudolf Wandl and Keith Watson.

Three Cities Create and Connect (supporting *Under Scan*)

Project Part-Financed by the European Union

European Regional Development Fund